DATE DUE

Regulatory Rights

Regulatory Rights

Supreme Court Activism, the Public Interest, and the Making of Constitutional Law

LARRY YACKLE

THE UNIVERSITY OF CHICAGO PRESS   CHICAGO AND LONDON

LARRY YACKLE is professor of law and the Basil Yanakakis Research Scholar at Boston University School of Law. He has taught and written about constitutional law throughout his academic career, and he is the author of five other books, including *Reform and Regret* and *Reclaiming the Federal Courts*.

The University of Chicago Press, Chicago 60637
The University of Chicago Press, Ltd., London
© 2007 by The University of Chicago
All rights reserved. Published 2007
Printed in the United States of America
16 15 14 13 12 11 10 09 08 07   1 2 3 4 5

ISBN-13: 978-0-226-94471-5 (cloth)
ISBN-10: 0-226-94471-9 (cloth)

Library of Congress Cataloging-in-Publication Data

Yackle, Larry W.
  Regulatory rights : Supreme Court activism, the public interest, and the making of constitutional law / Larry Yackle.
    p. cm.
  Includes bibliographical references and index.
  ISBN-13: 978-0-226-94471-5 (cloth : alk. paper)
  ISBN-10: 0-226-94471-9 (cloth : alk. paper)
  1. Constitutional law—United States—Interpretation and construction. 2. Police power—United States. 3. United States. Supreme Court. 4. Civil rights—United States. I. Title.
  KF4552 .Y33 2007
  342.73—dc22

                                                              2007005605

♾ The paper used in this publication meets the minimum requirements of the American National Standard for Information Sciences—Permanence of Paper for Printed Library Materials, ANSI Z39.48-1992.

FOR JEANETTE

Contents

Acknowledgments

Numerous friends and colleagues helped me with this project, among them Winston Bowman, Robert Brickman, Krikor Dekermenjian, Morton J. Horwitz, William Kaleva, Pnina Lahav, Gary Lawson, David Lyons, Tracey Maclin, Michael Meurer, Ryann M. Muir, Teresa Gallego O'Rourke, Mark Pettit, H. Jefferson Powell, David Seipp, Aviam Soifer, and Jeanette Yackle.

Introduction

Supreme Court justices are an aging tribe. Their longevity is a product of the legal safeguards established to ensure their independence. They are entitled to serve (and keep on serving) during "good behavior," which means (in practical effect) as long as they want to. And they invariably want to for a very long time. The justices now in place are an especially elderly lot. Then again, they, too, are mortal. Vacancies occasionally appear to be filled by comparatively youthful men and women whose nominations evoke heated debate. Most arguments regarding individual candidates are packaged as claims about Supreme Court justices' proper function once they are on the bench. We are told, in particular, that justices should not create constitutional rights; rather, they should enforce the rights the Constitution enshrines. In this book, I hope to convince you that arguments of that kind fundamentally misconceive the work justices do and, beyond that, the character of the American Constitution in whose name they do it. If we can once get the job description right, we will understand why battles over nominees are hard-fought and worth fighting. It *matters* who sits on the Supreme Court; it matters a great deal. It matters because the justices *do* create individual constitutional rights—the only rights we have, the only rights we have ever had, and the only rights we can hope to have.

I mean to argue that substantive federal constitutional rights draw their meaning exclusively from the great body of relevant Supreme Court decisions and that the only content those rights enjoy, abstracted from the Court's decisions, can be reduced to a single doctrinal idea: Government acts constitutionally if it acts instrumentally, adopting policy as a sensible means of achieving public ends. This is an unorthodox claim. I do not propose merely that instrumentalism figures in the common understanding of rights associated with the Constitution. No one doubts that. Scarcely any doctrinal formulation is more commonplace. Rational instrumentalism is ubiquitous in the Court's treatment of discrete provisions of the historical document adopted in 1789 (and subsequently amended twenty-seven ways), in the themes commonly inferred from the document as a whole, and in the underlying theories the document is said to embody. My argument runs deeper. With respect to the content of substantive individual rights, instrumentalism occupies the field entirely. Nothing else matters—not the textual provisions conventionally thought to establish rights, not the history behind those provisions, not the philosophical notions with which the Constitution is associated. I contend that rational instrumentalism is far more than a common element circulating through many bodies of constitutional law regarding substantive rights. Instrumentalism is the central doctrinal idea around which all else circulates.

I limit my claim to substantive rights—namely, rights that impede governmental action in the interest of individual freedom. Much the same argument might be advanced with respect to procedural rights, which generally govern the administration of substantive policies in particular instances. There, too, the text of the historical document does precious little work, rational instrumentalism a great deal more. But I make no effort to develop that argument. Nor do I contend that the text is irrelevant, and rational instrumentalism pervasive, with respect to constitutional concepts apart from individual rights. Provisions of the written Constitution do prescribe the basic nature and architecture of American government—for example, provisions explicitly calling for periodic elections and bicameralism in the legislative branch and implicitly for the separation of national powers and federalism.[1] I do think that when the Court takes up questions *about* those arrangements, the text itself offers little guidance. The answers the justices deliver rest on judgment, which, in turn, is often informed by means-ends instrumentalism.[2] But I do not press those arguments here.

My claim regarding substantive rights is conceptual in the modest sense that it locates constitutional significance at some remove from the document and its amendments. Yet I have no ambition to pitch instrumentalism at a level with any general theory of American constitutionalism. Theoretical arguments attend to antecedent questions much mooted in academic circles, among them the prerequisites of governmental legitimacy, the place of a higher form of law in a system that rests its legitimacy on political accountability, and the role of unelected judges in the implementation of that higher law. I scarcely mean to discount inquiries of that nature, but only to clarify where this book fits in the landscape. I do not believe that theoretical efforts seriously illuminate the American Constitution as it comes to life in Supreme Court decisions. I will have a little to say about the legitimacy of a Constitution fashioned by judges. But in the main I want to explore the Court and the Constitution in operation and thus to elucidate the substantive rights we actually have and whence they came. Finally, I also put aside the wealth of social science literature offering empirical data on the Supreme Court's behavior and attempting to explain substantive rights on grounds quite apart from legal reasoning.

Theorists who offer the best answers to conceptual questions typically contemplate a good deal of judgment for the Supreme Court to exercise, but stop short of exploring what the justices do with their authority. There are exceptions, of course. H. Jefferson Powell defines "[c]onstitutional law" as "an historically extended tradition of argument" that employs constitutional "words" to debate and (tentatively to resolve) public questions of the day.[3] I want to capture the doctrinal framework the Supreme Court employs to wrestle with modern cases touching substantive rights and to identify and analyze the many hard questions that doctrine calls on the justices to make in order to clarify the true meaning of the individual rights their decisions elaborate. I hasten to say that I do not condemn the Court for creating substantive rights. To my mind, there isn't any serious alternative to the hard-minded, problem-solving judicial judgment that gives rights their content. We have neither good justices who adhere to the Constitution nor bad justices who don't. We have only justices who exercise their best judgment in a system that counts that judgment as the Constitution. A good judge, in my view, is one who grapples seriously with real problems, honestly examines the relevant factors in the mix, tries his or her level best to come up with solutions that serve the country, and explains results realistically to the rest of us. This is the way things are and, I think, the only way things could be.[4]

We live in interesting times. Many observers detect a certain malaise in legal thought, linked to postmodern themes both in jurisprudence and in allied fields. To put the matter bluntly, we have lost faith in the idea that judicial decision making can be principled—that justices of the Supreme Court can rest their pronouncements of constitutional meaning on an objective foundation that cabins their personal predilections.[5] Mark Tushnet contends that we are experiencing a corresponding sea change in American thinking about the very nature and capacity of government.[6] We have, he insists, a new constitutional order in which our aspirations for government are much diminished, our hopes for prosperity seriously reduced.[7] The evidence is there for all to see in the behavior of the Congress and successive presidents.[8]

The Supreme Court has participated in this turn of intellectual events. The Court now sitting certainly is not the Warren Court of my youth—the Court that outlawed racial segregation in public schools, proclaimed the principle of one-person/one-vote, and put muscle in procedural safeguards in criminal prosecutions. This Court has established important limits on congressional power to regulate interstate commerce, recognized state sovereign immunity from some suits on federal claims, and announced related limits on congressional authority to enforce federal regulations against the states. Into the bargain, the Court has circumscribed Congress's capacity to enact and implement federal civil rights and environmental protection programs. At the same time, the current Court has declined (thus far) to abridge a woman's ability to choose whether to bear a child, upheld certain race-conscious admissions programs at the university level, and overturned state policies that penalize citizens on the basis of their sexual orientation.[9]

It is fair to ask whether we can explain this collage of decisions by reference to anything other than the justices' best judgments regarding the relevant considerations on each occasion—which judgments, in turn, are sometimes (though not always) different from the judgments the Warren Court would have made or, to be sure, the judgments that other men and women would reach today if they held seats on the highest tribunal in the land. I think not. Not, at least, where substantive rights are concerned. I don't suggest that the judgments the justices make are personal matters of taste. Justices of the Supreme Court are constrained by the conventions of legal practice, collegial decision making, and opinion-writing; by their own precedents; and, certainly, by the relative fragility of their position in relation to the other branches of the national government. But they are not seriously limited in the way that has conventionally been thought to be essential. They are not ruled by objective legal criteria that banish value judgments from their analysis; they do not enforce foundational law with an existence apart from their own decisions.

Legal scholarship has responded to the new constitutional order in general and to the Court's controversial decisions in particular. I do not say that the one has followed the other as action begets reaction. Academicians scarcely require worldly events to stimulate their creative energies. Still, the Court's decisions have reached down to the fundamentals of the system, making academic exploration of those regions more urgent. I scarcely propose in this book to engage the massive literature in point. Certainly, I have nothing to add to (or detract from) the work of theorists who would abandon the entire business of a constitutional system centered around the Supreme Court and focus, instead, on other forums in which the Constitution operates.[10] I lay aside Judge Easterbrook's insistence that the Court's preeminent voice with respect to the Constitution cannot simply be assumed and concentrate my attention on the Supreme Court's elaboration of constitutional meaning.[11] I *do* challenge the twin notions that the historical document and its amendments fix a wide range of policies in constitutional stone and that we are obliged to accept those policies as our own, unless and until we adopt additional amendments. By those accounts, the justices are neither charged to formulate constitutional law nor entitled to do so. Instead, they have the duty and responsibility to derive constitutional meaning from the document in its historical context. I critique strong arguments along those lines.[12] I acknowledge, of course, that other academic specialists adopt more complex, less absolutist, and thus more defensible positions regarding the value of text and history. Yet, in my view, sophisticated accounts of the place of the historical document in constitutional analysis largely drain textualism and originalism of consequence as serious restraints on modern policy in controversial settings.[13]

On the affirmative, my argument with respect to substantive rights is in keeping with theorists who regard the written Constitution as at best a point of departure, not one-stop shopping.[14] We must drop the pretense that the 1789 document and its amendments actually supply answers to difficult questions, as well as any claim that the intentions of the framers can be discovered and given effect. The Constitution is not an exclusively conservative constraining force, but primarily a positive empowering idea. In the main, it speaks to substantive policy not by announcing positions from which we cannot depart, but rather by inviting us to chart our own course. The words of the great clauses are inspiring, not confining. We cannot and we should not shrink from the specter of Supreme Court justices developing constitutional meaning on the basis of honest value judgments. If the Court's decisions are disquieting in whole or in part, it is not because the justices now sitting have forsaken an ambitious vision of the good society traceable to the written Constitution and substituted their own program. Where substantive rights are concerned, the Court is doing now what it has always done. The serious question is not *whether* the justices bring values to bear in constitutional decision making, but *what* values they choose to build into the meaning they assign to the Constitution and, importantly, their success in accommodating competing values. Our satisfaction with or disappointment in their performance must depend on that and that alone.

If we accept that the Court determines practical constitutional meaning, we are obliged to look hard at the doctrinal framework the justices fix as their guide and, in turn, at the way they resolve actual cases. Professor Powell has illuminated how Supreme Court justices and others struggled with important questions in the nineteenth century and in the early twentieth. After a fashion, I hope to pick up where Powell leaves off, examining modern Supreme Court decision making in one context. Along the way, I compare what I have to say with ostensibly similar treatments in the literature.[15] Suffice it to say now that, in the case of substantive rights, I argue that the justices rely on rational instrumentalism to realize the fundamental building blocks of modern constitutional jurisprudence. When they turn to specific cases, they deploy instrumentalism to marshal the relevant issues, albeit not seriously to predict the results they should reach. My argument proceeds in four stages.

In chapter 1, I explain that conventional thinking about the Constitution is crippled by the irrepressible misconception that the Constitution is one and the same with the storied document. It is easy enough to understand the document's appeal, and I explore a number of overlapping explanations. Yet I challenge the very idea that we are governed by a written Constitution. Relatedly, I explore the visceral insistence that the document specifies constitutional meaning by its literal text, either alone or in company with the intentions of its "framers." I canvass the many reasons why the text does not function in that way, but should be understood as a symbol of nationhood. The historical writing typically characterized as *the* Constitution casts a certain spell that has to be broken. That spell is of our own creation. American children are not born with a commitment to this old text any more than they arrive with cell phones already clapped to their ears. To borrow an apt phrase, they have to be carefully taught. I am much afraid that our reflexive invocations of the document (and our veneration of the men who wrote it) are doing the teaching. We relentlessly drum the supposed importance of the text and the framers into American culture. So we should not be surprised that we can achieve a more sophisticated understanding of reality only if we first pry ourselves loose from facile assumptions we have accepted without critical examination.

Despite the popular misunderstanding of the Constitution, and despite professional lip service to that mistaken view, there is a strong literature demonstrating its inadequacy. Truth is, the arguments for "textualism" and "originalism" have been demolished. Were it not for the Supreme Court's stubborn refusal to give them up, there would be no fish left in those barrels worth the shooting. Still, the Court does insist on citing the text of the document, together with its history, to justify constitutional decisions. That style of opinion writing (and I do think references to the text and its history are largely matters of style) encourages academics to try again (and again and again) to succeed where they and others have failed before. My aim is primarily to organize the arguments and counterarguments and to expose the pretense of a documentary Constitution for what it is.

We are beset by an awkward state of affairs. Serious academic observers recognize that the written Constitution contributes next to nothing to the resolution of hard constitutional problems. Yet most cling in some way to the notion that the document still signifies and that judge-made doctrine mediates between its text and the demands of particular cases. Perhaps Art Leff's lament hit the mark. It is "awfully hard to be a credible constitutional thinker by treating the Constitution as irrelevant."[16] I want to argue that in the case of substantive rights the supposed link between the document and the Court's work simply does not exist. The Court creates the real Constitution as it goes along, free of any serious connection to the text. Apart from the buildup of decided cases, we have only the doctrine the Court itself supplies, which operates (albeit roughly) to explain the Court's own decisions, to guide lower courts in the near term, and to channel the Court's approach to similar cases in the future. In turn, rational instrumentalism pervades substantive rights doctrine so completely as to dwarf any other factor in the mix. Virtually everything about substantive constitutional rights is doctrinal, and virtually everything doctrinal is instrumental.

In subsequent chapters, I make a sustained effort to establish rational instrumentalism as the doctrinal guide to the content of substantive rights. In chapter 2, I identify the jurisprudential foundations on which instrumentalism depends and for which it now operates. My principal mission in that chapter is to demonstrate that rational instrumentalism is nothing new, but draws on hard experience with alternative understandings of the way the Court should elaborate the content of substantive rights. To begin, I explain that courts (and the Supreme Court in particular) are not distinguishable from legislative bodies on the ground that they alone must have reasons for their actions. The duty to act rationally cuts across institutional lines and forms the doctrinal content of substantive rights against governmental power of any ilk. Then I collate various related strains in the development of the American political system, the confluence of which accounts for rational instrumentalism as the mainstay of constitutional doctrine regarding substantive rights.

There is a good deal of history in chapter 2, but I make no claim to a coherent linear narrative. Instead, I organize the materials around four overlapping themes: the rejection of natural-rights theory, the concomitant recognition that government is largely responsible for the measure of freedom that individuals enjoy, the acceptance of governmental power to regulate private activities for the larger social good, and the abiding effort to distribute authority between the Supreme Court and more politically accountable institutions. We cannot know precisely how the pieces fit together and when. But the culmination of events seems clear enough: The justices made peace with the general idea of governmental regulation, gave the states' regulatory authority a name (the police power), described the scope of that power (essentially as rational instrumentalism), and then defined substantive constitutional rights *against* regulation as a mirror image—namely, an entitlement to be regulated by means that rationally further the public interest. The variegated sources of rational instrumentalism explain why the Court is typically as generous to governmental action as it is. They also explain why the Court finds some regulation constitutionally wanting.

In chapter 3, I describe the reach of rational instrumentalism in the Court's development of substantive rights in order to explain and appreciate how thoroughly instrumentalism predominates. In one important sense, I challenge the way individual rights are conventionally conceived.

I explain that rational instrumentalism eludes the categories that academicians identify for constitutional checks on governmental authority—namely, "internal" and "external" restraints. I do not propose (with some libertarians) that the states are restrained by internal limits on their police power. But I do argue that the Court's doctrinal demand that the states act rationally cannot be understood as an external restraint, either. Neither label is apt. Doctrinally speaking, substantive rights boil down to a general entitlement to be regulated in a rationally instrumental way.

I focus in chapter 3 primarily on individual rights (against both federal and state governmental power) associated with the Due Process Clauses of the Fifth and Fourteenth Amendments and the Equal Protection Clause of the Fourteenth. But I also turn to the freedom of expression and religion generally ascribed to the First Amendment and to the substantive rights identified with the Eighth Amendment's prohibition of cruel and unusual punishments. I do not contend that the Court never articulates doctrine in any other way. Additional doctrinal wrinkles sometimes appear. I do claim, however, that if we parse the Court's doctrinal accounts of substantive rights, we find that rational instrumentalism provides the basic organizational design throughout.

In chapter 4, the heart of my project, I explore the Court's use of rational instrumentalism to arrange the issues that demand resolution in actual cases. The Court does not simply sift the interests at stake *ad hoc,* but employs rational instrumentalism to capture salient considerations for serious judgment. The headings of the analysis are easy to state. The justices must characterize the governmental action said to violate substantive rights, they must specify the individual interests affected, and they must assess the purposes offered to explain and justify the resulting distribution of costs and benefits. But the task of working those matters out is exquisitely difficult. At every stage, the justices wrestle with deeper problems that, in turn, leave enormous space for reasonable debate. As the justices face those problems and settle disagreements by majority vote, they create the content of substantive individual rights.

This is no occasion for regret. The issues the justices address pursuant to these arrangements are the right issues, representing long-standing insights concerning governmental power. The Court has not often reached the results I would have preferred—I'm a McGovern Democrat—nor come within striking distance of my preferences. I *do* regret many of the decisions I examine in chapter 4, though I am quite pleased with some.

Yet if substantive rights lack the content they should have, it is not for want of better controls on the men and women who exercise judgment, but only for want of better judgment from the men and women charged with the responsibility of decision. The message in chapter 4 is that we had best pick justices wisely, because we will get only the rights they allow us.

CHAPTER ONE

The Documentary Constitution

There is a certain disharmony in modern thinking about the United States Constitution. In popular conception, the Constitution is a particular text. The original document is under glass at the National Archives. Copies can be found at various state houses on the East Coast and at the back of most high school civics books. Justice Black used to carry a paperback version around in his vest pocket. This text is taken to be the blueprint for the political system we have. Its legitimacy is accepted without question and with a fair dollop of religious zeal. David Strauss puts it well: "To many people, allegiance to the Constitution and a certain kind of respect for the Founding . . . are central to what it means to be an American."[1] The place of the written Constitution in this culture is so pervasive, so profound, that academicians, too, feel compelled to kiss the book. Daniel Farber and Suzanna Sherry acknowledge certain propositions that virtually everyone endorses as "little more than common sense." First among them is the idea that "[t]he Constitution is a written document, drafted in 1787 and ratified in 1789, with [twenty-seven] amendments [since]."[2] Ronald Dworkin declares, "We have a constitutional text. We do not disagree about which inscriptions comprise that text; nobody argues about which series of letters and spaces make it up."[3] But this is only partially true and, in the main, misleading. Michael Moore has explained that those inscriptions exist in a basic "syntactic" sense only as so many "uninterpreted symbols" in a string.[4] If they are to have meaning, we must impose it on them. That meaning, in turn, is not merely a creature of language and grammar—the logical structure that distinguishes lines that human beings deliberately draw on the page (or in the sand) from those left behind by the wind and the waves.

Most Americans may think that the document (as amended) *is* the Constitution. But among specialists the popular understanding of the Constitution is problematic. William Harris says that "the presumption that a political world can be constructed and controlled with words" is preposterous.[5] It is hard to think that a few scratches on ancient pages can bear the necessary weight. The goal of university education on the subject is to dispel the simplistic assumption that the document alone resolves tough questions. As a matter of experience, we have never derived answers to the really difficult problems of government *from* this old writing. We have come up with our own answers and then, at most, ascribed them *to* it. We have done this largely through judicial decision making.

The trend around the world is toward written constitutions, not away from them. Perhaps emerging nations can draft good documents and then manage visible current problems via some kind of interpretation in the near term. Law is historically contingent. We need to understand, though, that other nations have not typically adopted documentary constitutions that contemplate anything like American judicial review.[6] European constitutional courts, for example, are not part of the ordinary judicial system. They do not bring the text of their constitutions to bear on ordinary disputes and employ it as a rule of decision, nor do they purport to articulate and enforce constitutional meaning as a working feature of everyday public law. Those courts do not superintend legislatures routinely. By contrast, they address constitutional issues in a much more distant and abstract posture, clarifying the landscape for the kind of preeminent legislative policy making that has prevailed in Europe since Justinian.[7]

In any case, this country has moved beyond the capacity to make do with a document, certainly a document as old as ours. Not that we need a new one. We most certainly do not. We need the mettle to treat the one we have according to its real value as a cultural icon. The development of our constitutional system does not tell a negative, even tragic story— namely, that the Supreme Court willfully refuses to adhere to the written Constitution, that the Court fails to implement the intentions of those who wrote and adopted it, or that the written Constitution simply does not supply the answers we need. The development of this system tells a

positive story—namely, that we manage to resolve the vexing problems
that arise without discarding the formative document and what we know
of its history, and that we can make some rough peace with that document even though it does not really determine the decisions we make.

Constitutional Law

Academicians have a way of defusing tension by drawing nice distinctions. In this instance, the common strategy is to bow to the popular
equation of the document with the Constitution, but then to distinguish
the Constitution, in turn, from constitutional *law*.[8] Only constitutional
law is said to bear any genuine operational consequences in the world.
That law flows from judicial decisions owing very little, if anything, to
the Constitution itself.[9] Nevertheless, and however much exegesis is required to move from the text of the Constitution to judicial decisions
about the text, theorists insist that the warp and woof of constitutional
law is still traceable to the written document—and must be, given that
the document and only the document counts as the Constitution.[10]

But this is sophistry and a pernicious brand of sophistry in that it generates misunderstanding and distrust. Ordinary people accustomed to
the ordinary use of language expect, naturally enough, that if the document is the Constitution, it must fairly control any constitutional law the
Supreme Court announces. And if it doesn't, something is amiss. The
justices must be dishonest. They must fashion law on their own without warrant in the authentic Constitution and perhaps in defiance of it.
The charge of duplicity is unwarranted. The Supreme Court *does* make
up constitutional law. That law is not illegitimate but rather forms the
only genuine Constitution we have. The popular obsession with the text
of the document conceals this fundamental fact of life. Better to apply
more discipline to the exercise, to recognize that the writing typically
called the Constitution is not what it's cracked up to be, and to put it in
its proper place. The document has enormous cultural significance as a
symbol; its existence helps to perpetuate the United States as a continu-
ous political entity. But when real decisions must be made, it has about
as much influence as the flag.[11]

Richard Fallon has advanced a more appealing argument for distinguishing the Court's decisions according to doctrine from the Constitution itself. Building on Lawrence Sager's work, Fallon posits that the
Court's function is not to "interpret" the written Constitution, but rather

to "implement" its "values" or "norms."[12] To do that, the justices need not (and should not) attempt to delineate constitutional values precisely in every case, but they can (and should) create doctrinal rules that only approximate what the justices regard as the Constitution's true meaning. The resulting distance between the Court's doctrinal formulations and the Constitution allows for reasonable disagreements between the Court and other bodies (especially legislatures) and also among the justices themselves. Moreover, doctrinal rules can be constructed pragmatically; they can be comparatively clear, for example, and thus easier to apply consistently and economically. Striving for the effective implementation of constitutional norms, the Court employs doctrine that either under-estimates or overestimates the confining force of the Constitution itself.

Professor Fallon's basic thesis is sound: We can best understand the Supreme Court in light of its responsibility to effectuate constitutional meaning in actual cases. But consider two objections to the notion that there is some genuine light between what the Court says and does, on the one hand, and the true Constitution somewhere in the background, on the other. Fallon himself concedes that, if he is right, we would ex-pect the Court to take up the key questions *seriatim,* first determining the "meaning" of a constitutional norm and then fashioning an appro-priate doctrinal "test" to implement that norm. In the event, the Court typically starts with the doctrinal question and, having settled on a rule, never reaches the "meaning" question at all—or, Fallon also concedes, the Court concerns itself entirely with doctrine as though it is indistin-guishable from meaning. As Robert Nagel has explained, doctrine con-ceived only to "supplement" the Constitution becomes the only "author-itative" way in which the Constitution is "explained to the public." And once that happens, prevailing judicial opinions are "incompatible" with "maintaining the authority of the original text."[13] Realistically speak-ing, any space between judge-made doctrine and the Constitution disap-pears. We see only the one, and the other (assuming it exists at all) has only aspirational significance.[14]

The other objection is more conceptual. Fallon offers his descrip-tion of the Court's work largely to account for the wide discretion the justices obviously exercise. Evidently, in his view, that discretion would be hard to justify if they were actually interpreting the Constitution. If, however, the justices are performing as practical lawyers, fashioning and enforcing doctrine to implement constitutional values, they may be al-lowed more flexibility to develop workable rules. Fallon dismisses claims that we must deduce the constitutional system we have from the text of the document, informed by its history. He argues, by contrast, that the Court can draw on extratextual sources in fashioning doctrine. Yet in the final analysis he, too, insists that the documentary Constitution is the wellspring. His analogy is theatrical and Elizabethan; Hamlet cannot proceed without its prince.[15] But we have to update our thinking. Let's get on with it; there's no use waiting for Godot.

Explanations

It is not hard to think of reasons for the persistent attachment to the text hammered out in Philadelphia. As illustrations only, consider two overlapping possibilities. One is the common notion that, to be taken seriously, a Constitution must be a written document that fixes our most fundamental values for all time and thus offers certainty in a chaotic world. The other is the belief that those values were democratically selected and thus formed the crux of a social compact that rightly rules us to this day. Neither explanation is satisfying. The first proceeds from a demonstrably false premise and carries on to a hopelessly naive impression of the way the American Constitution actually operates. The second is a plain mistake of historical fact.

The Constancy of a Writing

Writings have a power all their own. When Sir Edward Coke set out to identify restraints on the royal prerogative, he cited Magna Carta as a species of fundamental law that even the king was obliged to respect. That characterization was fabricated; the Great Charter was actually a laundry list of concessions wrung from King John by wealthy landowners. But the strategy worked. According to Edward Corwin, Coke's use of Magna Carta is "accountable in some indeterminate measure for the American idea that the constitution ought to be embodied in a fundamental *document*."[16] The French Revolution generated a documentary constitution setting down the basic tenets of the new arrangements. Thomas Paine insisted that only a text of that kind could count as a constitution, which he understood to describe the written work of "the people *constituting* a government."[17] Paine regarded subsequent foundational documents drafted in the early American states as paradigmatic constitutions. When a question arose regarding the extent of governmental power, it was common for officials to "take the . . . [relevant state] [c]onstitution out of their pocket" and consult the pertinent provision.[18] By Paine's account, the document developed in Philadelphia was of the same nature and thus was properly understood to be the new nation's Constitution.

But this conception of the Constitution is more familiar than it is telling. Paine's interlocutor, Edmund Burke, explained that the term *constitution* was not a name for any particular document, but rather the label applied to the "constituent parts" of the state (in the case of England, the Crown and Parliament). Before the Philadelphia Convention, that had been the general understanding. A society's *constitution* simply identified the laws, institutions, and related arrangements of which the society was *constituted*.[19] Now then, Burke has much to answer for: his celebration of religion as the foundation of civil society, his endorsement of the divine and hereditary right of English kings to rule, his promotion of accumulated wealth in the hands of the few, and above all his disdain for common people and for the idea of government by the consent of the governed. All those views offend any modern democrat.[20] Nevertheless, at the level of language, Burke's conception of a constitution comported with reality more than did Paine's. Burke was not at a stand when Paine challenged him to "produce the English Constitution" in "visible form" and insisted that, if he could not, he must concede that no such constitution existed. A constitution need not be, as Paine had it, a "thing antecedent to a government," which can be held in one's hands and quoted "article by article" to settle basic disputes.[21] The American Constitution does not work that way, and we should not make believe that it does.

Of course, there is no higher law in England of the same character as our American Constitution. Parliament's enactments are supreme, and courts are bound to give them effect, whatever the consequences.[22] Our written Constitution is conventionally understood to be different. Recall Gladstone's explanation of the distinction between the English Constitution and our own: "The one is a thing grown, the other is a thing made."[23] John Marshall anchored the Supreme Court's authority to determine the American Constitution's meaning in part in the idea that the Court is both suited and obliged to interpret a writing.[24] And many academics insist that the physical character of the document is central to its very nature and authority. The point is not just that a piece of paper is easier to find. Nor is it that a document is necessarily easier to understand. The point is that a writing represents a definitive political act that tradition and institutions do not. There is a case to be made, then, that the English experience (certainly Burke's estimate of it) has little bearing on the framework in this country.

One should consider, too, that this first explanation of the written Constitution's appeal rests on an attractive vision: human beings disclaiming the notion that they were bound either by divine will or by traditions they were not entitled to alter.[25] Jed Rubenfeld contends that when Americans wrote the Constitution down on paper, they faced and resolved the most fundamental question of all, ever-present but long-evaded—namely, whether human beings *can* govern themselves over time.[26] By his account, a documentary Constitution demands allegiance to a particular set of values (however roughly articulated), while an unwritten tradition only solicits respect for the past and invites participation in an ongoing enterprise. Since the American Constitution is written, so the argument goes, constitutional meaning must be determinate, and its pursuit an exercise in discovery rather than invention.[27]

All this sounds pretty good. With Paine (and *contra* Burke), Americans respond to the compelling spectacle of their forebears sitting down together, throwing off the past, and formulating prescriptions for their own future. Small wonder, really, that the document's reputation is nothing less than heroic. Once the Constitution was a thing made, it became a thing done—and once done, it was done well enough to leave alone. On this point, recall Gladstone's outlandish declaration that "the American Constitution is . . . the most wonderful work ever struck off at a given time by the brain and purpose of man"—the more so if he cribbed the line from an American jurist (Justice William Johnson).[28] Thomas Grey, Sanford Levinson, and others have explored the way in which the document has assumed religious significance.[29] It is entitled to deference, no questions asked, after the fashion of commandments fresh down from the mountain. Paine described a state's constitution as its "political bible."[30] And remember the speech that made Barbara Jordan famous: "My faith in the Constitution is whole, it is complete, it is total."[31]

Trouble is, the romantic image of Philadelphia and the ratifying conventions has precious little connection to reality. Many of the operative ideas in the 1789 Constitution had obvious antecedents in previous state constitutions, which, in turn, leaned heavily on English law and practice. Professor McIlwain once characterized the early state constitutions as "far less doctrinaire or *a priori* than those of France or the rest of

continental Europe."[32] There is considerable evidence that many contemporaneous observers frankly conceived that the document drafted
in Philadelphia was not especially novel but carried forward earlier conceptions of fundamental law.[33] As Lawrence Lessig explains it, some
provisions were "transformative" inasmuch as they were meant to change
older practices, but many were "codifying" inasmuch as they perpetu-
ated preexisting ideas.[34] Early amendments also came bearing their own
history. Even Akhil Amar, who chiefly celebrates the adoption of the
document as the nation's defining act, allows that "[m]uch of the First
Amendment . . . simply textualized the Federalist party line."[35]

There is also evidence that the Constitution was meant to serve for an
unforeseeable future.[36] In order to survive as a nation, we required elas-
tic ideas and a fundamental law that permitted those ideas to flourish.
Thoughtful people understood that at the time.[37] Our best jurists always
have. Morton Horwitz cites Brandeis: the Constitution "must have a . . .
capacity of adaptation to a changing world."[38] And Benjamin Cardozo:
"[t]he great generalities of the constitution have a content and significance that vary from age to age."[39] Justice Scalia, for his part, objects
that the meaning of the Constitution does not change with evolutionary
movements in society, though its significance may be affected by other
species of law that can and often do shift over time.[40] But that argument
defies observed experience. The Court has always been creative in assigning meaning to the Constitution.[41] The long line of Supreme Court
decisions since the formative period attests to Arthur S. Miller's conclusion: "'the' Constitution is more unwritten than written."[42]

Certainly, no one should believe that substantive constitutional rights
depend on textual provisions that brought them into being and without
which they would not exist. Hamilton and James Wilson famously argued that the Bill of Rights was a bad idea inasmuch as it might be read
to preclude by inference rights that were not explicitly stated.[43] Yet we
have never attached that kind of exhaustive significance to what is or
is not on the list of rights described (roughly) in the first eight amendments.[44] If the First Amendment did not exist, we still would ascribe
protection for the freedom of speech to the Constitution. By the same
token, if something else is important enough, we attribute it to the Constitution in the absence of any obvious basis in the text.[45] The document
we keep under glass figures prominently in our political culture. But its
written character does not, of itself, make it the real, working American
Constitution.

It is natural enough to hunger for certainty and clarity in human affairs. Social problems are ineluctably vexing, and all of us want something solid and uncontestable on which to depend. A definitive writing with a fixed and unchanging text virtually demands to be taken as the source of the constancy we crave. The alternative, by contrast, is unsettling and even frightening. If we relax our collective grip on the written Constitution, we fear we will set ourselves adrift to sink or swim on our own. Yet certainty is an illusion.[46] Law is not language; it is judgment exercised by flesh-and-blood human beings. When we treat the document itself as the Constitution, and when we in turn ascribe the Court's decisions to that document, we again invite the suspicion that the real basis of hard decisions is being concealed. Michael Dorf has explained that the effort to pin constitutional meaning on the text and its history "merely disguises the role of subjective value choice" and offers only a "false promise of predictability."[47] Mark Tushnet has put it neatly. We cannot have a "Constitution with the politics left out."[48]

The Legitimacy of a Compact

The social compact explanation for the written Constitution's appeal is equally flawed. Recall the argument: The historical document *is* the Constitution because it represents commitments we Americans made at the time.[49] As Edward Corwin once put it, the document's "claim to obedience is due to its source in a sovereign will—that of the people."[50] Some important modern observers (Bruce Ackerman and Akhil Amar among them) also begin with the proposition that the document has genuinely popular roots.[51] By this account, we not only decided to strike off afresh, choosing the governmental system under which we would live and making the enterprise effective by setting everything down in a definitive writing, but we also adopted that writing by a show of hands. Once parties enter into a written agreement, we typically don't let them wriggle out of it on the ground that they really meant to make some other deal.[52] The written Constitution is commonly regarded in much the same way, at least metaphorically.[53] In this instance, the idea is not that one party should keep the promises he or she made to someone else. If we Americans made commitments in the form of the 1789 Constitution, we made them to ourselves. Still, the suspicion persists that we are obliged to carry on with undertakings we adopted in the past.

But if we propose to govern ourselves, then we must do it. We cannot routinely shirk responsibility for serious modern problems by consulting a document pasted together by an older generation. Nor can we make important decisions and then insist that we are not really to blame because our forefathers made us do it. Democratic self-government demands a great deal of hard work and serious judgment in the here and now. Of course, we *do* shoulder that heavy burden. We should own up to it by acknowledging the machinery we actually employ to arrive at constitutional meaning: largely Supreme Court decision making. Academicians may contend that the written Constitution does not really override democratic sentiment but reflects and promotes elevated democratic judgments by the founding generation. But no one has made the necessary case. And no one ever will.

To begin, it is imperative to acknowledge that the written Constitution was not created by democratic means. There is no sense in asserting that it was, far less sense in constructing a theory of its legitimacy on the basis of a demonstrable falsehood. The document's true origin is not something to be noted in passing, then ignored in favor of intellectual accounts of political responsibility meant to substitute for actual self-government. We need to be honest about this. The 1789 document was drafted at the Philadelphia Convention and adopted thereafter by state ratifying conventions. Thus it *appears* to have been forged in a politically legitimate manner. Yet the hard facts of the matter defy any such understanding. To speak very bluntly, the Constitution was drawn up and approved by comparatively wealthy white men, chosen for service by a larger body of comparatively wealthy white men (not women, not people of color, and for the most part not people who lacked property).

Akhil Amar portrays the founding generation as republican and democratic for its time. And he scores fair points in that cause.[54] Yet there is no case to be made that eighteenth-century American society was egalitarian in any modern sense. Gordon Wood has explained that the men who dominated political affairs were ambivalent about human equality. Politics was not for the masses, but was to be conducted by the elite few who competed among themselves for the "wealth, power, and prestige" that came with public office.[55] The delegates to the Philadelphia Convention were selected by state assemblies. The members of those bodies, in turn, were chosen pursuant to local schemes that notoriously restricted the franchise (in the main) to adult, white, male property owners. The "freeholder" qualification reflected a number of related attitudes traceable to England and the American colonies. Men with property had a

personal interest in political affairs that translated into sensible participation; men without it were less interested and therefore less responsible.[56] Men with property had an economic base that ensured their independence; men without it were necessarily dependent on their employers
and landlords and thus subject to influence and intimidation. Women
were dependent on men and, in any event, lacked sufficient experience
in worldly affairs to participate in elections. Slaves, freedmen of African
descent, Native Americans, Catholics, and Jews were incompetent voters on still other (similarly benighted) grounds. If men without property,
women, and members of other excluded groups needed representation,
white, male freeholders supplied it "virtually."[57]

Professor Amar may be right that the process by which the 1789 document was ratified was democratic by the standards of the day. The delegates in Philadelphia specified that it was to be referred to state legislatures, but only so that it could be routed on to conventions specially
empowered to consider it. Jack Rakove explains that the idea was essentially to bypass both Congress and state legislatures in order to put
the new Constitution to the comparative "popular sovereignty" of the
people themselves.[58] Yet restrictions were everywhere apparent. The
delegates to state conventions were confined to the singular "legal act of
ratification."[59] They were allowed only to vote up or down on the document as a whole and thus were denied the opportunity to consider particular provisions separately, to adopt amendments, and to engage each
other in debates over the final product. They *proposed* amendments, but
that was quite another thing. Most important, the delegates to the state
conventions were not elected democratically, but were chosen by the
same white males who voted in other elections.[60] Amar fairly notes that
some (he thinks most) states dropped or adjusted the usual property requirements for voting. But it is scarcely reassuring to us now that his best
illustration is New York, which "*temporarily* set aside its usual property
qualifications and, for the first time in its history, invited all *free adult
male citizens* to vote."[61] In any case, by the best guesses, eligible voters
made up only about 20 percent of the population; no more than half of
them actually voted, and nearly half of those who voted opposed ratification.[62] Moreover, electoral districts were typically gerrymandered so
that the delegates who won election did not command a majority of the
freemen who cast ballots.[63]

Even if the process had been democratic, the basic question would remain: Why must we adhere to a text that a distant generation created?[64]
The document itself proclaims in its preamble to speak for "We the

People of the United States." But nobody argues that we are obliged to submit to what the framers wrote and ratified simply because they *said* we should be.[65] Why, then, does this writing have such a stranglehold on our national psyche? Academics offer various answers to the legitimacy question.[66] Some simply lay it aside, assume that the document *is* authoritative, and proceed from there. Henry Monaghan, for example, regards the Constitution's authority as "our master rule of recognition," behind which only political theorists need go.[67] Others do much the same thing, though with less candor. Still others hope to defuse the tension between the historical document and modern choices (however they are made) by ascribing democratic *bona fides* to value judgments made in 1789, notwithstanding the way the written Constitution was promulgated. On examination, however, no such argument is ultimately persuasive.

Consider Jed Rubenfeld's proposal that the occasion calls for an adjustment in the definition of democracy.[68] In his view, we should set aside any suggestion that simple majoritarianism provides the standard, as well as the suspicion that the Constitution must be antidemocratic because it presumes to override current majoritarian choices. Rubenfeld insists that no society can exist and purport to be self-governing if everything is constantly open to *current* majoritarian sentiment, without regard for anything settled previously. Human arrangements of all kinds (including any intelligible conception of democracy) must contemplate understandings that persist from one generation to the next. Democracy, according to Rubenfeld, is not "governance by the present will of the governed," but, instead, "a people's living out of its own self-given political and legal commitments over time—apart from and even contrary to popular will at any given moment." When we adopted the written Constitution, accordingly, we necessarily rejected the notion that American democracy means simple majoritarianism in a constantly shifting present.[69]

Rubenfeld reefs his argument considerably where individual rights are concerned, thus making his position more practical. He distinguishes between historical understandings of the practices that constitutional rights *prohibited,* on the one hand, and historical understandings of the practices that rights did not proscribe, on the other, and contends that we devoted ourselves only to the former. Since rights were not historically understood to prohibit very much, our constitutional commitments were correspondingly few (though solid in what they were). Accordingly, Rubenfeld can accommodate modern decisions about individual rights with no serious connection to any thinking ascribable to the founding generation. Those decisions invariably contradict only historical notions about what rights did *not* foreclose—that is, ideas to which we were never pledged in the first place.[70]

There is something to "precommitment" accounts of the Constitution. Ulysses tied himself to the mast so that he might hear the sirens' song without responding to their spell.[71] He committed himself to a course of action for some period of time and deliberately surrendered any ability to change his mind for the duration. By the same token, we commit ourselves to understandings about law over time. We do not live by impetuous, minute-to-minute bursts of majoritarian whim. We certainly bind ourselves by statutes enacted by modern legislatures. And we respect those statutes the day after they are enacted and for years to follow, unless and until they are changed by the ordinary process. Then again, statutes can be amended or repealed by a simple majority. That's not true of the Constitution. Article V establishes extremely onerous requirements for formal amendments. In part because of the difficulty of adopting amendments, the Constitution bids well to rule us a lot longer.[72]

Moreover, Rubenfeld's argument depends on our acceptance of the idea that Americans exist as a "people" in an actual (not symbolic) sense and that we are the same "people" we were in 1789. The people who were alive then no longer are, but Rubenfeld insists that "we" are still "they."[73] There's the rub. We're not. As Michael Klarman counters, "[T]he Framers are not us," and "in most ways the Framers do not even remotely resemble us."[74] The notion that our generation is one and the same with the people residing in these same parts two hundred years ago rests not on genealogy, nor on any understanding of the historical evidence, but on ideology alone. As Paul Kahn puts it, this is the "organic model of political order"—the extrahistorical thesis that human beings are of a piece with the state.[75] At best, Rubenfeld brings the debate over legitimacy back full circle to the mechanisms by which the 1789 document was written and adopted—mechanisms that were undemocratic by any modern measure.

A Constitution Made by Judges

Of course, the legitimacy question arises with respect to constitutionalism in any form. Even if the Supreme Court is not seriously bound by the 1789 text (as amended), it is obviously open to ask why unelected, life-tenured judges can set at naught the policy preferences of a current

majority. Alexander Bickel famously called this conundrum the "countermajoritarian difficulty."[76] Not only does the existence of a higher law
defy majoritarian rule, but in the American system the justices who divine its meaning are insulated from political accountability. There is an
argument that any concern about the Supreme Court's undemocratic
nature is beside the point. We do not have a simple democracy but a
constitutional republic that seems, sensibly enough, to require an institution like the Court to police majoritarian excesses.[77] Nevertheless, many
mainstream academicians have never been persuaded that the Court's
great power can be reconciled with basic democratic principles.[78]

On this point, however, modern scholarship provides fair answers.
Numerous observers have challenged Bickel's focus on the Court as
an aberrant institution in American public life—an autocratic pig in
the democratic parlor. Barry Friedman has demonstrated that legal academics early in the last century typically condemned Supreme Court
decisions for frustrating social reforms instituted by democratic means.
Later, in the 1950s, Bickel and others worried that Warren Court decisions they approved (promoting personal liberties and condemning racial segregation) were subject to the same critique. That concentration
on the Court and its behavior, largely to the exclusion of anything else,
led them to an "obsession" with the Court's apparently antidemocratic
influence, whatever the results.[79] Friedman and others, among them
Christopher Eisgruber and James Fleming, argue that the Court is not
so undemocratic as it may seem.[80] Justices are nominated by the president, they must be confirmed by the Senate, and they can be removed
by impeachment. So they are subject to at least some form of democratic
influence. Moreover, as successive presidents and Senates install new ap-
pointees to the Court over time, a form of popular democracy periodi-
cally asserts itself, leavening the Court's status.[81]

Supreme Court justices obviously cannot do whatever they want without regard for the political repercussions. As a matter of experience, they
manage to retain strong public support, even though occasional decisions
are unpopular in some quarters.[82] Often, the statutes that the Court invalidates reflect outdated policies, so that the justices are not actually at
odds with legislators currently in office.[83] When the Court does confront
contemporaneous majoritarian sentiment, its decisions typically affect
only the fringes of popular programs.[84] Were the justices to set themselves against the politically accountable branches routinely, they would
lose credibility and respect. And at a point soon after that, their orders

would cease to be enforced. In a real fight with the other elements of the national government, not to mention the populace at large, no one would bet his lunch money on nine old people wearing robes.

In the end, then, the authority of the Constitution and the justices who elaborate its meaning is not to be found in the document's formation but in its longevity, in its persistence. The Constitution is legitimate because we accept it as legitimate—today, in the here and now, though certainly not unanimously and perhaps more implicitly than explicitly. Larry Alexander contends that the "Constitution and the preconstitutional rules that give it meaning are authoritative only because we have decided for the moment that they shall be."[85] Michael Dorf equally rests the Constitution's modern authority on its "general acceptance" today rather than on its "adoption in 1787."[86] And Richard Fallon argues that "the status of the Constitution as law depends on contemporary practices accepting it as such."[87] I want to insist, though, that the Constitution we embrace is (or ought to be) not the historical document and its amendments but the Constitution we have forged anew in Supreme Court decisions. If legitimacy is implicit, then it must be found so in light of the real, working Constitution with which we actually live.

Textualism

The popular understanding that the historical document *is* the American Constitution at least implies that we can (and must) derive constitutional meaning via an interpretation of its text. After all, there are lots of documents to which we might look for guidance in establishing a governmental system and ordering our affairs under that system. If we seize upon this one exclusively as *the* Constitution, that judgment itself seems logically to entail making the text central to the analysis.[88] Even so, it is a mistake to think we can resolve serious constitutional questions simply by reading the text of the historical document. The problem at this level is not only that the characterization of the document as *the* Constitution is contestable, though that is reason enough to worry. It is also that the attempt to milk the text for the constitutional meaning we need is bound to be unsuccessful. It won't work, it has never worked, and we ought to stop insisting that it can work.

Textualism has had its ups and downs. Supreme Court justices have long insisted that the document *does* deliver answers to difficult problems. John Marshall explained that the Court's role was only to give the explicit "words" used by the Constitution their "natural" meaning.[89] There was a time a few years ago when many academics took a quite different view. Theorists that Thomas Grey called "non-interpretivists" owned that the Constitution depends on materials quite apart from the historical document.[90] Today, the "non-interpretivist" label is no longer in fashion. Grey himself disclaims it.[91] Once again, academics typically prefer to be regarded as "interpretivists"—most of them merely to acknowledge that they include the written document in their account of constitutional law,[92] some to convey the stronger message that the text is the exclusive source of constitutional meaning.[93] The most aggressive textualists are willing to consult external materials (like dictionaries) only insofar as they help to define the terms found in the document.[94] The reason for the turn back to the text is apparent. The current Court has declared its allegiance to the idea. Justice Scalia, in particular, insists that "the text is the law, and it is the text that must be observed."[95] Other justices are less adamant. Yet they, too, often purport to draw substantially more meaning from the text than the language can supply. Academicians accordingly feel compelled to credit textualism, notwithstanding its many and obvious shortcomings.

Caveat. There is a way in which textualism is (or can be) a formal analytical methodology, divorced from the origins of the text itself and from its authors. Lay aside the lessons of postmodernism and consider the strongest form of textualism in this legal context: Once the document to be interpreted is identified, it does not matter (or matters comparatively little) what anyone thought, or wanted, or hoped the law would be. It only matters what the law actually *is*. And we get *that* from the text we find within the four corners of the document formally adopted *as law*. On this basis, we can ignore all manner of evidence apart from the text, as well as any evidence of the meaning that anyone historically attached *to* the text. I want to be clear that this purist position is *not* common among advocates of a textualist approach to the written Constitution. By contrast, even the most dedicated proponents of the textualist creed think it only sensible to pay some attention to the people responsible for creating the 1789 document (and its amendments).[96] After all, to wrench the document away from the understandings of the drafters, the ratifiers, and the rest of the founding generation, is to exacerbate the tension between the Constitution and democracy. Those people may not have acted democratically. But it is a real threat to modern democracy to insist that the text of a particular document, existing apart from any decision-making process attributable to American politics, must somehow be respected as a higher form of law that vanquishes all in its path.[97]

Textualists, accordingly, are also "originalists."[98] In their view, the text of this document *is* the Constitution for the good and sufficient reason that it was written and adopted as it was by the "framers" acting for the community of which they were a part. Without that historical pedigree, the document would surrender its legitimacy.[99] Thus does textualism lead back to the discussion of the Constitution's democratic *bona fides* we just went through. Concomitantly, the Supreme Court scarcely ignores historical materials retrieved from the founding period. In company with their avowed adherence to the text, the justices routinely seize on evidence of that order, such as it is, as additional support for their decisions. I hasten to say that any attempt to read the document, its specific provisions, and its amendments in light of "original understanding" is problematic on independent grounds. But let me postpone discussion of those problems for now.

In the following pages, I sketch the numerous reasons why the text itself is an inadequate basis on which to explain the Constitution we actually have. I note, first, that the text fails to address some of the most important questions we face and speaks to others only vaguely. Then I argue that the terms found in the text bear no fixed meaning on which we can rely to resolve practical problems. Next, I show that the text of the written Constitution resists techniques devised for statutory construction. I demonstrate that it is untenable to infer constitutional meaning from the general political program outlined by the text and equally infeasible to interpret individual textual provisions by reference to others. Finally, I show that the text plays no serious, dispositive role in the Supreme Court's work. By contrast, the Court makes decisions on the basis of its own judgment about the most desirable results.

Yawning Gaps

The text of the written Constitution does not so much as acknowledge some of the most significant questions we have. In the great *Marbury* case,[100] for example, John Marshall conceded that nothing in the text speaks to the question whether the Supreme Court is empowered to decide what the Constitution means. Most modern observers agree, Justice Scalia among them.[101] The implications are significant. After all, the great body of judicial decisions on which we rely to settle constitutional questions depends on the premise that the Court is empowered to speak for the Constitution.[102] Notice, by the way, that it would scarcely make things easier if there *were* a provision in the Constitution specifying that the Court has the final say about the document's meaning. A provision like that would pose the same problem at a different level. We would still have to determine who gets to decide what that provision means. And if there were a provision specifying the Court for duty, we would still have to determine who gets to decide what that additional provision means. And so on.

Putting aside the "who decides" question, we might say (or maybe hope) that the text of the document addresses most other important matters and leaves us to worry about comparative details. But it is easier to argue precisely the opposite. David Strauss points out that on the rare occasions when the text *does* speak with sufficient specificity actually to drive results, it does so only with respect to the most trivial matters.[103] For example, a person must be thirty-five years of age to be president, and it takes two witnesses to obtain a conviction for treason.[104] The implicit point is not that it is crucial that we use those criteria. Quite the contrary. It's that we need *some* criterion in each instance, and the Constitution simply selects something suitable rather than squander time arguing over the best rule. There may be historical reasons why these two tests were adopted.[105] Yet the functional point of their specificity is apparent: clarity and efficiency regarding minutiae that do not warrant heroic effort to sort out. When, however, it comes to genuinely vital affairs, the Constitution is at best opaque and usually mute. Article I says nothing about congressional power to create an air force, but no one argues today that the Strategic Air Command is unconstitutional. The illustrations run on, and it appears once again that the text is doing no work when really significant problems must be resolved. In the end, then, we are left to find our own way without any fixed constitutional waypoints.

It is no good contending that textualism can work at least when the text itself invites attention to external materials. The example usually thrown up is the tired old Ninth Amendment, which proclaims that the "enumeration" of "certain" rights is not to be construed to foreclose "others retained by the people." Historians battle generally over what the Ninth Amendment was meant to achieve and specifically over what to make of "other" rights not "enumerated" in the Constitution.[106] By some accounts, we can be true to that particular amendment only if we identify extratextual rights and enforce them. But that argument is circular; it uses text as an excuse for ranging beyond the text. If we recognize and implement rights that are not "enumerated" in the Constitution (necessarily without guidance from any text), we cannot seriously propose that we are vindicating the text itself. This is why most committed textualists resist the attempt to draw any meaning at all from the Ninth Amendment. Remember Robert Bork's quip that we ought to treat that piece of text as though it were obscured by an ink blot.[107]

Nor can we produce the meaning we need from the text by combining its provisions with background themes that are not themselves explicitly stated. According to some theorists, the text of the Constitution may be understood to further political and philosophical values like democratic self-government, individual liberty, or the institution of private property. So the text may take meaning from yet other ideas not expressly articulated. This is ground over which countless battles have been fought in the last half century. The problem (the unavoidable and intractable problem) is that if we posit larger considerations that are not themselves prescribed by the text and assign meaning to the textual provisions we do have in the light of those ideas, we cannot remain true to textualism at all. Instead, we must abandon any genuine attempt to find meaning in the words actually contained in the document.

Vague and Ambiguous Terms

The spare terms to be found in the text of the documentary Constitution are not self-defining and thus cannot in themselves make arguments more analytically rigorous. Of course, the document provides at least some vocabulary in which to carry on public discourse. There is value in that, to be sure.[108] And no one seriously argues that words are conceptually unable to constrain choice.[109] Yet when a controversial interpretation is proposed, proponents and opponents alike can typically summon support from vague and ambiguous constitutional words and phrases, both sides insisting that the text (if not God) is on their side.[110] Consider, too, that the meaning of language can vary over time. A strict textualist might well insist on current definitions of constitutional terms.[111] Others, including Justice Scalia, prefer the definitions that were in place when those terms were inserted in the text.[112] Of course, that way lies originalism—a discussion I am postponing for the moment. Lawrence Lessig proposes to treat terms employed in the eighteenth century as belonging essentially to another language that must be translated for modern purposes.[113]

Even when the justices agree on the meaning of constitutional terms, they cannot use those terms successfully as operational legal standards for resolving cases. We learned that when the Court tried to explain its decisions as logical deductions from formal categories tracking constitutional terms like "Commerce . . . among the several States."[114] Today, the scope of Congress's power to regulate interstate commerce has little to do with the text of the Commerce Clause. The real explanation rests on a different, and much better, foundation. We have come to realize that in a system that purports to be democratic, economic policy is best left to politically accountable legislatures, even when federalism values are also at stake.[115] This understanding may not always produce satisfying outcomes. But we would hardly anticipate better results if judges were to try to determine as a constitutional matter whether and when wealth redistribution should occur. Painful experience explains the uproar over the suggestion in recent decisions that federal regulation can be confined (in some way or other) according to whether the activities to be regulated are, by nature, "commercial."[116] As we say in the American League, it's déjà vu all over again.

The Analogy to Statutes

Nor can we interpret constitutional terms in the same way we construe modern statutory language. Consider in this vein, Justice Scalia's contention that the interpretive goal is the same in both contexts and, moreover, that his own methodology for reading statutes supplies an explanation for taking the text of the documentary Constitution as the only source of constitutional meaning.[117] Scalia proceeds from the premise that a statutory text represents a compromise between adversaries in the legislative arena.[118] It often is not clear what that compromise was, and in many cases it is impossible to tell.[119] So a court should assume that a deal was struck and that the text of the enacted statute captures it. Then the court should give effect to the literal statutory language out of respect for the bargained-for policy it is assumed to represent. The bare terms of a statute may draw their meaning from external sources specifying generally accepted definitions—like, for example, dictionaries. But once defined by the lights of the relevant community (in the case of a statute, the legislature itself and the modern body politic for which it acts), statutory terms must be enforced as they stand.[120] On a parity of reasoning, Justice Scalia has it that if a constitutional provision is precise enough, the Supreme Court should interpret it literally on the same theory. The text of the historical document should simply be given the meaning it had in the relevant community (here, the framers and the founding generation as a whole).[121]

There are undeniable crosscurrents between the tasks of ascribing meaning to statutes, on the one hand, and identifying constitutional meaning, on the other. A realistic account of the way legislatures behave certainly has implications for constitutional analysis of any ilk, including (and especially) the Supreme Court's insistence that government must act rationally. I turn to those implications in chapter 4.[122] For now, suffice it to say that Justice Scalia's dogged textualism with respect to statutory construction is intensely controversial in its own country and that, transported to the business of attaching meaning to the written Constitution, his methodology is more dissatisfying still.[123] Everyone recognizes that the delegates in Philadelphia were engaged in politics, and most of us believe (or hope) they were doing serious deals.[124] Yet it is far from clear that those compromises are entitled to respect as the work of genuine law-makers. One need only recall that the ratifying conventions were not allowed to amend the document as drafted but had to vote it up or down in its entirety. That means, of course, that the conventions had no chance to negotiate over the details of particular provisions. Even if discrete provisions represented bargained-for settlements, those deals were made back in Philadelphia by the men who drafted the Constitution—not in the conventions where it was adopted into law. So it is a real reach to propose that the verbiage in the Constitution reflects underlying compromises with democratic credentials worthy of respect, such that the constitutional text is entitled to be enforced strictly according to its terms.[125]

The Text Writ Large

The strategy of inferring constitutional meaning from the general governmental framework established by the document also comes up short. The written Constitution does describe the basic elements of the political system we have, primarily by identifying the three branches of the Federal Government and by acknowledging (less specifically) a continuing role for the states. The independent executive branch distinguishes the

American scheme from a parliamentary system; the autonomous states distinguish our arrangements both from a traditional confederation of independent nations and from a centralized government operating through regional arms. Most observers think there is at least something to be gleaned from that basic configuration. Chief Justice Marshall engaged in structural analysis in the opinion widely regarded as his best, *McCulloch v. Maryland*.[126] Charles Black promoted a variant of that analysis.[127] Others, including Philip Bobbitt and Richard Fallon, have explored its features in some detail.[128]

But understand that decisions grounded in the political architecture outlined in the document are scarcely interpretations of its text at all. The Supreme Court's decisions on conflicts among the branches of the Federal Government, and equally its decisions on the relations between the Federal Government and the states, rest on ideas like the "separation of powers" and "federalism," which are only inferences from structure — better said, labels the Court itself supplies for themes the justices find implicit in the document. The justices admit as much. In *CFTC v. Schor,*[129] where the question was whether Congress had shoved independent federal courts aside in favor of an agency subject to political control, Justice O'Connor declined to rest judgment on the "language of Article III" alone.[130] And in *Printz v. United States,*[131] where the question was whether Congress had dragooned state officers into enforcing federal policy, Justice Scalia acknowledged that he had "no constitutional text" at all to work with.[132] My favorites are *Seminole Tribe*[133] and *Alden v. Maine,*[134] where there *was* an apparently applicable piece of text (the hapless Eleventh Amendment), but the justices explicitly set it aside in favor of a structural analysis they preferred. As a result, we have to suffer "state sovereign immunity" not because of the text of the documentary Constitution, but in spite of it. You have to love it: Chief Justice Rehnquist disclaiming "blind reliance" on the text that he and others typically purport to interpret.[135]

The Text in Context

It doesn't help to combine the strategy of drawing inferences from general structural arrangements with attempts to find meaning in particular constitutional terms. Textualist theorists under this heading contend that the trick is to read specific provisions not in isolation, but in company with others scattered through the full document. But that trick is tricky. It is one thing to assume that the political architecture framed by the Constitution must have some coherence: a national government with three branches living under the same roof with individual states having some measure of autonomy. It is another thing to assume that particular provisions bearing substantive content are integral to a single pattern. Each provision may be the result of a compromise unto itself, with no link to other provisions representing different bargains. Many provisions have no obvious intellectual connection with others but appear simply to be strung together by a single numbering system. Those provisions might well be read as atomistic units. The age requirement for becoming president and the two-witness rule for treason trials again provide illustrations. If we have provisions like that in mind, the document looks not like a skein of interrelated micro-compromises that together form a single macro-bargain, but like a basket of numerous, self-contained deals.

Akhil Amar insists that this won't do. His argument is simple: since the ratifying conventions had to accept the document in its entirety, the specific provisions of which it is comprised must have some unity.[136] But it is that argument that won't do. The take-it-or-leave-it way the document was presented to the ratifying conventions proves only that the conventions were forced to accept the provisions in the document *en masse*. It may be (I say it *may* be) that the drafters in Philadelphia thought the various elements of the document fit together in some way, but the men who voted it into law only bought the compilation, whatever its contents. It also may be, then, that the only macro-compromise represented is an implicit agreement to make this particular set of micro-compromises (reached back in Philly), none of which is necessarily linked to any other except in the sense that they all won acceptance as part of the package.[137]

Most observers treat the document as a single, integrated enterprise. Raoul Berger once said that "only a tyro" would do otherwise.[138] This, of course, is the kind of thing we associate with the civil law tradition.[139] Chief Justice Marshall took the holistic approach to the Constitution in *McCulloch*.[140] Recall his argument that the term *necessary* in the Necessary and Proper Clause could not mean "*absolutely* necessary," because the phrase "absolutely necessary" appears elsewhere (in a provision limiting the states' authority to levy duties on imports).[141] In order to give meaning to the "absolutely" modifier when it is used explicitly, Marshall explained that he could not read the Necessary and Proper Clause to be equally absolutist without it. John Ely picked up this kind of textualism,[142] and Professor Amar has pressed it to exhaustive lengths.[143] There are important limits to this interpretive technique. Adrian Vermeule and Ernest Young have pointed out, for example, that we cannot depend exclusively on supposed connections between provisions. We have to begin with some baseline view of a particular provision in order to be in a position to test whether that provision, so understood, is linked in some way to others.[144]

The real risk is that, assuming the document may sensibly be read as a unit, there is a tendency to go overboard with the idea. It is frankly unpersuasive to insist (as Professor Amar does insist) that the discrete provisions of the Constitution are not only reconcilable but are rigorously interconnected such that any and all elements of the text necessarily have some meaning consistent with the whole, and none is superfluous or, certainly, in conflict with the rest. Amar identifies numerous connections among ostensibly disparate provisions, always on the assumption that the document (and its amendments) form a coherent whole and, accordingly, that the meaning assigned to any particular clause must be established contextually. In his hands, constitutional interpretation resembles nothing so much as solving a jigsaw puzzle.[145] John Marshall's associations are hard enough to accept; Amar's meticulous cross-references, harder still. Human beings are imperfect, and the things they write often show it. Jack Rakove dismisses the idea that all the Constitution's "clauses were carefully framed and considered."[146] And he must be right. Even the French acknowledge that formal legal texts cannot possibly cover every contingency and that when judges fill in fissures they cannot simply apply logical rules of grammar but necessarily exercise their own independent judgment.[147] We don't expect perfection from other kinds of writings, and it makes little sense to expect it of this one.[148]

The written Constitution is a text, not a code; it is not a model of perfection and, in fact, reflects demonstrable drafting errors. Were we to apply rigorous grammatical rules to the Seventeenth and Twenty-Sixth Amendments, we would conclude that the one specified the direct election of senators only for six years following its adoption and that the other withdrew the citizenship of anyone under the age of eighteen.[149] At least, we may observe that Marshall's analysis in *McCulloch* was expedient. By declining a most inconvenient absolutist definition of *necessary,* he produced an account of congressional power that is genuinely workable. When Professor Amar engages his "intratextualism," he sometimes reaches conclusions that are neither convenient nor even plausible. He contends, for example, that since Article I comes before Article III, we can be sure that legislative power is prior to judicial authority in the different (and mightily important) sense that democratic politics forms the general foundation for the system. At least, in Amar's view, Congress is "first among equals."[150]

Whatever connections might exist among the provisions in the original document, the amendments necessarily alter the picture. They typically were adopted at different historical junctures, invariably speak to particular matters of interest at the moment, and do not (necessarily) share anything much in common with provisions already in place.[151] They may, of course, fortify some plausible sense of unity, but they may just as easily unseat earlier bargains, such as they were, by explicitly changing the constitutional treatment of the topics they address. It is when Professor Amar turns to amendments that his connect-the-dots approach goes to *really* implausible extremes. Amar argues, for example, that the Second Amendment (adopted in 1791 and having something to do with local militia and the "right to bear arms") teams up with the Nineteenth (adopted in 1920 and giving women the vote) to bar local police departments from discriminating on the basis of sex when choosing recruits.[152] Surely a more conventional analysis is far more persuasive. The Supreme Court would reach the same result in reliance on the Equal Protection Clause and, in so doing, would turn to rational instrumentalism as the core idea at work. In the end, it is futile to view the written Constitution as a perfectly elegant treatment of all that it covers—with a place for everything and everything in its place.

Negative Examples

Most telling, the Supreme Court only pretends to invoke the text of the historical document as the source of constitutional meaning and actually decides hard cases on the basis of pragmatic judgment. This is perfectly clear in decisions implicating individual rights that the written Constitution is said to vouchsafe. The Bill of Rights identifies various protections to which individuals are entitled, most of them procedural safeguards in criminal prosecutions. Yet a glance at the decisions in point reveals that the resolution of practical problems is the product of human judgment rather than deductions from textual language. When the text is invoked at all, it is almost always as make-weight. And even then it typically triggers a debate among the justices over the alternative interpretations available. The very existence of that debate demonstrates, in turn, both that the text supplies no definitive answer and that the Court's result actually rests on extratextual considerations over which the justices are also divided. Consider three Fourth Amendment cases.

In *Anderson v. Creighton*,[153] a private citizen sued an FBI agent for searching his home without a warrant. The agent responded, first, that the warrantless search was valid and, second, that even if the search was unconstitutional, he was entitled to immunity. On the question of immunity, Justice Scalia readily agreed that a law enforcement officer cannot be held liable for a violation of the Fourth Amendment if, at the time, he might reasonably have believed his actions were lawful. The plaintiff objected that it makes no sense to recognize immunity for "reasonable" violations of the Fourth Amendment, which itself protects citizens from "unreasonable" police behavior. Justice Scalia took the point. By his account, the agent could escape liability if his actions were "'reasonably unreasonable.'"[154]

Scalia explained, however, that the awkward idea of being reasonable and unreasonable at the same time is a function of the "*circumstance* that the Fourth Amendment's guarantees [are] expressed in terms of "'unreasonable' searches and seizures." If, by contrast, the Fourth Amendment had employed another "equally serviceable" term, the plaintiff's argument would disappear. Justice Scalia suggested, for example, that the Fourth Amendment might have barred "undue" searches and seizures, and, if it had, there would be no great difficulty conceiving that an officer might reasonably have concluded that a search was not "undue" in some particular context. Come to that, Scalia offered that the Due Process Clause might just as well have prescribed "*reasonable* process of law" rather than "due process." The terms in the constitutional text are not critical. "The fact is," Justice Scalia explained, "*regardless of the terminology used,* the precise content of most of the Constitution's civil-liberties guarantees rests upon *an assessment* of what accommodation between governmental need and individual freedom is *reasonable*."[155] Hold this thought. You will never find a more honest and accurate account of the "content" of substantive individual rights. Justice Scalia himself knows perfectly well that rights do not come from constitutional text. When he is honest about it, he says so.

In *United States v. Verdugo-Urquidez*,[156] federal agents conducted a warrantless search of a Mexican citizen's residence in Mexico. Writing for the Court, Chief Justice Rehnquist sustained their actions against a Fourth Amendment challenge. Initially, he explained that the Fourth Amendment explicitly protects "the people" and that the Constitution elsewhere uses that same phrase (that is, "the people") as a "term of art" connoting the "class of persons who are part of a national community or who have otherwise developed sufficient connection with this country to be considered part of that community."[157] While other provisions of the Bill of Rights extend protections to "persons" and thus may be available to aliens outside the country, the Fourth Amendment is more limited. Other justices rejected any such textual argument out of hand. Justice Kennedy (whose vote was necessary to the result in *Verdugo-Urquidez*) explained that he put no weight on "the people" as a restriction on the Fourth Amendment's reach and, by contrast, insisted that "the people" actually underscores that the Fourth Amendment, once adopted, extended well beyond the individuals who, as American citizens, "brought" the Constitution "into being."[158] Other members of the Court added their own explanations of the text.[159]

It seems clear that the Court would have reached the same result in *Verdugo-Urquidez* apart from the textual argument the Chief Justice offered. At least some precedents supported that result, and most of the justices agreed that it would be hard to administer the ordinary warrant requirement in a foreign country. Most important, the justices worried aloud about the next case—when they would be asked to force federal military authorities to adhere to Fourth Amendment standards and thus to be subject to judicial supervision with respect to the execution of foreign policy. This last was surely decisive. The *Verdugo-Urquidez* case was not about the text of the Constitution; it was about the justices' acceptance of the proposition that "the political branches" should be allowed to determine the standards that should govern search-and-seizure activities incident to the exercise of "armed" American "force" abroad.[160]

This same essential policy analysis is also dispositive on rare occasions when the text is ostensibly clearer. In *Groh v. Ramirez*,[161] a federal agent searched a private home on the strength of a warrant that failed to identify the items the officer was authorized to look for and seize. Writing for the Court, Justice Stevens started with the text and declared the warrant "plainly invalid," because the Fourth Amendment "states *unambiguously*" that "'no Warrant shall issue but upon probable cause, . . . and *particularly describing . . . the persons or things to be seized.*'"[162] Yet Justice Stevens did not stop there. He immediately went on to explain

that the "particularity" requirement has purposes: to provide the officer with clear guidance regarding his authority, to reassure the person
whose home is invaded that the officer is operating under the strictures
of law, and to supply reviewing courts with a paper record they can use
to determine whether the officer stayed within bounds. It is for those
reasons, not the text of the Fourth Amendment alone, that the Court
insists in *Groh* and other cases that warrants must name the items to be
seized. The Court would demand particularity (or something very much
like it) even if the Fourth Amendment were less explicit than it is—thus
to make the warrant requirement itself intelligible.

Justice Thomas and Justice Scalia dissented in *Groh*. On their different reading of the Fourth Amendment, the warrant's *existence* was
sufficient to make the search "reasonable," notwithstanding its lack of
specificity. The agent had told the magistrate what he was after, the magistrate had found cause to issue the warrant, the officer had explained to
the homeowner what he was doing, and, in fact, had limited the search to
places where the evidence might be found. In the final analysis, Thomas
and Scalia thought the purposes of the particularity requirement were
served well enough. Thus *Groh,* too, turned on the justices' assessments
of the interests at stake. Both sides began their arguments as reduc-
tions from text, but ended up somewhere else.[163] There are, to be sure,
instances in which the justices purport to rest judgment exclusively on
the Fourth Amendment's text. In a follow-on to *Groh, United States v.
Grubb,*[164] Justice Scalia's opinion for the Court approved a warrant con-
ditioned on a contingent event (the arrival of an incriminating package
at the suspect's home) and explained his result solely on the ground that
the Fourth Amendment neither prohibits anticipatory warrants generally nor requires that the contingent event be specified. In *Groh,* however, all the justices concurred, and there was no serious, policy-oriented
debate. Even at that, three justices warned that in cases presenting different facts, they might have constitutional qualms, notwithstanding
their interpretation of the warrant clause.[165]

Most of the time, the Court turns immediately to its precedents and
purports either to conform to what it has done in the past or to build
upon the past as needed for the case at hand. This is generally true in
the Fourth Amendment context and in other contexts, as well. A recent
Sixth Amendment case, *United States v. Gonzalez-Lopez,*[166] is but one
example among legions. The government acknowledged that the Sixth
Amendment generally entitles a defendant in a federal criminal prosecu-

tion to select his or her own lawyer (provided the defendant is able to pay the attorney's fees) and conceded that the trial judge below had violated that right. Nevertheless, the government contended that the resulting conviction did not have to be reversed in the absence of evidence that the error had prejudiced the defendant in some way. Writing for the Court, Justice Scalia held that no showing of prejudice was necessary. The right to choose one's own attorney, he explained, is not merely one of various procedural safeguards that together comprise the right to a fair trial. It is a free-standing individual right whose violation commands relief even if the right-holder receives effective representation from a different lawyer. Justice Scalia did not justify the decision in *Gonzalez-Lopez* on the basis of the Sixth Amendment's text—for the obvious reason pressed by Justice Alito in dissent. The Sixth Amendment does not say that a defendant gets to choose his own defense counsel, but only that he is entitled to "have the Assistance of Counsel for his defence."[167] Justice Scalia relied, instead, on the Court's own precedents. Those precedents were uncontested on their own ground, but (as usual) had to be extended to accommodate the problem in the case at hand.[168]

There are also instances in which the Court frankly ignores the text even as a starting point. Consider another case in which the justices were unanimous. In *Holmes v. South Carolina*,[169] a curious state procedural rule barred a criminal defendant from introducing evidence tending to show that someone else had committed the offense of which he was charged. Justice Alito upset the conviction on the straightforward ground that the accused in a criminal case is constitutionally entitled to "present a complete defense." That result was hardly remarkable. Nor was it remarkable (really) that Alito was indifferent to the source of the defendant's right. He said that it might flow from the Compulsory Process Clause or the Confrontation Clause, or it might arise "directly" from the Due Process Clause. But it mattered not. The right existed, and Justice Alito expressed it in instrumental terms: the state's rule prohibiting the defendant from offering his proof was "arbitrary" in that it advanced no "legitimate interests."[170]

The indeterminacy of the constitutional text is still more obvious with respect to the substantive rights on which I focus in this book: the amorphous rights associated with the two Due Process Clauses, one in the Fourteenth Amendment and the other in the Fifth; the Equal Protection Clause of the Fourteenth; the Free Speech and Religion Clauses in the First Amendment; and the Cruel and Unusual Punishment Clause in the Eighth. The vague and ambiguous terms in those provisions defy any definitive interpretation. The Court must *give* them meaning and, in so doing, must do something more than simply enforce them as written. I explain in chapter 3 that the Court has created the content of those rights via common law decision making and invariably offered rational instrumentalism as the guiding doctrine for the exercise of case-by-case judgment.

It may seem harmless enough if the Supreme Court seasons constitutional decisions with references to the language in the written Constitution. It may even be worthwhile to salute the documentary evidence we have that this is a continuing nation with a history, not a new one born every time we decide to make an adjustment. Paul Brest once quipped that arguing that a modern Supreme Court decision on a constitutional question rests on the 1789 document is rather like claiming that one of your ancestors came over on the Mayflower.[171] Yet it is deceptive and dysfunctional to pretend that Supreme Court decisions are genuinely interpretations of the written Constitution. They are not.

Originalism

The written Constitution is not made more serviceable if interpreted according to "original understanding." Many—I could safely say most—academics disparage the originalist project on a variety of grounds.[172] If history is to be consulted at all, one should think it must be the whole of our experience both before and since the document was adopted.[173] Yet originalism has always had some purchase on American thinking.[174] Even as John Marshall insisted that his task was to interpret the Constitution as written, he frequently considered extratextual materials as well, in part on the theory that they reflected original intentions helpful to an accurate understanding of the text.[175] I have already explained that modern textualists allow for some attention to the "framers" or the "founding generation" in order to justify the written document as *the* Constitution, entitled to be enforced as law.[176] There is a way, accordingly, in which textualism and originalism form a package that many Americans find irresistible.

Like textualism, originalism has had its peaks and valleys. A century ago, the Supreme Court explicitly disclaimed any attempt to read the Constitution this way.[177] More recently, originalism has enjoyed a resurgence, primarily because critics of the Warren Court adopted it as their methodology of choice.[178] The current Court often purports to give the constitutional text its original meaning. Justice Scalia, foremost of the Court's textualists, is equally committed to originalism. Scalia acknowledges the many pitfalls I am about to outline, but he insists nonetheless that originalism is a better bet than the alternatives, especially as a mechanism for constraining the power of unelected judges.[179]

I confess that I do not understand the staying power that originalism enjoys despite the powerful and, I should have thought, telling critiques that have appeared in print. Yet staying power it has in the minds of respected specialists.[180] So this kind of thinking about the Constitution must be engaged yet again. There is a large literature in point, and I cannot survey it all.[181] I describe the two principal forms that originalism currently takes and outline the reasons why neither offers a satisfying methodology for arriving at constitutional meaning by interpreting the written Constitution in historical context. Then I offer some illustrations of the Supreme Court's actual decision making—illustrations demonstrating that the Court only appears to invoke originalist methodology but, in truth, resolves constitutional questions on the basis of the justices' own sense of sound policy.

The Framers

The first general category of originalism holds (broadly speaking) that the written Constitution can and must be interpreted according to the understanding of its authors, called collectively (and ambiguously) the "framers." This is the brand of originalism we associate with Chief Justice Marshall, Chief Justice Rehnquist, Justice Scalia (on most occasions), at least some of the other justices now sitting (some of the time), and a coterie of academics.[182] Originalists of this sort take the text alone to be dispositive where its meaning is "plain."[183] But in the usual case in which the text is unclear, they insist that it should be interpreted in light of the meaning its authors assigned to it.[184] The task is to "enter the minds" of the framers, "see the world as they saw it," and "understand" that world in "their own terms."[185] By this account, there is no conflict between originalism and textualism; together, the two form a happy partnership. Recall that one of the difficulties with the most aggressive form of textualism is that it treats language in the abstract, divorced from those who wrote it. This version of originalism hopes to defuse that problem by taking the framers' intentions as evidence of the meaning of the text.[186]

This is not to say that originalists in this camp try to imagine how historical individuals would have resolved a modern constitutional question. Justice Thomas sometimes talks as though he sees his job that way,[187] but others take a more global approach. The Constitution is more than a list of its applications in situations that the framers had in mind or could envision. The originalist argument is only that we should endeavor to read the written Constitution in light of the meaning the framers attached to it.[188] For a recent illustration, consider *Crawford v. Washington*.[189] Writing for the Court, Justice Scalia began with the explicit text of the Confrontation Clause, quickly acknowledged that the text would "not alone resolve" the case, and then turned to "the historical background of the Clause to understand its meaning." On the basis of historical evidence, then, Scalia determined what the "framers" meant the Confrontation Clause to accomplish and resolved the ambiguities in its text in a way that conformed to that purpose.[190] Other justices quarreled with Scalia's reading of the relevant history, but they did not question his use of historical materials as evidence of the meaning properly to be ascribed to the text of the constitutional provision at hand.[191] This variety of originalism is familiar, but fraught with difficulty.

Initially, we may fairly ask why we should be bound by the intentions of the framers in any case. This question snakes back to baseline difficulties with the document's legitimacy.[192] Once again, the delegates to the Philadelphia Convention and the ratifying conventions were not chosen democratically. Once again, even if we assume counterfactually that they were, we had no say in the judgments they reached. It is hard to argue that we must adhere to what the framers thought because we respect them as visionaries whose judgments were simply better than any we might adopt today. If that is the idea behind originalism, it certainly is not democratic. The "great man" theory of constitutional meaning is akin to religious doctrines celebrating the teachings of prophets.[193] We need not disparage the demonstrable abilities of the men who were present at the creation to recognize that they produced a political document in the familiar pragmatic manner: "[I]n what must have seemed [to them] an endless process of give-and-take, they reasoned, cajoled, threatened, and bargained amongst themselves."[194]

It is hard, moreover, even to identify who the framers were: the principals at the convention in Philadelphia (who actually composed the document), the larger field of delegates (who only signed off on it), the delegates to the ratifying conventions (who actually adopted it)?[195] The framers of subsequent amendments are equally elusive. They would have been the drafters, supermajorities in the House and the Senate, and state-by-state majorities in local legislatures.[196] As to the original document, most originalists under this heading regard the ratifiers as the pertinent framers.[197] Yet they actually tend to rely on Madison, Hamilton, and a few others.[198] Those particular participants in the process may be important primarily because they wrote things down—that is, they drafted *different* documents that have survived to be seized upon as evidence of original understanding. It is argued on occasion that we can safely rely on what prominent individuals wrote on the assumption that others were moved by their arguments. But that suggests, again, that originalists lack solid evidence of the understanding of the many and must make do with what they can discover about the understanding of the few.[199] Michael Dorf proposes to resolve the identification problem by consulting everyone involved—all of whom participated as "ancestors" in framing the "*debate* about the Constitution."[200] That, too, is confession and avoidance. To define originalism at such an elevated level of generality is to rob it of any discernible character as originalism at all.

Consider, next, that author-focused originalism faces heroic logistical hurdles inasmuch as it demands that we identify and retrieve an accurate assessment of the thinking behind the document. Of course, no one seriously believes we can discover the subjective intentions of historical individuals.[201] Madison, Hamilton, and the other principals are no more transparent than anybody else, perhaps much less so. Moreover, it is impossible to say that an individual had any single reason for saying or doing anything in particular. This is one of the points Justice Scalia makes with respect to interpretation of any kind.[202] It is not only telling, but more telling than Scalia lets on. Psychologists explain the different layers of consciousness at work in the simplest human activities. We must distinguish, for example, between what an individual *believed* a term to mean and what he *expected* it would mean to others. And, in turn, between those things and what he *hoped* it would mean.[203] We cannot discover what the framers thought at the time. We can only "creatively construct it" for ourselves without pretense that we can arrive at any reliable determination of what they had in mind.[204] But, of course, if we do that, we abandon the originalist chase itself.[205]

Even if we could recover the framers' subjective intentions as a matter of historical fact, we would be hard pressed to show that many others shared those personal thoughts. Originalists thus typically insist that we try to capture more generalized understandings among the many people involved in the adoption of the Constitution. But the difficulties with recovering the framers' collective understanding are prohibitive. If it is hard to pin down precisely what an individual was thinking, it is much harder to say that a group of individuals had any single reason for a collective undertaking (like drafting and adopting a provision in the Constitution).[206]

Attempts to employ the techniques of professional historians are more appealing, but also disappointing. Professionals dismiss out of hand any attempt to present an objective account of history. For one thing, investigators inevitably bring their own ideological blinders to the job. For another, even the most scrupulous among them attempt to present an intelligible picture and thus necessarily shape historical events into a coherent story. Simply put, they seize upon data that suggest a pattern and discount the significance of contradictory evidence. As Jack Rakove has warned, "the ideal of 'unbiased' history remains an elusive goal" even among disciplined professionals.[207] The likelihood of bias is especially acute in the case of originalist approaches to the Constitution. Originalists do not pursue an objective account for its own sake. They examine the history behind the Constitution not as an academic exercise, but for the stated purpose of using historical data to interpret the document. The very essence of the project is tendentious. John Roche put it this way: We don't know much about what the framers actually meant, but we know a lot more (more than the framers themselves realized) about what they *"should have meant."*[208] We know about the modern problems for which we need constitutional answers, and so we "read the mystery story backwards" and impose intentions upon the framers that serve us well today.[209]

The practical problems run deeper still. Lawyers, judges, and legal academics alike begin their investigations of historical evidence with the mission to find support for the interpretative conclusion they want to reach. The investigation is then corrupted as evidence is screened in or out depending on its tendency to prove the point the enterprise was undertaken to demonstrate. Discussions of historical materials in briefs and judicial opinions typically fail to capture even the provisional objectivity that professional historians hope to offer. Martin Flaherty puts the scholarly standard somewhere below what we would expect from undergraduates.[210] It is not that historical materials are infinitely malleable; it is that this is "law office history"—legal arguments packaged as historical accounts in the hope of achieving a particular result regarding some modern question.[211]

The surviving evidence of original intentions raises additional logistical difficulties. Those documents are comparatively rare and, where they exist, demonstrably incomplete. Max Farrand seems to have done a creditable job of collating the materials from the Philadelphia Convention.[212] Yet Madison's famous notes on the debates are anecdotal at best. He himself described his work as merely a "sketch."[213] Professor Crosskey argued that Madison edited the notes after the fact.[214] Arnold Rogow has shown that Madison's perceptions and accounts of his own positions and speeches were often at odds with the impressions of others.[215] The question of perspective is crucial. Jack Rakove has warned that participants in historical events who paused to take notes necessarily brought their own attitudes, views, and beliefs to the task, robbing their product of any claim to genuine objectivity. Rakove relies on Madison to recreate "the *flow* of debate within the Convention." But by his own admission, Rakove reaches for Madison by default.[216] There being no better source, Rakove makes do with what he has. Finally, consider that the convention self-consciously tried to keep its deliberations secret. Nobody's illicit notes saw the light of day for many years. Since the delegates to the state ratifying conventions surely did not see those notes, they could scarcely have taken them into account in forming their own understanding of the document they were asked to endorse.[217]

The evidence regarding the ratifying conventions is extremely thin.[218] Yet it was at those conventions that the written Constitution received whatever imprimatur it enjoys as law. Originalists often rely on the Federalist Papers.[219] Justices of the Supreme Court certainly do so.[220] Yet those essays were works of advocacy addressed primarily to the New York convention in an effort to persuade the delegates to adopt the new Constitution wholesale.[221] They were the op-ed pieces of their day.[222] It is unlikely that anyone at the time regarded them as a reliable guide to what adopting the Constitution would mean.[223] Certainly, they were not (and did not purport to be) disinterested academic accounts of the proposed Constitution's text and structure. John Roche once said that the existence of the Federalist Papers proves only one thing: that "Hamilton and Madison were inspired propagandists with a genius for retrospective symmetry."[224] Of course, if we like *what* was said in the Federalist Papers, it may make no difference *why* it was said at the time. Then again, if we rely on the Federalist Papers simply because we find their content attractive, it seems we have abandoned originalism, the objective of which is to implement original understanding whether we like it or not.

Consider, too, that Madison's notes, the Federalist Papers, and other old instruments scarcely come to us bearing a perfectly clear meaning. Far from it. They are simply additional texts—ambiguous, vague, and inscrutable in their own terms.[225] Surviving documents of any kind must themselves be interpreted before they can be used to assign meaning to the text of the Constitution (the document that originalists regard as the one we really want to interpret). At best, then, originalism contemplates interpreting the document at one remove, first construing some piece of extra-document text and then using the resulting meaning (necessarily contestable) as an aid to assigning meaning to the language of the document itself. This is not to say that secondary sources are useless, but only to observe that they fail to supply anything approaching nail-it-shut certainty.[226]

In *Crawford* and other cases, the Court has attributed to the framers ideas about government that had evolved in England and in the colonies.[227] That strategy is at odds with the view that the adoption of the 1789 document was essentially a creative act rather than an event within a larger evolution of ideas about the way government should look and operate. Yet if we recognize that the document drew upon what had gone before (as we must), we have a much wider body of materials to consult for interpretive help. Unfortunately for originalists, that broader field is a mixed blessing inasmuch as it sweeps in the great body of English sources and thus introduces additional uncertainty. The Court sometimes allows for the consideration of events in the immediate aftermath of the Constitution's adoption. The Chief Justice did this in *Verdugo-Urquidez*.[228] The idea is still that only "original" (i.e., pre-adoption) thinking should count. But if the new Congress, the Supreme Court, and the president did something during the earliest days, we may infer that they thought it was constitutional to do it. That understanding, in turn, can be extrapolated back to the period prior to ratification.[229] Here again, though, originalists resort to assumptions in an attempt to compensate for want of hard evidence.

Finally, by all accounts, the delegates at Philadelphia and the ratifying conventions almost certainly understood that they were engaged in a great experiment, the future of which might depart from anyone's intentions, expectations, and hopes.[230] In this vein, Paul Brest argues that we should add to the mix whatever we know (or think we know) about what the people responsible for the Constitution wanted or expected later generations to do with it.[231] We should not assume that they regarded themselves as entitled to bind Americans to their particular perspectives on the Constitution for all time. Jeff Powell has unearthed a good deal of evidence suggesting that they anticipated that later generations would *not* be obliged to keep faith with original understanding, but would be free to assign quite different meanings to the text.[232] Recall that the convention decided against keeping an official record of its deliberations, perhaps to avoid creating materials that might be used (or misused) later to affect constitutional meaning. Remember as well that the text the framers chose was often so open-ended that it necessarily invited a variety of understandings over time. Keith Whittington is surely right that we cannot very well employ originalist methodology to determine whether the Constitution must be given an originalist meaning.[233] Yet it seems awkward to insist upon reading this historical document according to the understanding of authors who had enough sense to know that doing so would be a bad idea.

In the end, as Professor Brest puts it, our "understanding of original understanding may be so indeterminate as to undermine the rationale for originalism."[234] Originalists who hope to rely on the framers' thinking have more than epistemological difficulties to worry about in their quest for original understanding. There was no such collective understanding.[235] Listen again to Jack Rakove: "[T]he notion that the Constitution had some fixed and well-known meaning at the moment of its adoption dissolves into a mirage."[236]

The Founding Generation

The second form of originalism currently in fashion attempts to evade the difficulties with retrieving the framers' thinking by changing the subject. The idea here is that we should be interested not in what the authors of the Constitution thought they were writing, but rather in the meaning that the public at large took (or might have taken) from what was written. The question we ought to ask is what educated and informed people of the time would have understood the terms in the Constitution to mean—assuming that they were aware of the document and actually paused to consider it. This is Robert Bork's approach (though it was not always).[237] Justice Scalia sometimes endorses it.[238] And they have a handful of academic followers.[239]

Now then, this kind of originalism is notoriously artificial, and it is not at all clear that the Supreme Court is as enthusiastic about it as are its academic proponents. Its principal appeal is that it makes the leg-work easier. We need only look up the terms used in the document in the popular dictionaries at the time.[240] When, in *Crawford*, Justice Scalia turned back to the text of the Confrontation Clause and purported to square it with the framers' understanding, he relied on the 1828 edition of Webster's.[241] Consider, though, that the understanding of some vaguely defined consumers of the Constitution in society at large is ad-mittedly "hypothetical."[242] If we give the text of the document that kind of interpretation, we may end up with results that no one actually meant to achieve. That, in turn, undercuts the fulcrum on which originalists rest the claim that the written Constitution is legitimate—namely, the idea that it represents a set of judgments actually made (by someone) at the crucial juncture.[243]

More Negative Examples

All this said, we should not be surprised to learn that the Supreme Court's actual use of historical materials is thin to the point of trans-parency. Take, for example, two structural ideas with which the current Court is much taken: the separation of powers and federalism. Histori-ans report that neither of those ideas was formed, far less well formed, at the time of the Philadelphia Convention.[244] There is evidence that English judges had developed some sense of independence, but that idea, too, was embryonic in 1789.[245] In consequence, when the modern Court turns to the amorphous historical understandings of separated powers, it comes away with precious little genuine guidance for responding to hard questions. Nothing in that history says much about the gritty questions that now must be resolved. As a matter of fact, the Court makes of his-torical materials what it will and ends up presenting its own judgments as the product of historical understanding.[246]

Historical materials regarding federalism are no better. The jus-tices purport to see in the 1789 document the working out of a deep, systematic understanding of the relationship between the new national government and the preexisting states.[247] School children learn that Madison's "Federalist No. 10" described his grand vision of a complex power-sharing scheme that would discourage the corruption associated with factions. Yet sober observers entertain serious doubt that there was any such vision. By the best accounts, the delegates in Philadelphia regarded the framework established under the Articles of Confederation as unworkable largely because it left critical powers with the individual states.[248] Yet they understood that it would be impossible to obtain approval for a novel scheme that seriously subordinated the states to a new national government. In the end, it seems, they forged yet another set of compromises. They roughed out a scheme contemplating *both* the introduction of a more powerful central government *and* the perpetuation of the states. John Roche has described the result as a "make-shift affair," little more than "the farthest point the delegates felt they could go in the destruction of state power without themselves inviting repudiation." And it is "the irony of ironies" that Madison should come to be seen (along with Hamilton) as the architect of an elegant balance hailed as American federalism.[249]

When difficult modern questions arise touching the relations among the three branches of the national government or the interactions between the national government and the states, the Supreme Court typically selects the historical materials it likes from the long menu available, gives those materials the construction it chooses, and then packages its results accordingly. In *Alden v. Maine*,[250] for example, the question was whether Congress can authorize private suits for damages against the states in their own courts. Justice Kennedy conceded that there is no evidence that anyone so much as considered the effect the 1789 Constitution might have on any preexisting state immunity from suits of that kind. Yet he insisted that *silence* on the question justifies the inference that the "framers" meant not only to leave state immunity in place but to establish a federal constitutional prohibition on any attempt by Congress to authorize suits by legislation. Well. The "sounds of silence" may make for good popular ballads. But it is something else again to rest a decision striking down an enactment of Congress on the basis of what somebody might have said, but did not (so far as we know).

The Court employs historical materials in the same way when it turns to problems regarding individual rights. Consider *Verdugo-Urquidez* yet again.[251] Chief Justice Rehnquist offered no evidence that anyone actually proposed that the Fourth Amendment would *not* operate overseas, but only insisted that (in light of "available" historical data) "it was never suggested" that it *would*.[252] The really dispositive consideration in *Verdugo-Urquidez* was pragmatic. The justices were concerned about compromising the conduct of foreign policy. This is also the way to understand the *Crawford* case.[253] Justice Scalia purported to rely primarily on historical materials and offered his result as the best account of original understanding. Yet he was also moved by current policy considerations, including the administrative difficulties that the alternative analysis had created. Scalia's taste for formal rules to guide lower courts was very much in evidence beneath the surface of his originalist methodology.[254] The pattern is repeated in other cases in which results turn (as they should) on the justices' own best judgment rather than on anything genuinely traceable to original understanding. In *Georgia v. Randolph*,[255] for example, the difference between the majority and the dissenters came down to a debate about whether the majority's rule offered the police sufficient "practical guidance."[256]

In the cases on substantive rights in which I am interested, the Court routinely sets concerns for original understanding aside and takes up problems according to its own sights. In the gay sodomy case, *Lawrence v. Texas*,[257] Justice Kennedy did not say that the framers of the Fourteenth Amendment meant to establish an equality principle that would operate for gays and lesbians. He said something else, something that should pound in the ears of anyone who entertains for another moment the myth that substantive constitutional rights depend on original understanding. Kennedy said this: The men who drew up, proposed, and ratified the Due Process Clauses in the Fifth and Fourteenth Amendments understood that "times can bind us to certain truths and later generations can see that laws once thought necessary and proper in fact only serve to oppress." And he said this: "As the Constitution endures, persons in every generation can invoke its principles in their own search for greater freedom."[258]

Originalism utterly fails to explain the Constitution we have, much less important features of that Constitution that are plainly correct beyond cavil. Truth is, the Court's actual decisions regarding hard constitutional questions openly defy any sort of originalist foundation.[259] On this point, virtually everyone who writes in this field agrees.[260] If you like, consider better-known examples. The great *Marbury* decision proclaiming the Supreme Court's power to review legislation for constitutionality cannot seriously be defended on originalist grounds any more than it can be justified on the basis of the text alone.[261] The desegregation decision, *Brown v. Board of Education*,[262] equally eludes an originalist explanation.[263] Justice Scalia, for his part, admits that we cannot give originalism its head without courting unacceptable disruption. By his account, serious judges must live with "accepted old principles" but should hold the line there and forbear the creation of "new" constitutional rights.[264] Thus does Scalia, too, give up the game. Only the justices themselves are in position to say whether a proposition is entitled to respect because it is "old" and "accepted" or, instead, should be eschewed because it is novel.[265] At the very best, then, originalism is an incomplete analysis.[266] Honestly, with all due respect, it is no plausible analysis at all.

* * *

If the text of the 1789 document (as amended) does not operate as a working Constitution (and it does not), and if appeals to original understanding are unsuccessful in making the written Constitution serviceable (and they are), then the genuine, functional Constitution must be found elsewhere. That real Constitution is easy enough to locate. It resides in the stream of incremental judgments the Supreme Court makes in individual cases and in the doctrine the Court offers to organize its thinking. The quest for constitutional meaning is an ongoing, protean project by which judges make it up as they go along. Constitutional meaning lies in contemporary judgment, exercised by the men and women who sit on the constantly changing committee we call the Supreme Court. It's time we put aside distracting myths that things are or could be otherwise.

CHAPTER TWO

Constitutional Common Law

The Constitution is a species of judge-made law: an ever-growing body of judicial decisions stacked on top of one another. There is nothing especially novel in this. Most academicians concede, at least grudgingly, that constitutional law is neither more nor less than common law of a special order, albeit most insist that in some way or other the text and its history still "matter."[1] This is not to say that Supreme Court decisions stating constitutional meaning are no different by nature from judicial decisions creating non-constitutional common law.[2] And it is certainly not to say that the Supreme Court makes constitutional law in the manner that Congress and state legislatures create non-constitutional law by statute. There is a sophisticated jurisprudence exploring the wavering line between adjudication and legislation and, concomitantly, how they are associated, in turn, with the governmental entities involved.[3] Let me deal now only with a curious misconception that clouds clear analysis and postpone related discussions.[4]

It is frequently said that the Supreme Court makes constitutional law only when necessary to resolve disputes about constitutional meaning in particular circumstances and that the Court is duty-bound to explain its actions, but that Congress and state legislatures make non-constitutional law whenever they like, forging unilateral decisions about the proper policy to govern the future, and that they need not give reasons for enacting a statute. There is certainly something to this. The

Supreme Court does pronounce constitutional law in the context of particular, preexisting controversies and usually supplies opinions explaining its results. And Congress and state assemblies enact forward-looking statutes as a matter of choice (the former within the scope of its constitutionally delegated authorities and the latter on the basis of the police power). It is a mistake, however, to think that adjudication must rest on reason, but that legislation is purely a matter of will.[5]

Congress and state legislatures, too, must at least *have* reasons for their actions, even if those reasons are not articulated. The same is true of every other governmental entity or officer in the United States. This requirement of reasons is not intrinsic to adjudication and legislation in every political system imaginable. But it is a foundational idea in the American scheme of things. In truth, it is *the* foundational idea. Roscoe Pound declared as much nearly a hundred years ago: "Mere will, as such, has never been able to maintain itself as law. . . . There is no device whereby the sovereign, whether King Rex or King Demos[,] may put mere will into laws which will suffice for the administration of justice."[6] It is not the case, then, that only the Court is obliged to have reasons for its law-making. Legislatures are equally bound to act in a rationally instrumental manner. Government generally "must account for itself" if it presumes to adjust individual freedom.[7]

I hasten to say that the Court's law-making is constrained in other ways. The justices do their crucial work within the conventions of legal practice in courts of law generally and in the Supreme Court in particular.[8] Those conventions bear serious limiting consequences. Justices do not have to be lawyers with degrees on their walls. But they are. They think in the way that lawyers think, within the traditional confines of the legal profession. That is, they accept the responsibility to face up to issues, to examine relevant circumstances, and to consider opposing arguments. They genuinely analyze problems rather than forming opinions on the basis of ideology alone. At least, we expect them to do that, and we think and hope they do it (most of the time).[9] Moreover, the justices do not sit individually, but must reach some sort of consensus in order to act as a body. Collegial decision making entails further engagement as a check on a purely ideological agenda. Finally, again by tradition, the justices write opinions and distribute them to the rest of us. No one is especially satisfied that opinions really *justify* the Court's decisions, leaving no room for reasonable objection. But we do get at least the appearance of the justices' *explanations* of what they are about. And we, in turn, can evaluate and critique those explanations.

The justices do not resolve individual disputes *ad hoc*. They situate particular cases in context with other, similar disputes in the past and with still other cases likely to arise in the future. In any given instance, the Court's opinion typically dwells on precedents and attempts to reconcile them around some rationale that explains them all. Then, the Court engages that rationale in the case at hand. The effort to maintain consistency with prior decisions curbs the justices' personal policy preferences. Here again, we have to be realistic. The Court routinely distinguishes precedents away or, better said, pounds them into line behind propositions the justices find congenial at the moment. Still, the felt need to make some rough peace with what has gone before provides another check on judicial power, however feeble.[10]

When the Court explicates a rationale in specific terms, it supplies a fairly concrete doctrinal formulation. Doctrine is not simply a collection of precedents. Nor is it a restatement of the language in the written Constitution or an appeal to the original understanding behind the text. Doctrine is, instead, a verbal construction pitched at a level of generality beneath what is conventionally described as a principle, but not yet at the level of a precise prescriptive rule.[11] By some accounts, doctrine holds out the promise of certainty and objectivity inasmuch as it purports to confine the justices to the largely mechanical application of formulaic directives. We are due to be disappointed, then, when doctrine does not deliver on its promise, but only supplies the justices with jargon behind which they hide the judgments that truly determine results.[12] But that is not the way it works. Doctrine necessarily exists as a *formulation* of words, but provides no fixed *formula* for arriving at legal conclusions. Doctrine does not purport to lead the justices to correct answers to hard constitutional questions *without* the exercise of judgment, but only identifies the considerations that must be confronted *by* the exercise of judgment. When properly understood and sensibly deployed, doctrine does not conceal dispositive thinking; rather, it encourages an honest exchange of views.

Turn to the body of constitutional doctrine respecting substantive individual rights, and you will find rational instrumentalism at every turn. The idea that government must act instrumentally (adopting policy in the form of statutes, ordinances, and executive actions as a means to an end) runs through Supreme Court decisions regarding individual rights against both federal and state power. Of course, the Court sometimes offers different doctrinal formulations. Richard Fallon lists a handful of constitutional "tests" at work in the cases, none of them rational instrumentalism by name.[13] Yet in chapter 3 I show that in cases implicating substantive rights, those "tests" share instrumentalism as their common theme. The requirement that law must be rationally instrumental is not especially demanding. In most circumstances, government has little difficulty measuring up. I explore the reasons why this is so in this chapter. The same reasons explain, on the flip side, why some exceptional governmental actions do not pass muster. I consider those exceptional cases in chapter 3 and again in chapter 4.

I want to explain the foundations on which the general idea of rational instrumentalism rests, but I make no attempt to offer a linear narrative history. To try anything of the sort would be to commit the sin I have ascribed to academics who presume to recount the original understanding of the Constitution. No neat and tidy story ties the relevant thinking, thinkers, and events together in a coherent whole. If there is a knowable history here at all, it is intellectual history—perhaps the hardest history to master and present with anything approaching accuracy.[14] Different people (brilliant or simple, acting alone or in groups), struggling with their own immediate problems (laced with all manner of contingencies, fully understood or not), lifting thoughts (however grand, tentative, or confused) and snatches of language (however vague and ambiguous) from others, and adapting what they borrow (sensibly or not, and with great or little appreciation for what they are about), produce an admixture of data as perplexing as human frailty, ignorance, stupidity, cupidity, ingenuity, acumen, insight, character, and brilliance can deliver. There is no running it all to ground, bringing discipline to bear, and fashioning an intelligible picture about which we can be confident.

I do not mean to enter enduring debates among legal historians over the best accounts of roughly defined epochs and classic decisions. For example, I offer no firm view on whether the period conventionally called the Progressive Era marked a sharp break from an immediate libertarian past or, for that matter, whether the Formalist Era, as it is conventionally known, was all so libertarian (and formalist) after all. Rational instrumentalism was readily evident in the 1930s, but evidence abounds that similar thinking about individual rights had taken root earlier. Nor do I take sides on whether *Lochner v. New York*[15] deserves its unsavory reputation. Conventional attacks on *Lochner* have genuine power, but, there again, a more attractive (instrumental) understanding of individual rights seems clearly to have been at work in that case, as well. My message is only that rational instrumentalism is not something the modern Court has created out of whole cloth and sprung upon us without explanation. This doctrine has links to underlying ideas in American jurisprudence. I want to demonstrate that rational instrumentalism has a history, not that it has a history of any particular length. So I aim only to identify and characterize the relevant intellectual threads to elucidate the thinking that emerged from them.

There were times when at least some justices conceived that human relations were structured according to a natural order and that law, both the common law (with which they were familiar) and the Constitution (to which they had recently been introduced) embodied natural rights. There were also times when the justices conceived that the regulation of private activities by legislatures was alien to the state of nature, introducing coercion into an environment that had previously seen only free and voluntary private action. There was a tendency, then, to regard legislative regulation as unsettling *ab initio*—inconsistent with natural rights recognized by the common law and the Constitution and thus invalid. Nevertheless, and perhaps at the same time, the justices recognized that legislatures could enact regulatory measures where there was a genuine need. They named that authority the state's "police power" and described it as the ability to regulate in the interests of society at large.

The consequence, of course, was tension. In time, the justices reconciled the police power with the common law by conceding that legislatures could depart from previous arrangements devised by the courts alone. They squared it with the Constitution by defining constitutional rights *against* governmental power as rights to be free of "arbitrary" regulation—that is, regulation that was not warranted by the police power because it did not reasonably further the public interest. In effect, substantive rights were correlatives of the police power, the mirror image of government's legitimate regulatory authority. Government had police power to regulate as a means of achieving public ends; individuals had the constitutional right to be regulated only in that way. The justices experimented with a number of devices for restricting the police power. Ultimately, however, they conceded the run of choices regarding public policy to politically accountable institutions, that is, state legislatures and Congress, and fastened their own attention on governmental action that was not satisfactorily explained as a means of achieving social welfare.

Rational instrumentalism thus emerged as the organizing framework for judging the constitutional validity of governmental regulation affecting individual freedom.

I use four overlapping headings that delineate the underlying ideas on which rational instrumentalism rests. First, the rights that individuals have to order their own affairs are derived from government; there was no antecedent state of nature in which individuals enjoyed natural rights. Second, a regulatory policy instituted by government only adjusts the arrangements that previous governmental action or inaction brought about; there was no wholly private "free" market in which government had no role prior to the current regulation. Third, a regulatory policy can serve the public interest if it furthers an end whose value to society at large transcends the costs imposed on some individuals; government is not limited to policies that preserve preexisting natural rights, further particularly defined ends, promote private, self-interested market behavior, or allocate benefits and burdens to everyone in precisely the same measure. Fourth, politically accountable governmental institutions like legislatures are generally entitled to make public policy; courts ask only whether a plausible means/ends face can be put on what government does—thus to illuminate occasions when government regulates individual freedom for reasons that are *not* in the public interest because they do not allocate benefits and burdens in a rationally instrumental manner.

Rights

The first, and most basic, premise underlying rational instrumentalism is that individual freedom depends on the laws that human beings create for themselves—not natural rights from some other source, divine or secular. When individuals claim an entitlement to behave in some way, they may be called upon to cite the legal arrangements on which they rely. There is no appealing either to God or to the natural order of things. In common parlance, we often refer to the "rights" that individuals have to all manner of things—"rights" to engage in a range of activities or "rights" to be free from various forms of intrusion. But loose rhetoric about "rights" is misleading. We really want to describe "interests," but we use the label "rights" to introduce a (false) sense of entitlement and obligation and thus somehow to up the ante. Interests are real enough,

and they can be important. But they are not rights.[16] This does not mean
that individuals must always point to some species of positive law af-
firmatively authorizing the activity in which they wish to engage. Government recognizes all manner of unspecified freedoms simply by dint
of forbearance. The point, though, is that individual freedom is often
the default position because government often chooses to leave things to
private ordering.

It is unremarkable to say that natural rights have no genuine place
in the ordinary workaday world of contemporary American law and institutions.[17] Stephen Feldman counts "[f]aith in the existence of natural
law" as a defining "feature of *premodern* American legal thought."[18] As
Lloyd Weinreb puts it, the *modern* mind dismisses the idea of a "normative natural order" as "simply a fundamental mistake."[19] Recall that
some of the attraction of a written Constitution is that it appears to af-
firm that we can and do govern ourselves.[20] Still, if we are to understand
the origins of rational instrumentalism, we must examine the alternative,
natural-rights vision as it has figured in this culture historically, thus to
appreciate where we are partly by recalling whence we came. We need
not reach back to the Greeks and Romans. For our purposes, the relevant material begins with the great Enlightenment thinkers, especially
John Locke.

Natural Rights

Locke conceived of a state of nature (both historical and philosophical)
in which individuals had natural rights. He emphasized the dominion
over "property." Property, in turn, included an individual's own labor as
well as land and physical objects that he or she might own. Accordingly,
by Locke's account, property shaded into what we are inclined to call
"liberty"—a term that he used as well. In the forest, individuals enjoyed
a general freedom of action that could be maintained only by controlling
property. The content of that freedom was largely unspecified, though
it included a right of self-defense against anyone who interfered with its
exercise. Randy Barnett sums up Locke this way: Individuals were free
not because government typically allowed them a significant range of
personal choice, but rather because they naturally enjoyed a "private domain" where they were entitled to "do as they please[d]" so long as they
did not intrude upon the domains marked off for others.[21]

Lockean thinking plainly found its way into American law.[22] Natural-
rights rhetoric appeared in the Declaration of Independence: "[A]ll

men ... are endowed by their Creator with certain unalienable Rights. ... [A]mong these are Life, Liberty and the pursuit of Happiness ..."[23] John Marshall proclaimed that the individual "right to contract" was "anterior to, and independent of, society."[24] And in *Calder v. Bull*,[25] Justice Chase famously asserted that a statute presuming to excuse certain parties from adhering to a judicial decree was an offense to "natural justice." According to Chase, natural rights formed the backdrop of the Constitution, and the Supreme Court was obliged to invalidate statutes inconsistent with those preexisting entitlements.[26]

The telling point is the *way* American jurisprudence accommodated natural rights. Richard Epstein paints a simple picture. In step one, American courts incorporated natural rights into the common law. When courts decided cases, they did not presume to exercise any affirmative law-making authority. They were referees who resolved disputes over preexisting private rights. The content of those rights, in turn, mapped onto Locke's articulation of natural rights. That is why the common law proceeded from the premise that individuals were entitled in the nature of things to their own labor and to the land or objects they took into their possession. Step two followed logically enough. If common law rights were natural, then legislatures could scarcely have power to abridge them, and any statute purporting to do so must be unconstitutional. American courts thus conflated absolute natural rights with the common law and, in turn, collapsed both into the Federal Constitution. That is why governmental action curtailing liberty or property was constitutionally offensive.[27]

Others, most notably Edward Corwin, have explained the way American courts rationalized this conception of the Constitution with its text—specifically the Fourteenth Amendment's prohibition on deprivations of liberty or property without due process of law. Courts recognized that individuals could be deprived of liberty or property at the hands of government. That happened all the time when one citizen sued another on some common law claim, and a court (an arm of government) selected a winner and a loser and issued a remedial order requiring behavior to be altered or compensation to be paid. On those occasions, deprivations of liberty or property occurred *by* due process, that is, the process provided in court proceedings enforcing the common law. The justices were not accustomed to the idea that legislative regulation could have essentially the same effect in the absence of a violation of the common law as determined in judicial proceedings. They were wont to conclude, accordingly, that when a legislature unilaterally curbed the freedom that individuals previously enjoyed or diminished the value of their assets, it denied liberty or property *without* due process of law, that is, without common law proceedings in the courts.[28]

Of course, actual experience departed from this abstract conceptual account. Modern commentators have explained that state courts in the early nineteenth century often denied that the common law and natural law were congruent.[29] Some courts forged a collectivist vision of government's role in establishing a "well-regulated society" (justly called a "commonwealth") and linked that idea, in turn, to governmental responsibility for private rights. As early as 1851, Chief Justice Shaw declared that "[a]ll property" in the "commonwealth" of Massachusetts was "derived directly or indirectly *from* the government."[30] In 1871, a New York court said that property rights were not "absolute but relative" and "must be arranged to promote the general welfare."[31] Similarly, the Supreme Court recognized governmental power to alter common law arrangements. In the *Yeldell* case,[32] Justice Stone affirmed that the states could enact statutes establishing "new rights and duties for the prevention of wrong or for satisfying social and economic needs" and that the constitutionality of those statutes could "not be successfully challenged merely because a change in the common law [was] effected."[33]

Nevertheless, it seems clear enough that natural rights had some purchase on the Supreme Court's jurisprudence early on—at least enough to influence the development of rational instrumentalism by providing a foil against which to fashion a more viable understanding of public law, including constitutional law.[34] Justice Field invoked natural rights in his dissenting opinion in the *Slaughterhouse Cases*.[35] While the full Court sustained a Louisiana law giving a single company monopoly power, Field insisted that the statute violated "the inalienable right of every citizen to pursue his happiness"—a right that existed prior to the Fourteenth Amendment and was protected *by* it, "except" when government acted through "just, equal, and impartial laws."[36] And in yet another classic decision, *Allgeyer v. Louisiana,*[37] Justice Peckham declared that liberty was "deemed to embrace the right of the citizen to be free in the enjoyment of all his faculties; to earn his livelihood by any lawful calling; . . . and . . . to enter into all contracts which may be proper, necessary and essential to his carrying out to a successful conclusion the purposes above mentioned."[38] The terms *liberty* and *property* appeared in the Constitution, but the Constitution was not the source of either. Instead, liberty and property were previously existing ideas imported *into* the

Constitution—ideas that came with their own ready-made definitions, derived from natural rights and elaborated by common law courts.[39] Roscoe Pound once lamented that the natural-rights conception of law was preeminent well into the twentieth century "without a hint that any other might be tenable" and that, according to that orthodoxy, "the doctrines of the common law [were] part of the universal jural order."[40]

Rights and Formalism

By all accounts, then, the Supreme Court's decisions drew on natural-rights thinking in some measure.[41] In particular, the Court described liberty of contract as "among the inalienable rights of the citizen."[42] And famous cases involving more personal forms of liberty, among them *Meyer v. Nebraska*[43] and *Pierce v. Society of Sisters,*[44] may also have been anchored in natural-rights tradition. In part at least, the Court appeared to see its mission, and the mission of the Fourteenth Amendment, as the preservation of Lockean natural rights, reproduced in common law arrangements.[45] And, for a season, the Court relied on a categorical definition of "liberty" (particularly "liberty of contract") as the starting point for formalist deductions.[46] The conventional example is *Lochner v. New York.*[47] Historians debate whether *Lochner* lends itself to this understanding. I will come to other perspectives on the case in a minute. Fights over precisely what the Court did or meant to do in that particular instance can distract from what is genuinely important: an exposition of the ideas with which *Lochner* is associated. Nevertheless, *Lochner* is the classic vehicle, and like everyone else I will use it.[48]

The New York "Bakeshop Act" required the proprietors of bakeries to maintain equipment properly, to keep plumbing in good repair, and to provide sanitary water closets for employees. In addition, the statute provided that no employee could be "required or permitted" to work more than ten hours a day or sixty hours a week. An operator in Utica, Joseph Lochner, was convicted of violating the provision on working hours. He sought review on two theories. First, he contended that the work-hour provision violated the Equal Protection Clause inasmuch as it singled out "a certain number of men employing bakers" while permitting others "similarly situated" to "work" their employees as long as they liked.[49] Second, he argued that the work-hour limit invaded the "rights of person and property."[50] Writing for the Court, Justice Peckham set the equal protection claim aside and overturned Lochner's conviction on the basis of the second theory. The point of contention is what Peckham understood that second theory to entail.

By one common account, Justice Peckham thought Lochner's claim was grounded in natural rights that were incorporated into the common law and thus constitutionally immune from governmental regulation (at least in the absence of exigent justifying need). Peckham's general approach to Lochner's argument suggested the natural-rights ideas that Peckham himself had expressed for the Court in the *Allgeyer* case. He explained that the liberty at stake was the "right of contract"—both Lochner's right to contract with his workers and the workers' right to contact with him. Focusing on the workers' side of the ledger, he described "the general right to make a contract" as the "right of the individual . . . to enter into those contracts in relation to labor which may seem to him appropriate or necessary for the support of himself and his family[.]"[51] Peckham did not deny that the New York Legislature could regulate private activities; he evidently had no difficulty with the rules regarding sanitary conditions at bakeries. Yet he insisted that the work-hour limit was different and could be sustained only if it survived careful scrutiny. Arguably, then, he rested his decision disapproving that aspect of the statute on libertarian, natural-rights grounds assimilated in some way into the Constitution.[52]

To the extent Peckham's opinion in *Lochner* stood on natural rights, it invited and immediately evoked a withering counterattack. Justice Holmes contended that judges who professed to "believe in natural law" mistook circumstances with which they were familiar for arrangements having universal significance.[53] By his account, moreover, it was impossible to deduce appropriate results in cases from categorically defined concepts like "liberty." According to Holmes, formalist legal analysis ignored the judgment the law required: "General propositions do not decide concrete cases."[54] Pound, for his part, famously derided formalist analysis as "mechanical jurisprudence."[55]

The Positive Present

The Court ultimately repudiated the idea that it must recognize and enforce natural rights that preexisted government.[56] Law, including constitutional law, is not a creature of nature. Cass Sunstein has put it this way. The Court now acknowledges that rights are not prior to government; they are not "pre-political."[57] With Chief Justice Shaw, the Court recognizes that individual rights owe their existence *to* government. The institution of private property is the classic illustration. Property is not a feature of a natural world existing before individuals came together and formed government. Property was never prior to law, but has always been created by law. It is not a unitary relationship between an owner and some thing of value; it is a web of legal relationships that government establishes between potential claimants. Individuals can sensibly maintain that land or chattels belong to them not because they seized them before anybody else and own them in some natural sense, but rather because government's laws recognize the interests of those in possession and protect them against others. None of this is jarring, of course. Barbara Fried and Morton Horwitz, as well as Sunstein, have described historical efforts to make it the stock and trade of economic analysis—as it surely is today.[58]

Small wonder that these ideas figure in the current Supreme Court's formulations of constitutional doctrine, chiefly rational instrumentalism. In particular, the Court now disclaims the notion that a regulatory policy may be invalid because it violates liberty of contract, understood as a feature of natural rights. The only standards that governmental action must satisfy are the standards the Court ascribes to the Constitution. Chief Justice Hughes spelled this out in *West Coast Hotel*,[59] when he upheld a minimum-wage law against the charge that it violated freedom of contract. Hughes explained that the Constitution refers to "liberty," but prohibits only deprivations of liberty (or property) "without due process of law." There is no liberty of contract arising from a previous state of nature. There is only the constitutional right to due process of law, triggered by a deprivation of life, liberty, or property. This positivist understanding of rights pervades the modern system.

There are times, to be sure, when a yearning for natural rights resurfaces. Even today, both Supreme Court justices and academic commentators occasionally use "liberty" and "right" as though they are interchangeable.[60] This despite the understanding settled since *West Coast Hotel* that liberty is not a free-standing right at all, but an interest that can activate the right to due process of law. Libertarians like Barnett and Epstein explicitly rely on Locke's world view. On occasion, public figures also invoke natural rights. During the hearings on Judge Robert Bork's nomination for a seat on the Supreme Court, Senator Biden professed to believe that human beings enjoy rights apart from positive law.[61] Yet the mainstream commitment to positivism prevails. When Justice Thomas appeared before the Senate Judiciary Committee for hearings, Biden questioned him sharply about his commitment to natural-rights thinking, now widely disclaimed.[62]

The subsequent history of the abstract categorical logic associated, rightly or wrongly, with *Lochner* is more mixed. Justice Holmes denounced the Old Court's formalism: "The provisions of the Constitution are not mathematical formulas having their essence in their form."[63] Today, the justices (or most of them) take a decidedly more pragmatic approach to their duties (most of the time). By common account, constitutional law is not a creature of logic or language, but is rather a matter of judgment in light of actual, empirically demonstrable conditions in the world. Accordingly, when the justices rely on rational instrumentalism to work their way through difficult cases, it is that kind of judgment that determines results. Nevertheless, formalist thinking occasionally resurfaces and, very occasionally, commands majority support. Justice Scalia famously promotes rule-based jurisprudence as a sensible methodology whose chief function is to cabin judicial discretion.[64] Where once formalism was a weapon by which the Court protected liberty from governmental regulation, formalism now is more commonly deployed to protect governmental regulation from the Court.[65]

Markets

The second idea embedded in rational instrumentalism is that ostensibly private market arrangements depend on government to give them effect. Just as there were no natural rights prior to government, there was no entirely private and "free" market apart from government, either. To deny the one is also to disclaim the other. Governmental action or forbearance creates the environment in which private ordering takes place. Instrumentalism acknowledges as much by positing governmental involvement in any given state of affairs and attending to the way government sets about its responsibilities. Here again, there is much in our intellectual history touching alternative understandings. We can only understand current thinking against the backdrop of those alternatives and an appreciation of why they have been abandoned.

The Unregulated Baseline

According to Lockean theory, natural rights recognized by the common law formed a kind of "original position."[66] Individuals fended for themselves—laying claim to property, protecting that property from interlopers, and exchanging goods and services for mutual advantage. No one could force anyone else into a bargain; everyone was entitled to choose for himself whether to accept a proffered deal. Employment is the traditional illustration. Within the Lockean vision, individuals could not be compelled to surrender their property right in their own labor. But they might agree to place themselves in someone else's service in exchange for wages. If they did so, they must have done it freely and voluntarily. Forced labor was a breach of natural rights and an offense to the common law, thus justifying an appropriate remedy in court. If, however, workers were not physically compelled but accepted employment, they were taken to have done so in the exercise of their own free will, that is, in the exercise of their natural and common law rights. To suggest otherwise was to deny the existence of the baseline natural right to choose.[67]

Within this framework, government was conceived to come late to a natural status quo ante—an environment that was by hypothesis entirely voluntary and free. If government presumed to regulate private relationships, it must necessarily introduce coercion for the first time. A statute fixing employment terms necessarily forced the parties to depart from the positions they had voluntarily assumed for themselves and to proceed, instead, under arrangements that government prescribed. Governmental coercion could only reduce the parties' preexisting natural rights to bargain freely among themselves. Regulation of the previously free and wholly private market for labor was thus in violation of the natural order.

Cass Sunstein, Owen Fiss, and others identify these ideas at the bottom of prominent Supreme Court decisions.[68] The famous example is, again, *Lochner.*[69] Justice Peckham recognized that the work-hour limit in that case might be a "labor law," that is, an intervention into the labor market on the side of workers to assist them in their dealings with employers. He acknowledged that the legislature might have concluded that employers were compelling workers to put in long hours and thus might have straightforwardly forestalled that practice by starting the bargaining process from a different baseline—a statutorily determined restriction on the hours that employees could be required to serve. Peckham understood that the case at hand was very much about coercion. Lochner had concededly "required" his employees to stay on the job by contracting with them for extended hours.[70] Nevertheless, he had used no physical force, and that omission was dispositive. Peckham saw nothing to suggest that bakers were unable to care for themselves "without the protecting arm of the state, interfering with their independence of judgment and action."[71] If bakers remained on the line after ten hours, it followed that they did so voluntarily and, importantly, as an exercise of their constitutional right to decide for themselves what to do with their own labor.

Sunstein, Fiss, and others contend, then, that Peckham actually decided the *Lochner* case on the assumption that the market for bakers' labor in New York was wholly private and "free" prior to the work-hour statute.[72] Lochner had done nothing wrong simply by driving a hard bargain with his workers—nothing, that is, that the common law regarded as wrong. For that reason, there was no basis for judicial relief. For the same reason, there was no basis for the legislature's attempt to upset the bargain by statute. Government had no power simply to interfere with the free market, imposing burdens on some and conferring benefits on others, taking from A and giving to B, and thus redistributing wealth.[73]

This account of *Lochner*, too, may be mistaken or, at least, misleading. Recall that the Court recognized state authority to regulate markets.[74] William Wiecek identifies two competing streams of precedent during the Formalist Era—one condemning regulatory measures, the other largely sustaining them.[75] It seems clear nonetheless that many observers at the time understood the Court's analysis in *Lochner* in precisely the way that Sunstein and Fiss suggest. Horwitz and Fried have described the attempts by economists to respond to the Court by illuminating government's role in establishing the foundation for commercial activity.[76] The concerted attack on *Lochner* as bad economics was all the more telling as time wore on.

The Regulatory Present

Conventional wisdom now regards the very existence of a "free" market as illusory. There is nothing natural about the distribution of wealth. Instead, private players depend on government in the crucial sense that the laws made by government create the necessary backdrop for their activities.[77] Here again, government is responsible for the measure of liberty that individuals enjoy and for the property interests they may successfully assert. In every context, private freedom does not precede government, but relies instead on governmental policy in the first instance. Corporations need government to supply them with charters authorizing their operations. Merchants (corporate or not) need government to provide the background legal rules against which they bargain among themselves, with their employees, and with the public at large. And the obvious illustrations go on.[78]

It follows that governmental regulation of the market does not contemplate some diminution of the individual freedom that the unregulated market respected. There was no previous, unregulated market. When government enacts a regulation, it does not enter an independent private sphere for the first time, limiting preexisting choices. Government only makes an adjustment in the arrangements that government itself established by dint of prior policy judgments to permit or encourage private action. Government cannot avoid regulating for distributive effects. According to conventional wisdom, the very point of government is to distribute and redistribute wealth in service of social welfare goals. Most modifications of the status quo cannot be regarded as constitutionally troubling, but rather are matters for politically accountable judgment.[79]

It is equally illusory to conceive that private participants in a pregovernment natural market acted voluntarily, unless and until government brought coercive power to bear.[80] Private economic power, too, is coercive. It can, and routinely does, force conditions on comparatively weak players that they in no sense accept of their own free will. Harsh employment arrangements of the kind implicated in *Lochner* provide a good example. If workers are forced to choose between laboring extremely long hours and going hungry, they are functionally coerced just as effectively as if they were lashed to their stations.[81] Economic relationships may have been simpler in earlier times, allowing for more individual choice. But the Industrial Revolution changed all that. Collective working arrangements in factories linked everyone's fortunes together, foreclosing any serious option to refuse and go elsewhere. In the modern environment, those with economic power are in a position to exploit the weak. And governmental intervention in support of the exploited may only help to balance the scales.

This has been the Court's thinking at least since the 1930s. In *Home Building & Loan Ass'n v. Blaisdell*,[82] Chief Justice Hughes acknowledged that in "earlier days" the Court had thought that "only the concerns of individuals or of classes were involved" in market relations and that government was "touched only remotely." Hughes explained, however, that the question in regulatory cases was "no longer merely that of one party to a contract as against another, but of the use of reasonable means to safeguard the economic structure upon which the good of all depends."[83] Three years later, in *West Coast Hotel*,[84] Hughes made it clear that the Court appreciated the implications of government's paramount role. If government allows employers to pay low wages and drive their workers onto the relief rolls, the effect is to subsidize employers at the expense of the public at large. If, instead, government requires employers to pay a minimum wage, it simply eliminates the subsidy and, into the bargain, spares society the relevant costs. Since *West Coast Hotel*, what previously was disclaimed as constitutionally impermissible (taking from A and giving to B) has been understood to be the inescapable function of government: the distribution of wealth, for which government is in any case responsible.

The Public Interest

The third underlying idea driving rational instrumentalism is that government is free to make regulatory adjustments in the interests of society as a whole. This familiar proposition seems self-evident, but its firm foothold in modern thinking was built from unsuccessful intellectual experiments with alternatives. To fill in the gaps, I sketch two related understandings of governmental authority—each of which once had some currency, and neither of which any longer does. Initially, I take up the idea that government can regulate only to further natural rights enjoyed by individuals in the state of nature. That notion could not survive the demise of natural-rights thinking itself and the consequent recognition of the state police power. Then, I turn to the idea that the Court should recognize a wider police power but should circumscribe it in other ways. As the Supreme Court has rejected each of these contentions, it has embraced in their stead the proposition that government is free to adopt regulatory policies whose public-regarding value transcends the costs imposed on affected individuals or groups. That proposition, in turn, explains why the Court generally indulges governmental means in the service of plausible public goals.

Natural Rights (Again)

The notion that government is empowered to regulate only in order to advance natural rights can be traced to a familiar source. John Locke allowed that individuals in the state of nature might join together to protect their natural rights from invasion by others and thus might surrender some rights to be taken up and protected by government. He acknowledged, for example, that individuals exchanged the natural right of self-defense for a guarantee that government would punish wrongdoers. Yet no individual would enter a compact that made him worse off than he was previously, but only one that would transfer to government the responsibility to protect rights that he chose no longer to defend for himself. Locke granted that the creation of government necessarily entailed positive (as opposed to natural) laws and, concomitantly, socially justified limitations on individual freedom. Yet the "common good" extended only to the maintenance of preexisting natural rights that individuals created government to safeguard. By Locke's account, "the preservation of Property" was the very "end of Government."[85]

Richard Epstein has explained how this understanding entailed the integration of natural rights and the common law. Individuals in an original, pregovernment posture could surrender to government only enough authority to provide remedies for violations of the natural rights they would otherwise have protected on their own. The right of self-defense passed to government was merely the authority to remedy violations of other natural rights not similarly given up. Government could punish one individual for interfering with another's property—that being a "wrong" recognized by natural law and, in turn, the common law. Thus if A trespassed on B's land, government (in the form of a court) could take wealth from A and give it to B as compensation. By contrast, government could not punish anyone who had not committed a wrong known to the common law and, therefore, had not opened himself to any penalty. Government (acting now in the form of a legislature) could not take from A and give to B simply because officials thought the public interest would be served by a different allocation of wealth.[86]

By conventional account, these ideas figured significantly in early American thinking about the scope of government's regulatory authority. Jennifer Nedelsky reports that in 1789 "every major political figure in America treated property as at least one object of government."[87] In his *Calder* opinion, Justice Chase suggested that Locke's notion of the common good should do service in American constitutional law. Chase conceded that individuals entered into a social compact in part to "promote the general welfare." Yet he insisted that the general welfare meant the preservation of individual natural rights, chief among them the right

of "private property." To illustrate, he said that a statute offends "all reason and justice" if it "destroys, or impairs, the *lawful private* contracts
of citizens" or "takes *property* from A and gives it to B."[88] According
to Chase, a people would not have created a government with powers of
that character. To do so would have been inconsistent with the very purposes for which government was established in the first place. Chase
therefore denied that the Constitution authorized such laws.[89]

   The picture that Chase painted of marginal legislative authority to
create a night-watchman state was impossible to reconcile with the political system already taking shape at the time. The idea that government
was limited to protecting private liberty or property competed with an
alternative conception of governmental action in the general public interest. Gordon Wood has shown that even some Revolutionary War figures understood that government's purpose was not to advance private
rights, nor even a collective public interest defined as the aggregate of
private interests. Instead, government's mission was to overcome tensions among private interests in service of a unitary public good shared
by all.[90] Morton Horwitz has explained that over the course of the nineteenth century common law courts discarded the notion that their task
was merely to find the law as it existed in the state of nature and instead embraced the understanding that they were entitled to forge legal
doctrines to further sound social policy.[91] Judicial decisions in aid of the
public interest invited the exercise of legislative power for the same ends.
Predictably, Chief Justice Shaw said that property (itself the creation of
government) was "held subject to those general regulations, which are
necessary to the common good and welfare."[92] Shaw plainly did not define the "common good" in line with Locke. He declared that legislatures could "make, ordain and establish all manner of wholesome and
reasonable laws, statutes and ordinances . . . not repugnant to the constitution, as [the legislature] shall judge to be for the good and welfare of
the commonwealth."[93] Both courts and treatises gave that kind of regulatory authority a name: the state "police power"—the power to regulate
instrumentally in the public interest.[94]

The Police Power

The evidence is mixed regarding the police power in its infancy. According to some sources, government's regulatory authority was sharply
curtailed. Thomas Cooley and Christopher Tiedeman argued that the

police power was derived from the common law of necessity and was therefore confined to regulations addressed to a "noxious use" of property.[95] Apparently operating from that premise, some decisions limited regulatory measures to emergency circumstances and thus invalidated policies that we would easily accept today.[96] Relatedly, some early decisions cabined the power of eminent domain on the ground that governmental takings were "not of a public nature" if private property, once seized, was transferred to other private individuals. Invoking the classic formula, courts sometimes held that government did not put land to a public use if it "should take the property of A and give it to B."[97] Others, most notably Ernst Freund, insisted that the police power was considerably more muscular. Freund identified contemporary cases in which courts sustained regulations so long as they were "reasonable."[98] And, by some accounts, a regulation *was* reasonable unless it was shown to have been enacted by "mistake, or in a spirit of fraud or wantonness."[99] According to Chancellor Kent, many courts generally left it to the "wisdom of the legislature, to determine when public uses require[d] the assumption of private property."[100]

The Supreme Court had no immediate occasion to elaborate the nature and scope of the emerging police power. Congress was not thought to have any such general regulatory authority, but rather had only the more limited powers enumerated in the 1789 document.[101] And, in any event, Congress rarely enacted statutes that called on the Court to explore the confines of federal legislative action.[102] After the adoption of the Fourteenth Amendment, however, the Court was obliged to formulate authoritative, federal constitutional standards—and did so readily. On the surface, the Court's doctrinal statements allowed the states considerable room in which to operate. In *Coppage v. Kansas*,[103] the Court described the police power in the language that would become classic— namely, as the general authority to superintend private activities in service of the "public health, safety, morals, or general welfare."[104] And in *Adkins v. Children's Hospital*,[105] the Court explained that the power could be used to regulate even the vaunted "liberty of contract" so long as the regulation was not "unreasonable."[106]

Nevertheless, in *Coppage, Adkins,* and other decisions, the Court held police power measures invalid ostensibly because they did not reasonably serve the public interest as the Court then understood it. Those decisions reflected three related themes: the idea that the objectives for which government could regulate (i.e., the public health, safety, morals, and general welfare) were formally defined and sharply limited; the idea that government could regulate only to facilitate private, self-interested market behavior; and the notion that government could impose regulatory burdens on some only if equal burdens were imposed on all. None of those themes has survived, but, here again, we can understand the Court's modern approach only by examining how and why earlier ideas were discarded.

FORMALISM (AGAIN).   By some accounts, the Court attempted to turn the affirmative definitions of the police power's ends into significant limits on government's regulatory authority. The public "health" was one thing, the public "safety" another, and the public "morals" still another. In any given instance, the Court parsed those categories to determine whether a statute served one or more of them reasonably. The last traditional objective, the "general welfare," appeared to consume the other three and, into the bargain, to establish an amorphous assembly of interests that would defy judicial assessment. The Court would have none of that. Instead, the Court insisted that the first three items on the prescribed menu (health, safety, and morals) had independent meaning and were not deprived of their constraining power by the addition of the open-ended "general welfare" category.

Here, too, the *Lochner* case is commonly seen as illustrative. Justice Peckham acknowledged that the state could regulate liberty of contract pursuant to the police power. But he explained that, to be valid, a regulation must have "a more direct relation, as a means to an end, and the end itself must be appropriate and legitimate." [107] Taken literally, that sounds like the very rational instrumentalism the Court embraces today. But in *Lochner,* Peckham may have meant that a state's means must serve one of the traditional ends of the police power identified in the Court's decisions. [108] He declared that a limit on workers' hours "involve[d] neither the safety, the morals nor the welfare of the public." Accordingly, he focused on the possibility that it might serve the public health. The state contended that the statute protected the health of bakers themselves in the near term and, in the longer term, ensured that healthy bakers produced wholesome bread for the public. There was evidence to support those arguments; Justice Harlan relied on that evidence in dissent. But Peckham found the connection tenuous. The work-hour rule appeared actually to be a "labor law," which placed it outside the traditional ends of the police power. The necessary link between the statute and the one legitimate end in sight was not made, and liberty of contract prevailed.[109] Understood this way, Justice Peckham departed from Locke's common good inasmuch as he acknowledged that government's end need not be the preservation of natural individual rights exclusively. Yet he insisted that only the governmental interests the Court had pigeon-holed as the public health, safety, morals, or general welfare would do. And in any given case the Court itself would determine whether a statute furthered one of those distinct interests.

The idea of limiting the police power to particular ends captured in traditionally recognized categories was never entrenched. Justice Holmes arguably disposed of the idea in *Noble State Bank v. Haskell:* "It may be said in a general way that the police power extends to all the great public needs. . . . If then the legislature . . . thinks that the public welfare requires the measure under consideration, analogy and principle are in favor of the power to enact it."[110] Justice Douglas explained in *Berman v. Parker*[111] that "[p]ublic safety, public health, morality, peace and quiet, law and order" are only examples of legitimate police power objectives. They "merely illustrate the scope of the power and do not limit it."[112] In any case, the Court has long since discarded the idea that the police power is restricted to the pursuit of categorically defined objectives. In its place, the Court has refashioned the description of regulatory power into a far more generous, regulation-friendly check on governmental authority—namely, rational instrumentalism. There *are* limits on the police power, but only the now-familiar limits. Whatever government does, it must do as an instrumental means of achieving genuine public-regarding goals. I explain in chapter 4 that rational instrumentalism helps to identify governmental action that does not serve public welfare writ large.

Just as the Court has abandoned any attempt to curb the police power by limiting its reach to prescribed objectives, the Court has also discarded any allied attempt to place limits on what counts as a public purpose within the meaning of eminent domain doctrine. In *Hawaii Housing Auth. v. Midkiff,*[113] the lower court invalidated a scheme forcing large landowners to sell individual parcels to tenants on the theory that it was "a naked attempt . . . to take private property from A and transfer it to B solely for B's private use and benefit."[114] In the Supreme Court, Justice O'Connor dismissed that argument in reliance on *Berman*. There are dissents from this development. In the *Kelo* case,[115] some justices resisted the idea that virtually any disposition of property that government determines to be in the "public interest" must count as a public "use." At least, they argued, government should have rather more explaining to do if the property it takes ends up in the hands of private developers.[116] Yet a majority of the justices acknowledged that a taking to promote "economic development" is for a public use, even though the public neither owns nor uses the property in question. Writing for the Court, Justice Stevens made the reason crystal clear: If the Court were to enforce a fixed doctrinal definition of "public use," it would risk being drawn back into superintending the objectives that government can select in pursuit of public welfare. Stevens explained that in modern times the Court has "eschewed rigid formulas and intrusive scrutiny in favor of affording legislatures broad latitude in determining what public needs justify the use of the takings power."[117]

In eminent domain cases, too, there are still limits. Justice Stevens confirmed in *Kelo* that government cannot take property as a pretext for showering special benefits on a "particular private party."[118] Justice Kennedy wrote separately to encourage lower courts to detect and disapprove attempts to use the eminent domain power to "confer benefits on particular, favored private entities, and with only incidental or pretextual public benefits."[119] Yet those caveats only flag the possibility that in some instances (extremely rare instances in the case of eminent domain) government may yet take action that cannot be regarded as rationally instrumental in service of the public welfare. In the final analysis, then, both in police power cases and in eminent domain cases, government generally is entitled to wide discretion.[120]

LAISSEZ-FAIRE.   The *Lochner* case is also commonly regarded as an illustration of another, related attempt to curb state power by circumscribing the ends that states may pursue—namely, an effort to prescribe *laissez-faire* as the only economic policy compatible with the Constitution. The story lies not so much in Justice Peckham's treatment of the argument that the work-hour law was a health measure, albeit the kernel of it was there. It rests more prominently in Peckham's rejection of the argument that the statute might be sustained as a "labor law." He evidently meant a straightforward regulation of the market for bakers' labor—a statute that intervened in the relationship between employers and employees on the side of the latter, protecting workers from a harsh bargain. That, Peckham intimated, was not a policy the state was entitled to legislate. The point was not just that a pure regulation of labor contracts could not count as a health measure. It was that legislation interfering with labor contracts the state found objectionable was independently invalid as an affront to underlying constitutional commitments to capitalism.[121]

On this reading, Justice Peckham reached back, again, to natural-rights tradition and combined it with Social Darwinism, then very much in vogue. Put baldly, he adopted the premise that the same natural laws that controlled biological life also governed human social and economic relations.[122] In human affairs, too, the strong could and *should* exploit the weak so that only the fittest survived. Accordingly, when government presumed to limit the ability of employers to exercise their economic power out of self-interest, it compromised the competitive environment on which social welfare (naturally) must depend. As long as employers had committed no common law wrong (by physically coercing their workers), they had done nothing to violate the natural rights of others and render themselves liable to their victims. It followed that they were entitled to drive any harsh bargains they liked, justifying the result on the basis of their employees' formal willingness to agree. Taking from A and giving to B in the absence of common law liability was not merely poor policy—it was tampering with the foundations of the universe. A policy of that kind could not be successful and must be unconstitutional.

If this was Justice Peckham's position, it was plainly unsound. Justice Holmes famously cried foul: "This case is decided," he said, "upon an economic theory which a large part of the country does not entertain. . . . The 14th Amendment does not enact Mr. Herbert Spencer's Social Statics."[123] Other critics followed suit.[124] Judge Hand charged the Court with bias toward industry and the wealthy,[125] and a sizeable academic literature took essentially the same view.[126] Morton Horwitz has explained that the *Lochner* decision galvanized an aggressive assault on the premises of classical conceptual analysis.[127] That campaign contributed to the development of the quite different approach to regulatory action with which we are familiar today.[128]

To be sure, there is reason to doubt that Holmes had Peckham quite right. Recent observers question whether the link between *laissez-faire* and Social Darwinism was as close as Holmes suggested, whether the great body of decisions in the period reflected a genuine commitment to either, and whether many of the justices actually found either attractive.[129] Certainly Holmes himself was as enthusiastic about Social Darwinism as were his colleagues.[130] Then again, it probably makes no great difference whether *Lochner* was correctly understood at the time or even representative of the Court's thinking generally. For our purposes, it is only important to observe that, for a very long time now, the Court has routinely disclaimed any suggestion that economic policy is unconstitutional if it departs significantly from *laissez-faire.* Writing for the Court in *Nebbia v. New York,*[131] Justice Roberts declared that the Constitution allows a state to "adopt whatever economic policy may reasonably be deemed to promote public welfare." Courts are "both incompetent and unauthorized" to second-guess the "wisdom" of the policy adopted.[132] The view that government could not regulate in a way that "took from A and gave to B" was relegated to the dissent.[133] Later, in *Williamson v. Lee Optical,*[134] Justice Douglas was clearer still. "The day is gone," he said, "when this Court uses the Due Process Clause to strike down state laws, regulatory of business and industrial conditions, because they may be unwise, improvident, or out of harmony with a particular school of thought."[135]

CLASS LEGISLATION.   Recent scholarship suggests that in *Lochner* and other cases the Court enforced a third limit on the police power—namely, a general requirement of equality.[136] By this account, the Court meant to say that government could regulate private activities only in a formally egalitarian way, such that all citizens enjoyed the same benefits or suffered the same burdens. Partial or "class" legislation that distributed largesse unequally was invalid, because it did not serve the *public* interest but only the interests of those with the political capacity to obtain the government's assistance.[137] Howard Gillman quotes *Lawton v. Steele:* "To justify the State in . . . interposing its authority in behalf of the public, it must appear, first, that the interests of the public generally, as distinguished from those of a particular class, require such interference."[138]

There is a good deal to be said for this revisionist thesis—enough, perhaps, to give it precedence over the more familiar *laissez-faire* account.[139] It would be nice to think that the Court did not simply seize upon the Constitution as a means of helping well-heeled interests frustrate market regulation, but instead addressed itself to the classifications government employed in distributing benefits and burdens. And it is plausible to think that the Court may have distinguished on that ground between health and safety rules that applied to all, on the one hand, and labor regulations that shifted economic value from employers to workers, on the other. That might explain why, in *Lochner,* Justice Peckham found no constitutional difficulty with the state's regulation of sanitary conditions at bakeries, but faulted only the work-hour rule. Of course, some of the Court's contemporaneous decisions were grounded in the Equal Protection Clause, which would account for judicial attention to the way state regulations classified.[140] Yet *Lochner* was not among them, and therein lies the import of this revisionist explanation of the Court's work.[141]

The argument advanced is not that the Court referred to due process but really meant to rely on the equal protection feature of the Fourteenth Amendment. It is that the justices carried forward an aversion to class legislation stretching back to colonial times. Early state constitutions contained provisions insisting that government was instituted for the "common good" and not for the "private interest or emolument of any one man, family, or class of men."[142] Those provisions shared an intellectual affinity with Justice Chase's natural-rights discussion in *Calder* and Madison's warning about "factions" in "Federalist No. 10."[143] In this vein, consider that the statute in *Calder* intervened in ongoing litigation and allowed some of the parties another chance to make their case.[144] Taking from A and giving to B may have been offensive not (only) because A suffered a significant loss, but (also) because B received a corresponding gain.

If, however, decisions like *Lochner* were anchored in ancient egalitarian ideas of that order, they represented an untenable revival of Lockean natural-rights thinking.[145] Recall that Locke's idea of the common good contemplated only governmental actions vindicating the natural rights that all individuals enjoyed.[146] Government was therefore constrained to extend benefits to, or to demand sacrifices from, all or none without qualification. Everyone had to be treated in precisely the same way, according to a single, unifying standard provided by the definition of the individual natural rights to be vindicated. There was no occasion for varying anyone's treatment on the basis of government's notions of good public policy. That conception of the police power was unrealistic. It contemplated, again, a natural and wholly private environment that government was unable to upset.[147] Once the Court disclaimed any such private market and, concomitantly, acknowledged that government was responsible for whatever state of affairs existed at the moment, the Court could scarcely maintain that government was nonetheless bound to perpetuate any fixed status quo.

Moreover, the proposition that government must treat everyone in precisely the same way would produce paralysis. It would deny to govern-

ment the instrument crucial to the modern regulatory state: the authority to do quite the opposite. Government must have the ability to treat
people *differently*—thus to create incentives that move the individuals
affected to change their conduct, thereby channeling behavior into socially desirable paths and promoting the general public interest. In this
vein, Professor Gillman argues that the Court's real blunder was to perpetuate the Lockean vision that regulatory legislation must operate with
perfect distributional equality in a world in which industrial relations
pitted the weak against the strong and thus created a need and justification for governmental regulation that Locke never imagined—regulation
that deliberately distributes benefits and burdens unequally in order to
achieve public-regarding ends.[148]

If the Court was chiefly concerned about class legislation, any genuine enthusiasm for the idea soon lost momentum. The Court ultimately
acknowledged that government *could* take from A and give to B. That
is what the emergence of democratic regulation in the public interest
was largely about. Today, certainly, we may cluck a bit when government legislates special arrangements or subsidies for certain individuals,
groups, or companies. Recall, too, that the Court condemns the taking
of property for the sole purpose of benefiting a favored private party
(with no compensating public returns).[149] But in the main, decisions to
move economic wherewithal around form the routine province of government.[150] Government can properly decide that some citizens should
suffer a diminution in their freedom or wealth in order that others may
enjoy a corresponding expansion. All that is necessary is that the con-
sequential burdens and benefits together serve the long-term interest of
society as a whole.

This understanding is essential to modern rational instrumentalism.
Government conventionally regulates by very deliberately treating individuals and classes differently in order to encourage people to behave
in ways that government considers to be for the social good. That is the
occasion for the generosity that instrumentalism shows to governmental
decision making, whether judged under the heading of due process or
equal protection. There are, of course, circumstances in which the modern Court finds regulation to be constitutionally invalid for failure to
square with the public interest. But those are not cases implicating economic arrangements; they are not cases in which government chooses
to take from A and give to B. Instead, they are cases about vital ways
in which government falls short of its responsibility to uphold the public

interest—cases in which government penalizes individuals not for what they have or what they do, but for who they are, what they value, and what they say.[151]

Efficiency and Elections

The fourth idea reflected in rational instrumentalism is common to the first three, but deserving of separate treatment: judicial deference to legislative policymaking. On one level, the idea is to leave decisions to the body most competent to make them. By some accounts, *Lochner's* celebrated ruin was a consequence of the evolving recognition (associated with the Legal Process School) that the Court was not positioned to make "scientific" judgments about social policy and that legislatures were better suited to identify social ills and to fashion sensible solutions.[152] Recall another caution from Justice Holmes: "[I]t must be remembered that legislatures are ultimate guardians of the liberties and welfare of the people in quite as great a degree as the courts."[153] Stated bluntly, the sentiment is that courts "ought to be very slow to declare that [a] state legislature [is] wrong in its facts" and thus to second-guess legislative understandings of the existence or gravity of social conditions.[154]

In *Lochner,* Justice Peckham was unimpressed with the New York Legislature's determination that limiting the hours bakers could be forced to work was a sensible means of protecting the public.[155] Today, the Court routinely accepts legislative estimations of whether particular measures can be successful.[156] In point of fact, the Court adopted its modern, deferential approach in at least some cases following closely on *Lochner's* heels. Frankfurter attributed the advance in some measure to Louis Brandeis's brief in *Muller v. Oregon,*[157] where the Court bowed to the economic analysis supporting a similar work-hour limit for women.[158] After *Muller,* courts in general were more willing to judge the validity of economic regulation "in the light of a realistic study of the industrial conditions affected" and to permit legislatures to view society as a "whole community" rather than as "independent individuals dealing at arms' length with one another."[159] In *McLean v. Arkansas,*[160] the Court articulated the modern view in strikingly modern language. Justice Day explained that a regulation is "not to be set aside because the judiciary may be of opinion that [it] will fail of its purpose or because it is thought to be . . . unwise." The statute in *McLean* undoubtedly helped workers in their dealings with their employers. But that alone could not condemn it: "We are unable to say, in the light of the conditions shown . . . that this law had no reasonable relation to the protection of a large class of laborers in the receipt of their just dues and in the promotion of the harmonious relations of capital and labor engaged in a great industry in the state."[161]

The Court's deference to legislative authority also responds to democracy. The basic idea is simple enough. Legislatures should generally make public policy for the good and sufficient reason that they were elected. Courts, by contrast, should keep their law-making functions to a minimum for the good and sufficient reason that they have no similar electoral warrant. James Thayer articulated this theme early on and even then insisted it was well settled already and wanted only for more attention.[162] Judicial decisions upsetting legislation in the name of natural rights and "free" markets, or on the basis of various limitations affixed to the police power, obviously neglected it. Yet thinkers commonly associated with the Legal Process School erected their account of public institutions around a basic commitment to legislative policymaking and judicial restraint—both to distribute institutional authority according to comparative capacity and to promote democracy.[163]

The turning-point decisions were candid about this. Recall that in *Nebbia,* Justice Roberts disclaimed any judicial warrant to examine the "wisdom" of a legislative policy.[164] In *Williamson,* Justice Douglas declared that "this Court" no longer uses the Constitution to override legislative policies it regards as "unwise" or "improvident."[165] Douglas's opinion in *Berman* was even more emphatic: "[T]he legislature, not the judiciary, is the main guardian of the public needs to be served by social legislation."[166] Most of the justices on the current Court agree. Writing for the majority in *Kelo,* Justice Stevens described the Court's modern "policy of deference to legislative judgments" regarding whether takings of private property serve a "public purpose."[167]

This is grossly oversimplified, of course. The point of chapter 1 was to explain that courts necessarily make a lot of law, including constitutional law, and thus participate actively in making public policy. Nevertheless, with the benefit of hindsight, it is easy to discern a prodigious educational experience for the Court. The justices learned that law cannot be reduced to logical deductions from conceptual categories, that the real toss and tumble of life must be acknowledged, and that in a nation that professes to be democratic it is largely the function of politically responsible institutions to select the means of advancing social welfare. As the Court's sophistication increased, so did its commitment to defer whenever possible to the judgments of elected officials.

The acknowledgment of legislative authority takes many forms, most obviously the process-based jurisprudence promoted by John Ely and others.[168] Ely's "process-purification" explanation for valid constitutional decisions is less prominent in academic circles today than it was a generation ago. Still, the basic ideas at work enjoy real staying power and often show up in Supreme Court opinions elaborating substantive rights according to rational instrumentalism. Once a politically accountable institution has taken a position on a matter of public policy, the Court ordinarily defers to that judgment for the very reason that it represents a politically accountable choice. If affected citizens don't like it, they are best advised to employ political avenues for effecting change. There are exceptions, of course, when disaffected individuals are not redirected to politics but receive a sympathetic hearing in the judiciary. Even as the justices have acquired an appreciation for democracy, they have also developed an understanding of their own role in this complex constitutional system. Briefly stated, they have recognized that role to be the discovery of *non*-instrumental impositions on individuals. Some actions taken by politically responsible institutions are unconstitutional, because they cannot be shown to be related to the public welfare (as an instrumental means to a public-regarding end). I elaborate in the chapters to follow.

*   *   *

Rational instrumentalism emerged from the nation's experience with alternative understandings of governmental power. The Court came to understand that there are no natural rights and no entirely private markets free of government involvement. Instead, rights and the private relations they entail are ascribable *to* government. Regulation is not alien to the natural state of things, but the bedrock of civil society—an endless series of adjustments in arrangements for which government is ineluctably responsible. The Court also learned that it could not (and should not) attempt to superintend routine regulatory authority by confining the public interest to any fixed menu of approved ends, to any particular economic policy, or to a perfectly even-handed distribution of burdens or benefits. So far from being invalid *per se,* governmental wealth transfers are inevitable—the very point of government. Finally, the Court came to appreciate its role in a democratic society. That role is not generally to second-guess the wisdom of the policies selected by more politically sensitive institutions, but to ensure that governmental action genuinely serves the public interest. All these ideas combined to produce rational instrumentalism as the core doctrinal content of substantive rights.

This is scarcely to say that all is well, that the justices have now found the right track, and that it is easy to decide cases about substantive rights against a rich experiential backdrop and the doctrine it has produced. It is only to say that the ideas sketched in this chapter give meaning to rational instrumentalism, which has developed into the Court's best doctrinal tool for elaborating the content of substantive rights. These underlying ideas continue to nourish and refresh rational instrumentalism as the doctrinal account of rights today, infusing instrumentalism with the energy needed to contend with a polyglot of actual cases in which individuals tangle with government and its minions. As the justices proceed within the framework rational instrumentalism supplies, they constantly refer back to these themes. I will have occasion to do the same.

CHAPTER THREE

Regulatory Rights

S ubstantive constitutional rights are not discrete entitlements established by the written Constitution and its amendments that capture
for the ages precisely the protections that individuals should enjoy. Nor
are they individuated spheres of personal freedom into which government is forbidden to intrude in some absolute sense.[1] Substantive rights
are a function of protean Supreme Court decisions that constantly make
and remake the arrangements between individuals and their government. The Constitution *is* what the Court makes of it in the long series
of actual cases decided. It is common to regard the task as striking (and
restriking) the proper balance between individual freedom and governmental power. That is misleading. The justices do not decide when
and where government's efforts to regulate for the public interest must
be subordinated to an individual's self-centered concerns. They decide
whether governmental action sensibly allocates burdens and benefits
in ways that promise to achieve discernible public objectives. In so doing, they draw upon the background ideas I sketched in the last chapter,
ideas that produced the fundamental understanding that government
acts constitutionally when it acts instrumentally in the public interest.
The substantive rights we enjoy coalesce in an entitlement to be regulated in that way and no other. This is not much to go on. But it is all we
have and, frankly, all we can hope to have.[2]

Rational instrumentalism comes bearing significant challenges. The analysis required to determine whether governmental action is instrumental in the necessary sense reproduces (on a different level) many of the same problems that attend failed efforts to interpret the written Constitution. Even as the justices abandon any serious attempt to derive constitutional meaning from the text of the 1789 document and its history, they still must ascribe meaning to statutes and other forms of governmental behavior—and not just any meaning, but meaning in light of underlying purposes, hypothesized or proven. This is so even though in many instances we may have serious doubts that such purposes exist and, if they do, that they can be discovered. I touched on these points in chapter 1 in connection with Justice Scalia's methodology for statutory construction and its potential extension into an originalist approach to constitutional interpretation.[3] I take them up in earnest in chapter 4.[4]

My objective in this chapter is to demonstrate that we can find instrumentalism in all the doctrinal formulations the Court offers for substantive rights. It is conventional to group Supreme Court decisions about rights under headings drawn from the written Constitution. We are said to have decisions about the meaning of due process, equal protection, freedom of expression, cruel and unusual punishments, and so on. And when we follow the Court as it moves from one context to the next, we expect to find the justices grappling with the peculiar questions entailed in the elaboration of each text-based right in turn. On examination, however, the Court actually wrestles with the same questions in each conventional category—namely, the questions that rational instrumentalism brings to the fore. This common doctrinal design cutting across familiar borders makes it possible to dig much more deeply into the way the Court actually decides constitutional cases about substantive rights.[5] I begin with some clarifications regarding rational instrumentalism. Then I turn to categories of substantive rights as they are conventionally understood and locate rational instrumentalism at the bottom of them all.

Preliminaries

Restraints Neither Internal nor External

The understanding of substantive rights as rational instrumentalism resists the dichotomy between "internal" and "external" restraints on governmental power. Instrumentalism fits neither category, but simply addresses itself to government's agents, federal or state, and explains how power at either level is to be exercised. This will sound jarring to specialists familiar with the jargon. By conventional account, Congress has two constitutional hoops to jump through. First, Congress must act within the internal restraints of some discrete power conferred by the Constitution; then, Congress must negotiate any relevant external restraints imposed by the Constitution as a further check.[6] The easiest illustrations are instances in which Congress plainly enjoys some affirmative power to act but in which the particular statute enacted violates substantive individual rights. Congress has power to regulate interstate commerce and thus can prescribe operational rules for railroads, but a statute mandating that passenger cars be racially segregated would violate individual rights ascribed to the Fifth Amendment.

The states, by contrast, are understood to enjoy a general authority to forge whatever policies they deem proper.[7] That power was not established by the 1789 document, but owes its existence to the legitimacy of the state entities and officers who exercise it—namely, to the sovereign *bona fides* of state government.[8] It follows, so the argument goes, that a state legislature has only one federal constitutional hoop to manage. Since the states do not depend on the Federal Constitution for their lawmaking authority, there is no occasion for identifying wherein the 1789 document confers a discrete power and deciding whether the limits internal to that power have been breached. Whatever a state does is fine insofar as the Federal Constitution is concerned, unless the state violates a restraint external to its general authority to make law. Here again, the most graphic illustrations implicate substantive individual rights. A state statute mandating racially segregated seating would violate rights attributed to the Fourteenth Amendment.[9]

However familiar this general orientation may be—it can be traced all the way back to John Marshall[10]—it is mistaken or at least misleading inasmuch as it conceives that states are empowered to do what they will unless and until they violate individual constitutional rights. That suggests, in turn, that rights have a certain content as orbs of individual freedom. And the question whether a species of state action is constitutional turns on whether it pierces one of those protected bubbles. Yet when the Court offers doctrine to elaborate the content of substantive rights, it supplies rational instrumentalism. On the one hand, instrumentalism cannot be understood as an internal restraint on governmental authority, federal or state. It is not entailed in the definition of the affirmative power said to be at work—either one of Congress's enumerated powers or the general state police power. On the other hand, instrumentalism cannot be characterized as an external restraint, either. It does not presuppose governmental power unless and until some independent check is brought to bear. Rational instrumentalism does not describe the contours of individual rights so much as it simply imposes a fundamental requirement (substantive rationality) on whatever actions government may take.

I explained in the last chapter that the Court fashioned rational instrumentalism as the doctrinal content of substantive rights from early accounts of the affirmative scope of regulatory authority. One theme in that mix was the notion that the traditionally identified ends of the state police power (health, safety, morals, and general welfare) constituted internal restraints inasmuch as they restricted government's regulatory reach without reference to anything in the Fourteenth Amendment. Some aspects of Justice Peckham's opinion in *Lochner* suggested that kind of thinking.[11] Yet the idea that instrumental governmental means must aim to achieve particular, formally bounded objectives did not survive. The moral of that story is that the Court developed the more familiar and generous rational instrumentalism in operation today partly as a rejection of any such internal restraints on the police power.

Some libertarians argue that there *are* internal federal constitutional restraints on the police power that can condemn a state policy apart from any external limit. Randy Barnett contends, for example, that the Supreme Court need not explain decisions overturning state statutes restricting individual freedom as violations of specifically defined Fourteenth Amendment rights. Instead, the Court may hold, as an antecedent matter, that laws limiting liberty or property simply extend governmental coercion beyond the authority the police power establishes and thus beyond constitutional limits implicated by that power. Barnett does not propose to revive the police power ends analysis suggested in *Lochner*. Instead, he would have the Court protect "liberty" independently.[12]

Professor Barnett argues that if the Court were to adopt his position, real consequences would follow. State laws that now survive on the theory that they do not violate Fourteenth Amendment rights would be struck down on the ground that they are not justified by the police power in the first place.[13] The only recent decision Barnett offers in support of his view is *Lawrence v. Texas*,[14] in which the Supreme Court invalidated antisodomy statutes. But in that case, the Court's own explanation of its analysis was quite different—consonant with the account I want to offer.

At most, Barnett offers an alternative way the Court might have written its opinion. I take up *Lawrence* in chapter 4. It is true that some justices have generated formalistic stratagems for grappling with controversial cases involving sensitive individual interests. But those devices are not meant to recognize internal limits on governmental regulation of liberty; rather, they are employed to discipline the Court's discretion to find governmental regulation invalid.[15]

I argue that rational instrumentalism provides the essence of the constitutional doctrine governing substantive rights both with respect to enactments by Congress and with respect to state police power measures. But I do not contend that rational instrumentalism operates as an internal restraint on state action. Again, rational instrumentalism wears neither label. I hasten to say that nothing would change (necessarily) even if the Court were to reconceive the police power by making rational instrumentalism an internal restraint. It seems perfectly clear that the Supreme Court reaches the results it thinks best and that anything short of a radical adjustment in its articulated doctrine would make no difference. That, after all, may be part of the explanation for the Court's recurrent reliance on rational instrumentalism to form the content of substantive rights. The justices do their level best to fashion appropriate constitutional meaning as they go along, maintaining a measure of continuity with the past and offering a measure of predictability for the future. We should not expect them to depart significantly from the body of their work on the ground that Professor Barnett advocates or, for that matter, on any grounds whatsoever.

Regulatory Rights in the Literature

Echoes of the conception of substantive rights I want to describe have appeared in the literature. In amazing lectures published thirty years ago, Anthony Amsterdam distinguished two models of the Fourth Amendment.[16] Under the conventional model, the Fourth Amendment recognizes individual "atomistic spheres of interest" and establishes limits on the ability of law enforcement officers to intrude into those spheres; under the "regulatory" model, by contrast, the Fourth Amendment simply establishes standards for police conduct. Amsterdam's regulatory model suggests in microcosm the basic conception of rights on which I want to build—namely, the idea that the content of substantive rights is best understood as a general standard of conduct for government to observe.

I should be clear that Professor Amsterdam focused exclusively on the Fourth Amendment (which has both substantive and procedural components), that he suggested the regulatory model as a means of addressing problems peculiar to that setting, and that, into the bargain, he claimed a textual basis for the model in the Fourth Amendment itself.[17] Nevertheless, his regulatory model conceives of at least one right as an affirmative direction to government about the way to behave. That conception, in my view, has a wider and far more significant application. We have individual rights, and we can talk about them *as* rights. But we should understand that the Court develops their content not by identifying individual capsules of liberty and specifying whether and how government may constitutionally puncture them, but by telling government forthrightly what governmental action must be. Contrary to conventional thinking, rights do not restrict government negatively; they impose positive requirements for any action the government undertakes.

Much more recently, Richard Pildes has argued for a "structural conception of rights" that also borders on the "regulatory rights" idea I want to offer.[18] Pildes, too, resists the traditional understanding that rights are "atomistic" spheres of individual freedom enjoying a privileged status as against the common interest. Instead, by his account, rights are mainly constraints on the *"kinds of reasons"* for which government can take action. This, according to Pildes, is why the Supreme Court does not (really) fix boundaries around individual rights and proclaim that any governmental incursions across those boundaries must necessarily be unconstitutional. It is also why the Court attends to the reasons behind governmental action. If rights were immunities from interference, it would not matter *why* government invades the individual's province. Since government's reasons *do* matter, it follows that rights must have a different character. Pildes contends that rights are best understood as "tools" the Court employs to "police the kinds of purposes government can offer to justify its action."[19]

There is a lot to like in what Professor Pildes has to say. He plainly rejects the conventional understanding that individual rights are external restraints on governmental power (though not in so many words). He also recognizes that the real meaning of rights lies in "actual constitutional practice" wherein the Supreme Court orchestrates the relationship between individual freedom and governmental authority by ensuring that government regulates for acceptable reasons. Pildes insists that rights are not individualistic imperatives, the public be damned, but are instead devices for achieving collective interests. When we say that rights are violated, we mean (or should mean) that government has taken action that does *not* promise to achieve public ends. Pildes recognizes that the content of rights turns on "value-laden" judgments that the justices make in the great variety of contexts in which arguments over the public interest occur.[20]

Professor Pildes fails fully to appreciate, however, that rational instrumentalism is the Court's way of elaborating substantive rights. He sees the means/ends focus of the Court's doctrine as evidence that the justices neither insist that individual rights override social welfare nor somehow balance individual rights against governmental interests. And he dismisses the Court's articulations of doctrine as distractions from the reality of rights jurisprudence. At most, Pildes argues that his conception of rights helps to explain key features of the Court's work that do not comport with the conventional "atomistic" model—namely, the Court's failure actually to enforce rights-absolutism and its concentration on government's reasons for curbing individual freedom. I do not argue that the justices self-consciously conceive of substantive individual rights in the "regulatory" way I describe. I recognize that they take seriously the attempt to package their analysis as appeals to textualism and originalism. Certainly, I concede that when they invoke rational instrumentalism, they are inclined to present their work as more constrained than it is. I do set aside the various "standards of review" the justices purport to apply in individual rights cases. But rational instrumentalism itself is the doctrinal reflection of the intellectual history traced in chapter 2. That doctrine is not distracting at all, but right on target. Moreover, I think the justices recognize as much—and say so expressly in cases in which their responsibility for judgment is most apparent.[21]

Professor Pildes's project is analytic, essentially ahistorical. He fails fully to appreciate that the conception of rights he calls "structural" and I call "regulatory" is not really new, contributed by academicians as an account of rights superior to what the justices have thought to be the case. This understanding of rights has been around for a good while and has been knowingly acted upon by justices with a sense of history and, more to the point, a sense of the lessons of history for modern American constitutional government. Professor Pildes fortifies his treatment by useful references to actual Supreme Court cases, but he makes no sustained attempt to follow his conception of rights into the larger run of decisions and thus to explore the implications. I make that attempt, both in this chapter and in the next, and in so doing I hope to reveal just how much judgment is required of the justices in order to deliver decisions about substantive individual rights.

Steven Smith has developed the argument that the Constitution in general is best understood as a demand that government conform its behavior to reason.[22] According to Smith, the Constitution rests on two conceptions of reason, the one tied to classical thought and the other to a more modern-looking rationalism associated with the Enlightenment. Smith contends that the fundamental point of the Constitution is to demand that we govern ourselves according to the kind of "reason" for which we ourselves are responsible—rather than trusting to the "supposed wisdom of past generations" or to "ignorance, credulity, and superstition."[23] While he disclaims both textualism and originalism, he nonetheless ascribes the Constitution's commitment to reason to the "founding generation." By his account, the "framers" primarily hoped to control the Federal Government by enumerating its powers specifically, but they also anticipated that internal restraints alone might not suffice and thus added individual rights as a backstop. Smith insists that by taking upon ourselves the "activity of reason," we have rejected the framers' undertaking that reason was "supposed" to reside in the text of the document.[24]

Professor Smith also acknowledges points that are consistent with my thesis. He accepts that justices may be able to ascertain values that are shared widely enough to serve as moral "conventions" and that justices can ask (and resolve) difficult questions about whether governmental policy genuinely respects those conventions and operates within their framework in a consistent way. Smith calls this judicial duty "regulatory reasoning," that is, reasoning systematically about governmental behavior against the background of conventions the justices themselves do not establish but only accept for purposes of analysis. And like so many others, he recognizes that when the Supreme Court applies regulatory reasoning to governmental action, the Court explains its analysis in the language of rational instrumentalism. Smith concludes that regulatory reasoning is unsuccessful in that it cannot account for variations in plausible moral beliefs. He suggests that judicial decisions rationalizing results may be worthwhile, but he laments that "reason" is often only the label we attach to the views of cultural elites.[25] Of course, I am more optimistic.

David Beatty argues that when constitutional courts in Europe and Asia determine the meaning of rights-bearing provisions, they typically employ methodology we associate with English common law and that their decisions tend to emphasize a single core idea: proportionality.[26] By his account, this is true of the major European constitutional courts, the European Court of Justice, the European Court of Human Rights, and the Supreme Court of Japan. In some respects, Beatty's comparative study of those tribunals parallels my own provincial treatment of the American Supreme Court. Beatty himself largely faults our Court for clinging to the myth that interpretivism can resolve hard problems, while central courts in the rest of the world acknowledge the severe limits on textual analysis. But he also acknowledges corresponding themes. He links proportionality with the means/ends formulation in American decisions, identifies essentially equivalent doctrinal approaches to apparently distinct rights, and urges American judges to think of themselves as pragmatic problem-solvers.[27] Those points seem right to me. Proportionality is plainly an intellectual cousin of the rational instrumentalism I think dominates the Supreme Court's doctrinal framework for analyzing substantive rights problems.

Or perhaps, I should say, proportionality is a constituent element of rational instrumentalism. Consider the message that the injunction "Be reasonable" genuinely conveys—not, surely, that all is well so long as agents of government don't take leave of their senses. Much more is implicated—attention to the personal and governmental interests at stake, to the care government takes in crafting a means of achieving its ends, and, surely, to a fair sense of proportion. If a trolley can take only a few more passengers, it would be rational (in a minimally logical and functional sense) for the platform captain to tell all the women in the queue that they must wait for another car. But that would not be anybody's idea of a *reasonable* way to allocate scarce space. The idea that moves constitutional courts of justice elsewhere thus collapses into the doctrinal framework the American Supreme Court uses to elaborate substantive rights, which doctrinal framework (again) illuminates relevant considerations that, in turn, drive results. Illustrative cases bear this out.[28]

The prevalence of rational instrumentalism in the American Supreme Court's explanations of substantive rights can scarcely be questioned. Numerous academic observers have remarked on it.[29] Twenty years ago, Cass Sunstein pointed out that the Supreme Court uses virtually the same doctrine to determine the validity of governmental action under various clauses of the Constitution.[30] The reason, he inferred, is that while those clauses have "different historical roots and were originally directed at different problems," they respond to a "single underlying evil." Sunstein identified that evil as governmental action on the basis of "naked preferences," by which he meant the political capacity of private interests to use the levers of government to achieve the "distribution of resources or opportunities" they desire. He explained that the clauses he identified share a common concern with the objectives (rather than the effects) of governmental action and are largely aimed at "discrimination" for the "impermissible purpose" of advancing private preferences rather than some "public value." Sunstein argued that when the justices interpret those clauses, they employ a "number of devices—most prominently the required showing of some degree of means-ends connection and the identification of a category" of "impermissible ends" to "filter out naked preferences."[31]

Over the years, Professor Sunstein and others have developed these initial thoughts in an impressive and influential body of scholarship, some of which I rehearsed in the last chapter. I want to adopt the idea that various strands of constitutional law, often thought to be distinct, are actually animated by a single doctrinal framework on which the Court consistently relies for guidance. Nevertheless, my project is different in a number of important respects. In his initial essay, Sunstein attempted to draw meaning from explicit provisions of the written Constitution and, moreover, to rest in some measure on the original understanding of the historical document (together with its amendments). He contended that the document reflects an aversion to governmental action in furtherance of private interests, and he associated that underlying idea with the "framers' hostility toward naked preferences"—demonstrated by Madison's concern that government not be captured by "factions" and by "the Constitution's roots in civic republicanism."[32] Sunstein thus joined company with many other academics who persist in the notion that the text of the document, colored by original understanding, genuinely shapes Supreme Court decisions about constitutional meaning.

I take a different view. Professor Sunstein rightly went looking for the ideas embodied in the doctrine the Court articulates. But he mistook the source of those ideas. I grant that the account of substantive rights I describe is very much the product of American political history, some of it reaching back to the eighteenth century. But the Court has not labored to realize any original vision, however vaguely formed; instead, it has jettisoned the ancient aversion to class legislation (tied as it was to natural-rights thinking) and substituted the understanding that government can create classes, as long as the public interest is served.[33] Rational instrumentalism is the product of disappointing experiences with alternative accounts of governmental authority and a consequent wisdom about what American constitutional democracy should be. Sunstein worried aloud that judicial enforcement of the constitutional "principle" he identified allowed "enormous room for judgment," and he was nervous about the judicial "creation" of theories regarding impermissible ends, "especially when they shift over time or can be tied only with difficulty to the text and intended function of the relevant clauses."[34] Those are not my concerns.

Sunstein's argument (in 1984) was at once more expansive and more limited than my own. He was clear that he meant to be largely descriptive. Yet he couldn't help but be more ambitious. Thus he suggested that the "principle" he identified might be a "candidate for a unitary theory of the Constitution"—reaching many other clauses he did not discuss, as well as the Constitution's "structural provisions." I do not foreclose the possibility of extending rational instrumentalism to other contexts. But I do mean to limit myself to a discussion of substantive individual rights. Professor Sunstein also excluded certain individual rights from his general principle, explaining that those rights restrain governmental power in the absence of any impermissible purpose. By way of example, he cited the "right to 'privacy'" in *Roe v. Wade*.[35] He acknowledged that it might be possible to "collapse rights constraints and theories of impermissible ends," but he insisted that the "focus" in each context "is very different." I argue, by contrast, that, *doctrinally speaking,* there is little to choose among substantive rights. They all operate in much the same way, demanding that government use rationally instrumental means in the pursuit of public ends.[36]

Sunstein's basic thesis was that the clauses he discussed make it impermissible for government to adopt policies for the purpose of shifting economic wherewithal to some at the expense of others, with no public payoff. There was something to that argument. Sunstein and others later expanded on it, I have already noted it, and I will address it further in due course.[37] It does seem fair to say that the Supreme Court once invalidated at least some economic regulatory legislation on that theory or something very much like it.[38] But the next step in Sunstein's argument was problematic by comparison. Having argued that the distribution of wealth for private ends is impermissible, he extended that idea to the distribution of "opportunities" according to private desires. By his account, statutes imposing burdens on the basis of race or gender can equally be condemned on the theory that they, too, serve impermissible ends.[39]

Here again, I want to differ. There is reason to believe that, for a time, the Court thought it was illegitimate for government to redistribute wealth in *many* circumstances (apart from the ordinary operation of the common law), even when there was a plausible basis for concluding that the costs imposed on the few were offset by the gains for the public at large. If so, however, the Court has long since discarded any such proposition.[40] Modern governmental action that visits non-instrumental burdens on racial minorities and women is invalid for want of a legitimate explanation, all right, but not because the Court draws an unbroken line between race and gender decisions and long-rejected thinking in economic cases. The justices have quite different reasons for holding that punitive measures on the basis of race and gender are constitutionally unacceptable. I mean to explore those explanations and, in so doing, I again invoke Professor Sunstein's more recent scholarship.

Finally, Sunstein noted but did not develop the many vexing problems entailed in the application of means/ends scrutiny. That is where I mean to concentrate my attention in chapter 4. I will not worry over those problems in an effort to demonstrate flaws in rational instrumentalism, far less to condemn this basic doctrinal framework for failing to restrain the Court's judgment. I examine the difficulties rational instrumentalism raises to prove that it only marshals relevant considerations. Instrumentalism provides a serviceable organizational structure because it carries forward powerful lessons learned the hard way in the history of American public law.

My argument is that rational instrumentalism is the basic doctrinal definition of substantive rights. I aim to prove this by addressing the rights Americans enjoy under four headings pegged, by tradition, to the text of the historical document. I begin with the right to due process of law and the right to equal protection of the laws. Then I examine rights in two other categories articulated in the Bill of Rights: freedom of speech (and religion) and freedom from cruel and unusual punishments.[41]

Due Process

Rational instrumentalism plainly supplies the core of substantive due process analysis. Illustrations are everywhere about us. Any governmental activity that adjusts individual freedom (of any kind) presents the question whether it deprives the persons affected of liberty without due process of law. Typically, governmental action does *not* because, *ceteris paribus*, it constitutes an instrumental means of achieving public-regarding objectives. This is bedrock, or at least ought to be bedrock, and would be bedrock if the justices were only clear about what it is they actually do in relevant cases.

Trouble is, the justices often are not clear at all, but rather leave the erroneous impression that so far from deploying substantive due process (thus rational instrumentalism) as a routine touchstone of constitutionality, they resist due process entirely (and, perhaps, rational instrumentalism along with it). In run-of-the-mill cases involving market regulation, the justices are wont to suggest that substantive due process no longer supplies any limits at all on government's behavior. They do so in reaction to perceived excesses in the Court's past and in recognition of an appropriate deference to legislative economic policy in modern times.[42] In cases implicating especially sensitive human interests, they are wont to suggest again that due process has no application, but that other, independent "fundamental rights" are in play. For all the world, it appears that substantive due process is reserved for a third category of cases in which executive officers are alleged to engage in especially abusive behavior, and even there supplies only a modest check on egregious violence. I want, first, to get straight how and why the Court located substantive curbs on governmental action in this unlikely place—namely, in the idea of due *process*. Then I turn to the decisions in these three theaters and argue that, accurately understood, they are all illustrations of substantive due process and, importantly, that the substantive due process they illustrate is rational instrumentalism.

The Substance of Process

The phrase "due process of law" was not original with the Fifth Amendment (where the Constitution first used it) nor, certainly, in the Fourteenth Amendment (where the Constitution employed it again). By common account, "due process" was Lord Coke's rendition of key language in the thirty-ninth chapter of Magna Carta, which declared that the Crown could take no action against a free man "except by lawful judgment of his peers or by the law of the land."[43] The complex history of due process in English law is obscure, the subject of much continuing debate. For my purposes, it is enough to examine American materials.[44] I began this discussion in the last chapter.[45] Some state courts invoked due process provisions in state constitutions to upset state laws well before 1868.[46] The Supreme Court decided *Dred Scott*[47] on the basis of substantive due process derived from the Fifth Amendment. The Court also found a few state statutes invalid before 1868 and thus may have anticipated the substantive limits on state behavior that the Due Process Clause of the Fourteenth Amendment would make available.[48]

Nevertheless, there were powerful arguments to the effect that due process was exclusively a matter of procedure.[49] A legislature might violate due process by prescribing that a statute would be enforced in individual cases without a fair hearing to determine the facts. But due process had nothing to say about the validity of the statute itself, apart from its enforcement.[50] That is probably why John Campbell, counsel for the plaintiffs in the *Slaughterhouse Cases,* placed primary reliance on the Privileges or Immunities Clause.[51] In the event, the Court gave that clause an extremely narrow construction that has crippled it ever since.[52] Pausing only briefly over due process and equal protection, Justice Miller confirmed that the former reached only procedure and insisted that latter addressed only racial discrimination. The notion that state regulation could deny due process of law apart from the procedural means by which it was enforced appeared in *Slaughterhouse,* but only in the dissenting opinions filed by Stephen Field and Joseph Bradley.[53]

The dissenting view in *Slaughterhouse* ultimately prevailed. Recall that in *Lochner* Justice Peckham arguably treated liberty (in the form of the "right of contract") as a free-standing natural right, antecedent to the Constitution and independent of it.[54] Yet he invoked the Due Process Clause of the Fourteenth Amendment as the textual basis for his decision. The employer in *Lochner* did not complain about any want of *process* in his treatment; he did not argue that he had been denied a fair trial. He contended that the statute limiting bakers' hours was itself unconstitutional, even if it was rationally and fairly applied in his case. The *Lochner* decision and many others in the period are thus rightly regarded as illustrations of the Supreme Court's reliance on due process to examine the validity of substantive regulatory measures. Notwithstanding much confusing rhetoric, the justices readily acknowledge today that due process has a perfectly legitimate substantive dimension.[55]

Of course, constitutional doctrine need not respond to anything in the written document and very often does not. Moreover, the line between substance and process is notoriously thin.[56] Courts employ process to enforce a substantive rule, thus hoping to bring consistency to the resolution of what would otherwise be isolated cases. And by resolving ostensibly disparate cases, courts generate a substantive rule that hopes to reconcile them all. Still, the very idea of *substantive* due *process* sounds oxymoronic.[57] There are two explanations for the Court's acceptance of the argument that Field and Bradley advanced, one conceptual and the other practical. We have been through the conceptual explanation. The Court apparently conceived that a statute that diminished an individual's freedom or assets as a matter of legislative policy alone violated due process in that it deprived the individual of liberty or property in the absence of a common law wrong determined by the process afforded in the courts.[58] The practical explanation is obvious. The Court soon recognized the need for some substantive restraint on state regulatory authority. Since *Slaughterhouse* had largely eliminated the Privileges or Immunities Clause and the Equal Protection Clause as possibilities, modifying due process was the only game in town.[59]

Market Freedom

After its birth of necessity, substantive due process operated as a matter of course in cases involving ordinary regulatory legislation. It might seem that the conceptual explanation for a substantive dimension to due process in the first place proved too much. Any regulatory statute must necessarily affect liberty or property without the process entailed in the judicial resolution of private disputes according to the standing common law. Therefore, any statute should have been unconstitutional. Yet the justices were never so dogmatic. Recall that they tolerated adjustments in the content of common law arrangements.[60] The challenge was to allow legislatures a measure of maneuvering room while preventing them from upsetting any and all familiar arrangements without substantive constitutional restraint.

In the earliest cases, the justices declared (ambiguously) that due process would not countenance "arbitrary" laws.[61] Later, in cases like *Lochner,* they merged the negative constitutional limits that substantive due process placed on governmental action with the affirmative scope ascribed to the police power.[62] That move rendered a substantive check on legislative power, articulated in the language of instrumentalism: Legislatures were free to regulate, but only as a reasonable means of furthering the general social welfare. Recall that in *Lochner,* Justice Peckham explained that a regulatory statute was valid if it constituted "a means to an end" and "the end itself [was] appropriate and legitimate."[63] Peckham's analysis in *Lochner* has been criticized on many counts, but rarely for recognizing a substantive side to due process and stating its requirements in that classic way. Having embraced the idea of substantive due process (at least implicitly), Peckham needed some content to pour into that idea and, sensibly enough, borrowed from the precedents describing the police power.[64]

Roosevelt's first appointee, Hugo Black, pressed a radically different agenda. According to Black, due process had no general substantive content at all and thus supplied no constitutional tool with which the Court could superintend regulatory legislation.[65] Other justices rejected that idea and continued to mouth much the same doctrinal formulation for due process that Peckham had articulated. In *Nebbia v. New York*,[66] Justice Roberts explained that due process demanded that a governmental means "shall have a real and substantial relation to the object sought to be attained."[67] In *Ferguson v. Skrupa*,[68] where Justice Black attempted to sustain a regulatory measure on the theory that due process had no application at all, Justice Harlan wrote separately to explain that the statute in that case was valid only because it was a reasonable means of achieving the state's ends.[69] Harlan's account, not Black's, reflected the prevailing view.[70]

To be sure, in economic regulation cases today the Court largely leaves it to politically accountable decision makers to determine both public goals and the appropriate steps to take in achieving those goals. The Court has not relied on due process to invalidate a regulation of business for many years.[71] On rare occasions when the justices fault ordinary regulation, they prefer to invoke the Equal Protection Clause, instead (perhaps for reasons I will take up in a minute).[72] The justices sometimes talk and act as though Justice Black has won in the end and there is no substantive due process left—except for cases in which the liberty at stake is "fundamental."[73] Nevertheless, the conduct of business activities remains a form of liberty, the regulation of which triggers dues process. It is just that government is free to regulate market behavior in the interests of the general public welfare, and the justices, again, are content that in the run of cases there is nothing to suggest that elected officers are doing anything else. The analysis in *Lochner* is dead only in the sense that the Court's *application* of substantive due process in that case is now uniformly disclaimed. But the *Lochner* analysis is very much alive in the sense that substantive due process remains intact (along with the rational instrumentalism that supplies its doctrinal content). If this were not true, the equal protection decisions the Court occasionally delivers in this context (decisions that might just as easily wear the due process label) would be unintelligible.[74]

Fundamental Interests

Substantive due process also addresses governmental action with respect to sensitive individual interests—generally speaking, interests associated with the intimacies of personal life. The justices sometimes shrink from this reality. Here again, they occasionally talk and act as though due process has no significance of its own force. The difference is that, with respect to these human interests, due process has not been abandoned entirely, but functions as a vehicle for bringing other "fundamental rights" to bear. It appears necessary, accordingly, to apply whatever doctrinal content those discrete rights have in order to decide cases. Writing for the Court in *Cruzan*,[75] Chief Justice Rehnquist assumed the existence of a "constitutionally protected *right*" to decline lifesaving medical care.[76] In *Glucksberg*,[77] he framed the issue as whether there is a "*right* to commit suicide which itself includes a "*right* to assistance in doing so."[78] Similar accounts pepper prominent decisions. In *Roe v. Wade*,[79] Justice Blackmun rested, in part, on a supposed "*right* of privacy."[80] In *Casey*,[81] the joint opinion reaffirmed "the *right* of [a] woman to choose to have an abortion before viability."[82] And in *Lawrence v. Texas*,[83] Justice Kennedy said that the "liberty protected by the Constitution" permits gays and lesbians "the *right*" to choose the sexual partners they will.[84] Other illustrations abound.[85]

This "rights" rhetoric gives rise to another linguistic curiosity: the idea of "unenumerated rights."[86] We might have anticipated that only libertarians would argue that "unenumerated" rights exist and must be judicially enforced. Yet in these cases the Court's conservatives are also active proponents. Chief Justice Rehnquist acknowledged that "fundamental rights" have no footing in the Bill of Rights and, in truth, have no serious textual foundation at all.[87] If they are rights, then, they must be "unenumerated." David Strauss has declared flatly that substantive due process is now only "the name given to the idea that the courts may recognize rights . . . that do not have an explicit textual basis in the Constitution."[88] I explain in the next chapter that some justices refer to "fundamental rights" for tactical purposes. They do not countenance the recognition of other independent "unenumerated" rights at all, but hope to restrict rigorous due process review to the human interests identified as "fundamental" in the Court's precedents.[89] Here, I want only to clarify that references to "fundamental rights" in due process cases are not to be taken seriously but endured as a distraction.

The justices do not really mean that substantive due process serves only to introduce other independent rights into the mix. They mean (or should be understood to mean) that the right to be enforced is the right to due process itself, and they only confuse matters by using the terms *right, liberty,* and *interest* interchangeably. In *Cruzan,* even as Chief Justice Rehnquist acknowledged a constitutional "right" to refuse medical attention, he explained in the same breath that the plaintiff claimed a *"liberty interest"* in declining treatment.[90] In *Glucksberg,* he said that substantive due process protects "fundamental *rights* and *liberties.*"[91] In *Roe,* Justice Blackmun allowed that the "right of privacy" at stake could be found in "the concept of personal *liberty.*"[92] In *Casey,* the joint opinion explained that "[c]onstitutional protection of [a] woman's decision to terminate her pregnancy derives from the Due Process Clause" and that the "controlling word is . . . '*liberty.*'"[93] And in *Lawrence,* Justice Kennedy recognized that the plaintiffs wished only to "exercise . . . their *liberty* under the Due Process Clause."[94] Here again, countless other illustrations are available.[95]

The idea of "fundamental rights" has a familiar history—yet another illustration of the gallant efforts the Court has made to construct workable constitutional doctrine despite unruly constitutional text. Let's recall that history under three headings. First, the Court developed the proposition that the Fourteenth Amendment incorporated the "fundamental" procedural rights specified in the Bill of Rights for application in state criminal cases. Second, the Court held that the Fourteenth Amendment similarly absorbed the freedom of expression associated with the First Amendment. Third, the Court attempted (for a time) to ascribe Fourteenth Amendment protection to an additional band of personal interests on the theory that they, too, were adopted from the Bill of Rights. These stories help to explain both how the label "fundamental rights" came into use and why that label is no longer serviceable—except as a strategic device. When the justices are careful with language, they explain that the task is to elaborate the right to due process "on its own bottom"[96]—not "fundamental rights" with an independent existence of their own. Here, as elsewhere, the doctrinal meaning of substantive due process is rational instrumentalism.

PROCEDURAL RIGHTS.   Early on, the Court held that *procedural* due process in state criminal prosecutions meant "fundamental" fairness.[97] That understanding proved dissatisfying. State procedures for criminal cases were appalling, and, in the 1960s, the Court was ready to administer stronger medicine. Justice Black famously seized the chance to assault substantive due process from the flank. Black contended that the drafters of the Fourteenth Amendment had meant simply to incorporate the Bill of Rights.[98] That meant that all the procedural rights catalogued in the first eight amendments were applicable to state criminal prosecutions and that the (comparatively few) substantive rights on the list, most notably freedom of speech in the First Amendment, were equally applicable to state as well as federal action. For Black, however, the negative implication was equally significant. Once the Bill of Rights was exhausted, there was no residual due process for the Court to deploy as a check on state regulation of economic affairs.[99] Therein lay the basis for Black's scheme to at last forestall further resort to the substantive due process associated with *Lochner*.[100] Black's position did not prevail in the thoroughgoing way he hoped it would, but some justices adopted variants on his basic theme.[101]

Against this background, it is easy to understand why the Court might describe the content of the general right to *procedural* due process by reference to the independently specified rights contained in the Bill of Rights. According to incorporation theory, those rights only restated the right to due process in a more particularized way. These events also help to explain references to discrete *fundamental* rights. The Warren Court ultimately reached a compromise position—namely, that the Due Process Clause embraced those procedural rights contained in the Bill of Rights deemed to be "fundamental" to a fair trial, as well as other procedural rights not included in the Bill of Rights but nonetheless equally "fundamental."[102]

SUBSTANTIVE RIGHTS.   A similar analysis surfaced with respect to freedom of expression. Early in the last century, the justices began to fashion doctrine elaborating the right of free speech established by the First Amendment, itself applicable only against the Federal Government. Soon thereafter, they contrived to read the Due Process Clause of the Fourteenth Amendment to justify applying the same doctrine to censorship at the hands of the states. The syntax was more challenging. Freedom of speech was substantive. It could not be characterized as another fundamental procedural right contained in the Bill of Rights that, in turn, formed one of the procedural safeguards making up the process due in state proceedings. If the justices recognized that difficulty, they hid it behind another perplexing obfuscation. They simply noted that the freedom of expression the First Amendment protected against national power was "among the fundamental personal *rights* and *'liberties'* protected by the due process clause of the Fourteenth Amendment from impairment by the States."[103]

It would have been neater to explain forthrightly that freedom of speech counted as *liberty* and that governmental action limiting an individual's freedom to speak (like the freedom to carry on a business) brought the right to due process into play. And not only the right to procedural due process (should government engage some fact-finding proceeding meant to identify a speaker for punishment), but also substantive due process: the substantive right to be regulated with respect to expression in a rationally instrumental way. Then again, if the Court had taken that route, it would have reproduced (on a different level) the very puzzle the justices had created in the procedural due process context. Treating expression as a form of liberty protected by due process might suggest that the discrete right of free speech grounded in the First Amendment would not extend routinely to cases involving state power. Instead, any freedom individuals had to express themselves would be developed as an aspect of due process alone. The Court would do with respect to the substantive matter of expression what it originally did with respect to procedural safeguards in criminal cases. The working idea would be due process and only due process—not the First Amendment freedom of speech also protected against federal authority.

Some justices leaned in that direction.[104] But the full Court soon explained that in this context due process would serve as a conduit for applying to the states the same restraints the First Amendment imposed on the Federal Government. In modern cases, the Court recognizes a single body of free speech doctrine and brings it to bear on both state and federal action without distinction. I return to freedom of speech below. For now, it is only important to understand that in free speech cases the working idea is not substantive due process, but the freedom of speech identified with the First Amendment. Due process is not itself the rule to be applied in a speech case, but only the package in which the rule arrives for application.

BEYOND THE BILL OF RIGHTS. With the criminal procedure and free speech "incorporation" cases on the books, it is hardly surprising that when the justices turned to especially sensitive human interests with no obvious analogue in the Bill of Rights, they were inclined to say, again, that due process was only a shell surrounding other discrete rights, which do the real work. The best illustration is *Griswold v. Connecticut*,[105] where Justice Douglas insisted that various provisions of the Bill of Rights *implicitly* recognized a "right of privacy" that, in turn, was incorporated by the Due Process Clause for application to the case at hand.[106] Black objected that the very point of incorporation theory was that only an explicit Bill of Rights provision would do, else the negative restraining force of the theory would be lost.[107] The other justices rehearsed positions on incorporation borrowed from the procedural due process context. Importantly, though, every member of the Court wrote or joined an opinion articulating the question in *Griswold* as whether the statute touched a "right" of some ilk, evidently independent of due process yet in some way subsumed by it. Justices who subscribed to incorporation theory in some form did it. And justices who rejected incorporation (at least in *Griswold*) did the same.[108]

In light of the *Griswold* experience, justices today may be forgiven for using the rhetoric of "fundamental rights" in the run of substantive due process cases. Yet the fact remains that the "rights" of which they are wont to speak outside the free speech context are really liberties— that is, interests. The only right in view is the right to due process itself. That right protects not other discrete rights but a spectrum of liberty interests. And its operative power turns on the nature of the individual interest at stake in any given instance. When only market freedom is implicated, the justices typically have no reason to doubt that a governmental regulation serves some public objective. When "fundamental" interests—Again, I say *interests,* not *rights*—are at risk, the justices *do* have reason for doubting that governmental regulation furthers social welfare and are thus much harder to please. The Court typically reveals these inclinations expressly by varying the standard of review under which government's regulatory behavior is to be tested. Always, though, substantive due process analysis rests on the basic model that rational instrumentalism supplies. There is a good deal more to say about the Court's use of rational instrumentalism in the analysis of disparate cases, especially about the Court's largely unsuccessful efforts to explain its behavior on the basis of different standards of review. I pick up this conversation again in the next chapter.[109]

For now, suffice it to say that substantive due process in "fundamental rights" cases is no different in kind from substantive due process anywhere else. These cases are distinguishable from *Lochner* not because they involve different rights independent of due process but because they implicate different individual interests. If *Lochner* was wrongly decided (and virtually everyone concedes it was), it was not because Justice Peckham enforced the wrong right (due process) with the wrong doctrinal content (rational instrumentalism), but because he made the wrong value judgment about the interests that due process and rational instrumentalism brought into view.[110] When the justices are careful to explain that the right at work is due process itself, and equally when they suggest that some other right is implicated, they invariably invoke rational instrumentalism. Chief Justice Rehnquist approved the statute in *Cruzan* on the theory that the state could sensibly restrict a surrogate's ability to act for an incapacitated person in order to further the state's benevolent interest in ensuring its citizens' ability to make their own decisions about medical care.[111] He sustained the ban on physician-assisted suicide in *Glucksberg* because it was "rationally related to legitimate governmental interests."[112] Justice Blackmun struck down the anti-abortion statute in *Roe* because it was not "narrowly drawn to express only the legitimate state interests at stake."[113] The joint opinion in *Casey* sustained most of the provisions of Pennsylvania's abortion law because they served a variety of purposes without visiting an "undue burden" on a woman's ability to choose abortion before viability.[114] And Justice Kennedy invalidated the sodomy statute in *Lawrence* because it furthered "no legitimate state interest" sufficient to "justify its intrusion into the personal and private life of the individual."[115]

Abusive Behavior

Rational instrumentalism also orchestrates substantive due process analysis when executive officers employ brutal methods to enforce otherwise valid laws. At first glance, to be sure, the Court appears to vary its approach in this third body of cases, ostensibly to ensure that constitutional claims grounded in due process do not routinely substitute for ordinary tort actions against misbehaving officers.[116] In the leading case, *Lewis*,[117] Justice Souter explained that the Court first determines whether the executive action in question is "covered" by some independent provision of the Constitution—typically a right (substantive or procedural) listed in the Bill of Rights. If so, the Court interprets that provision to occupy the field to the exclusion of any claim under "the more generalized notion of 'substantive due process.'"[118] If not, the Court allows that a due process violation may appear, but only if the action complained of fails an exceptionally charitable test: the officer's behavior must be so "brutal" and "offensive" that it "shocks the conscience."[119]

On the face of it, this approach to abusive behavior cases seems problematic for my thesis that rational instrumentalism supplies the doctrinal basis for substantive rights of any kind. When the justices insist that due process claims are unavailable where other constitutional provisions operate, they appear to proceed from the premise that it makes some difference *which* substantive right is at work. Yet that difference need not contemplate a shift to a fundamentally different doctrinal framework. In substantive due process cases involving actions by executive officers, the familiar demand that government must serve the public reasonably remains paramount. The *reason* that shocking behavior is unconstitutional is that it is "arbitrary in a constitutional sense,"[120] which is to say it is "the exercise of power without any reasonable justification in the service of a legitimate governmental objective."[121] In an ordinary police misconduct case, the governmental ends are obvious enough: making an arrest, avoiding flight, or eliminating a threat to the public. Officers may well need to use force to subdue a suspect, perhaps extraordinary or even lethal force. If, however, they take extreme measures out of proportion to anything sensibly justified to get the suspect under control (read measures that "shock the conscience"), their actions are not in aid of the public interest and therefore are invalid.[122]

The point in the cases on police brutality is that *specific* tactics must have some justifying purpose—not merely the generally articulated public interest in crime control, but a near-term objective that warrants the particular violence in which the police engage. Thus officers may conceivably justify extreme force to subdue a dangerous assailant in the street, but will find it more difficult to explain the continuation of that same force once the suspect is in handcuffs. There is an argument, of course, that harsh interrogation techniques may be instruments for obtaining a confession needed for a conviction and thus rationally related to crime control. There is even an argument that torture may sensibly be employed in furtherance of national security. Yet neither instance requires going beyond rational instrumentalism as the framework for analysis. I would not be surprised if, in a torture case, the Court were to talk as though some tactics are unconstitutional in any circumstances (i.e., without regard to any means/ends analysis), in the way that Justice Scalia has said that the "rack and thumbscrew" can never constitute a valid

punishment for crime.[123] But the real working doctrine is still the injunction that governmental action must be reasonable, and that requirement
calls on the justices to exercise judgment in context. If special doctrinal
wrinkles show up, they do not cabin that judgment in any different way.

In this particular instance, there is less in the Court's doctrinal analysis than meets the eye. The alternative constitutional provision in view
is usually the Fourth Amendment prohibition on unreasonable searches
and seizures. That "reasonableness" standard incorporates the same root
doctrinal idea: rational instrumentalism.[124] In truth, then, the "shock the
conscience" test for substantive due process violations does not distinguish due process from the Fourth Amendment; rather, it effectively
conflates the two. The justices have generally addressed police abuse under the heading of the Fourth Amendment and have built up a sizeable
body of precedents that, together, define what counts as "reasonable" in
this context.[125] They plainly worry that if substantive due process claims
are added to the mix, lower courts and the rest of us may get the idea
that attaching the due process label to a claim can trigger a different
analysis and, perhaps, a different result. But that is not true. Where substantive rights are concerned, labels linked to particular textual provisions make no real difference at all. That is the signal we should take
from the Court's announcement that only shocking police behavior violates due process, that is, behavior that would also typically run afoul of
the Fourth Amendment.[126]

I do not want to overstate my case. Obviously, the whole point of introducing the "shock the conscience" test is to signal that police violence
is generally to be tolerated, even if an ordinary means/ends analysis
might conclude that officers were needlessly physical. And decisions regarding what counts as a "search" or a "seizure" occasionally may foreclose reliance on the Fourth Amendment and channel attention to due
process as a backstop. The *Lewis* case is an illustration.[127] Still, when the
question is whether police violence offends substantive rights, the basic standard is always essential reasonableness and, accordingly, rational
instrumentalism.

Equal Protection

Rational instrumentalism is also the doctrinal anchor in equal protection
cases.[128] Equal protection of the laws is scarcely self-defining. It begs for

some interpretive exegesis, pedestrian or grandiose, which promises to elucidate the idea of equality for constitutional purposes. Kenneth Karst contends that equal protection embodies a broad commitment to equal citizenship.[129] Owen Fiss argues that equal protection is not concerned with equality at all so much as with the subordination of groups historically identified by race.[130] The Supreme Court's account of equal protection has no such systematic philosophical character. But at the level of doctrine, the Court's explanation of this substantive right is familiar. Government discrimination must be rational in the sense that it constitutes a means that genuinely promotes social welfare.

Equality and Purpose

Equal protection cannot mean simply that government must adopt and enforce laws of "general applicability," such that everyone is subject to the same rules.[131] The Court sometimes suggests that is true, but then immediately acknowledges that the abstract question whether governmental action treats classes of individuals equally is unintelligible standing alone.[132] Recall that, by some accounts, the Court once conceived that governmental regulation *could* affect everyone in precisely the same way and was invalid if it did not.[133] In that context, identical treatment was defined by reference to a supposed natural-rights backdrop. Everyone was entitled to like treatment in the sense that government had legitimate authority only to vindicate natural rights that all individuals voluntarily surrendered to its care. Once natural-rights thinking was discarded, a substitute baseline was needed to take its place—a different and more sensible standard against which equal treatment might be determined. The question whether a regulatory measure dispenses equal treatment necessarily elicits another: Equal with respect to what? If not natural rights that everyone enjoys, then what?

The answer, of course, is the purpose for which a regulation is established. To put the point in the conventional way, the Court now has it that equal protection requires only that government treat *similarly situated* people equally. And people are similarly situated only with respect to the purpose for which they are sorted.[134] All rules classify and on that basis treat people or classes differently.[135] That is the point of rules. Government plainly has authority to separate individuals into classes and dispense different treatment to each class, so long as the individuals grouped together in a class are similarly situated with respect to the governmental purpose in view. This understanding corresponds, in turn, to the instrumental way that government is supposed to regulate. Government typically hands out disparate treatment to the members of different classes in order to encourage behavior that government prefers or to discourage behavior that government disdains. A rule that mandates certain conduct and imposes a penalty for violations necessarily puts those who comply in one category and those who do not in another, and then treats the members of the two classes differently. That different treatment comports with equal protection, *ceteris paribus,* because the members of the two classifications are not similarly situated with respect to the purpose the classification is meant to achieve.[136]

The Overlap with Due Process

But you see the implications. As soon as equal protection analysis introduces government's purpose into the mix, what follows is indistinguishable from the rational instrumentalism associated with substantive due process.[137] Here, too, the operative question is whether government's means furthers some purpose in the public interest. The only difference is that in equal protection cases the means is described as the basis on which government classifies. But the description of rules makes no analytical difference. The rules the Court typically addresses under the heading of substantive due process can just as easily be attacked as discriminatory, and rules the Court treats as classifications under the heading of equal protection can just as well be challenged as arbitrary.[138]

In *Lochner,* for example, the work-hour limit in the Bakeshop Act distinguished between employers who let their workers go home after ten hours and those who did not. Justice Peckham might well have focused on that classification, applied an equal protection analysis, and resolved the case that way.[139] If he had taken that course, however, his analysis would not have changed a bit. The due process analysis he actually employed inevitably entailed an assessment of the classification built into the work-hour rule. Under either heading, equal protection or due process, the constitutional question was whether New York's unfavorable treatment of employers who violated the work-hour provision (and its favorable treatment of employers who complied) amounted to a rational, instrumental means of accomplishing the state's ends. The overlap between equal protection and due process is everywhere apparent in the Court's case law. When Chief Justice Warren brought due process to bear on race discrimination in *Bolling v. Sharpe*,[140] he recognized that the Due Process Clause of the Fifth Amendment contains an "equal protection component."[141]

By some accounts, there is a difference in focus between these two great clauses in the Fourteenth Amendment. Cass Sunstein contends that due process is essentially backward-looking inasmuch as it preserves traditionally valued understandings of individual liberty from the excesses of modern legislative policy, while equal protection is forward-looking inasmuch as it self-consciously departs from the past and establishes new standards for government to meet.[142] Recall that "due process" was nothing new when it was injected into the American Constitution. By contrast, the phrase "equal protection of the laws" was original with the Fourteenth Amendment. In Lawrence Lessig's terminology, the Due Process Clauses were "codifying" features of the Constitution, but the Equal Protection Clause was "transformative."[143] Accordingly, equal protection is the more likely basis for finding practices unconstitutional notwithstanding that they were accepted historically. There is something to this. I have just explained that the Court gets serious about due process primarily in cases implicating "fundamental" individual interests, and in the next chapter I explore the role that tradition plays in determining whether any particular interest counts as fundamental for those purposes. Still, the backward-looking/forward-looking distinction won't do.

Some justices, notably Justice Scalia, *do* regard due process as a static concept, a constant reminder of the way things were and a summons back to better halcyon days.[144] But the more conventional view is that due process is a protean idea contemplating development over time. William Eskridge quotes Justice Frankfurter: "'Due process' is, perhaps, the *least* frozen concept of our law—the *least* confined to history and the *most* absorptive of powerful social standards of a progressive society.'"[145] Moreover, the Court has invoked both due process and equal protection to take and hold new ground. That was true in *Bolling,* of course.[146] The *Roe* and *Casey* cases were decided under the heading of due process, *Romer* relied on equal protection to invalidate a ban on anti-discrimination laws protecting gays and lesbians, *Lawrence* switched back to due process, and no other illustrations are needed.[147]

Justice Jackson offered a different argument for distinguishing between due process and equal protection. In the old *Railway Express* case,[148] he contended that due process applies a heavy hammer inasmuch as it prevents government from regulating an activity at all, while equal protection offers a lighter touch: government may regulate, but only if it distributes benefits and burdens more evenly. There is something to this, too. If government can pursue an objective only by means of a policy that imposes burdens on everyone similarly situated, it follows that more people will be affected and, accordingly, that the political check on government will be stronger. Equal protection thus fortifies democratic responsiveness. If, by contrast, government could charge the brunt of the costs to relatively few citizens, it would be able to pursue an objective that bears fewer public rewards. Concomitantly, if government misallocates the costs of achieving some end, and the Court finds fault only on equal protection grounds, government can react by spreading burdens more widely and still (perhaps) pursue its original goal.[149] Nevertheless, Jackson's argument sees a difference between due process and equal protection where, in truth, there is only a difference between levels on which rules can be arbitrary or discriminatory. Irrespective of whether due process or equal protection is said to be in play, the same questions about governmental means arise, and the same rational instrumentalism can do service.

The ordinance in *Railway Express* barred commercial vehicles from displaying advertising unless the ads promoted a firm's own product. The exception privileged newspapers, which had lobbied for it in order to preserve the ability to paste current headlines to the sides of their delivery trucks. By Jackson's account, it made sense to upset only the exception for self-sponsored ads—thus to force the city to ban ads on all commercial vehicles, thus to bring newspapers within the prohibition, thus to give them an incentive to oppose the ban for everyone, thus to bring about a political resolution. That analysis assumed, at least implicitly, that a more sweeping prohibition would be valid for want of the particularly troubling classification entailed in the exception for self-promoting ads. Maybe so. Yet it is also available to argue that a ban limited to commercial vehicles is unconstitutional because it prefers private automobiles, that a prohibition on ads affixed to all vehicles is unconstitutional because it prefers stationary signs, or, for that matter, that a ban on advertising is invalid because it prefers other forms of expression.

If classifications at those higher levels of generality are constitutionally acceptable, it can only be because the Court thinks, in each instance, that the means is sufficiently related to the governmental interest in view (i.e., traffic safety). And at each level, in turn, it makes no difference whether a challenger characterizes a rule as arbitrary (and thus a violation of due process) or discriminatory (and thus a violation of equal protection). Either way, the same rational instrumentalism supplies the doctrinal framework for determining whether the city's means comports sufficiently with its public-regarding ends. This is only to say that rational instrumentalism allows for the consideration of all the factors relevant to a serious examination of governmental action, including Jackson's point that some rules are especially troubling because they dilute incentives for political reform.

When we come to refinements of the instrumental framework, we may have occasion to consider whether one or the other, due process or equal protection, is the more suitable textual starting point. Take, for example, the perennial debate over whether regulations of abortion should better be addressed under the equal protection heading. Donald Regan argued early on that limitations on abortion draw an indefensible classifying line between those who wish to avoid unwelcome childbirth and those who wish to be treated for other conditions.[150] Yet if some limit on abortion is struck down, it is likely to be because the Court doubts that the heavy burdens it imposes on an especially sensitive liberty operate instrumentally to promote the public welfare and suspects, instead, that it simply saddles women with responsibility for childbearing, without recourse. The instrumental calculus is the same under either label, due process or equal protection. Of course, lots of people contend that anti-abortion statutes bear so obviously on women as a class that they should be placed in the category with explicit gender discrimination and thus condemned as classifications according to status.[151] There again, however, the same basic doctrinal framework answers as usual: status classifications are troubling because they are not instrumental means by which government may sensibly try to channel behavior.[152] In this vein, it is well to note Justice O'Connor's discussion of the effects of abortion regulation on women— delivered in the course of her substantive due process analysis in *Casey*.[153]

The *Lawrence*[154] case similarly illustrates the essential fusion of equal protection and due process. Texas made sodomy a crime only if the participants were of the same sex. Everyone acknowledged that the statute primarily affected gays and lesbians and thus regarded it as a classification on the basis of sexual orientation.[155] Justice O'Connor, for her part, found that classification irrational and would have held it unconstitutional as a violation of equal protection.[156] Writing for the Court, Justice Kennedy chose to treat the statute as a classification between those who commit sodomy, on the one hand, and those who do not, on the other. Still recognizing that sodomy is an offense primarily implicating gays and lesbians, however, Kennedy insisted that the statute classified according to sexual orientation, even if its explicit limitation to same-sex behavior was set aside.[157] Discrimination on the basis of sexual identity is obviously subject to an equal protection challenge, and there is no doubt at all that, if Justice Kennedy had examined the Texas statute through an equal protection lens, he would have found it wanting on that theory. He decided, instead, to strike it down as a violation of substantive due process. Gays and lesbians, too, have liberty interests in choosing their sexual behavior and partners and, concomitantly, in forming the close personal bonds to which sexual intimacy is often related. A statute that systematically makes those choices criminal infringes liberty without due process of law.[158]

Justice Kennedy explained his reliance on due process in part on practical grounds: he did not want to leave the false impression that a general sodomy statute, applicable on its face to everyone alike, would be valid.[159] But there was no need to shift constitutional theories to clarify the holding in *Lawrence.* Kennedy was crystal clear that a facially neutral sodomy statute nonetheless classifies according to sexual orientation, and he could easily have explained that such a statute would violate equal protection.[160] Then again, his approach in *Lawrence* is entirely understandable. The Court had grounded the decision in *Hardwick*[161] (sustaining a similar state law) on due process and had explicitly footnoted equal protection out of the picture.[162] If Kennedy had relied on equal protection in *Lawrence,* he might have been understood to leave *Hardwick* intact. That, in fact, is what Justice O'Connor would have done.[163] By resting on due process, Kennedy put himself in position to overrule *Hardwick* squarely.[164]

The justices acknowledge that governmental action in a single set of circumstances can implicate more than one constitutional right. When that happens, they sometimes purport to take each possibility in turn, moving from one to another until some decision proves dispositive.[165] Police brutality cases are an illustration.[166] Yet when the meaning of one substantive right is largely congruent with the meaning of the next, it is hard to take any kind of *seriatim* approach seriously. Knowledgeable litigants articulate their arguments both ways. And if anyone presses only one theory, the Court explains that the choice doesn't matter.[167] This kind of redundancy might be worrisome if constitutional meaning were derived from the text of particular provisions of the written Constitution. But since that is not the case, doctrinally interchangeable rights are

not troubling at all, but only to be expected. Typically, alternative textual labels affect only the Court's frame of mind as it proceeds according
to the same doctrinal framework: rational instrumentalism.

Classifications

Several bodies of Supreme Court case law are conventionally regarded
as illustrations of equal protection doctrine in action. I want to discuss
a few of these briefly, in order both to demonstrate how closely equal
protection analysis tracks with substantive due process and to anticipate a more general treatment of rational instrumentalism later. First,
I take up equal protection cases in which the Court is readily satisfied
that discriminatory policies further social welfare, ostensibly because
the justices are not seriously concerned that government is doing anything out of the ordinary. Next, I look quickly at equal protection decisions that parallel the "fundamental interest" due process cases we just
went through. Finally, I account for cases in which government classifies
individuals according to status (e.g., race or gender) and thus raises the
suspicion that no public-regarding goals are served.

ORDINARY CLASSIFICATIONS.   I explained in the last chapter that many of
the Court's early decisions on "class legislation" were actually decided
on the basis of the Equal Protection Clause.[168] The result was a body of
equal protection cases tracking due process decisions like *Lochner* and
articulating the same means/ends doctrine. In *F. S. Royster Guano Co. v.
Virginia*,[169] Justice Pitney explained that a classification "must be reasonable, not arbitrary, and must rest upon some ground of difference
having a fair and substantial relation to the object of the legislation, so
that all persons similarly circumstanced shall be treated alike."[170] And
in *Lindsley v. Natural Carbonic Gas Co.*,[171] Justice Van Devanter upheld
a state law because he could conceive of a set of facts under which the
statute could rationally serve a legitimate purpose.[172]

Just as due process decisions came under attack, so did equal protection decisions engender the same criticism. Justice Holmes ridiculed
equal protection as the "last resort" of constitutional arguments.[173] And,
in time, the Court became ever more generous to economic regulatory
measures, judged under either heading. In *Williamson v. Lee Optical*,[174]
for example, Justice Douglas declared that legislatures are expected to
make discriminating choices according to their estimate of the public

interest and that they may address one phase of a social problem while ignoring others they think less urgent. That view holds true today, enriching the meaning of the general understanding that a governmental classification is valid if it is "rationally related to a legitimate state interest."[175] The Court occasionally invalidates social welfare regulation on equal protection grounds, and in so doing makes it appear that rational instrumentalism is not the same amiable fellow here that he has now become in the substantive due process context.[176] But the better explanation is that the justices are more comfortable with the equal protection label because it seems less tainted by memories of *Lochner.*[177]

FUNDAMENTAL INTERESTS (AGAIN). Equal protection doctrine also sports its own parallel track for cases implicating "fundamental" human interests. This line of decisions began early. In *Skinner v. Oklahoma,*[178] Justice Douglas invalidated a state statute authorizing sterilization of persons convicted of multiple felonies involving moral turpitude. He acknowledged that the legislature was entitled to "deference," but he insisted that sterilization implicated procreation, "one of the basic rights of man"—"*fundamental* to the very existence and survival of the race." Since the statute burdened a "basic liberty," it could be sustained only if it survived more rigorous examination.[179] Building on *Skinner,* the Warren Court developed a considerable list of "fundamental rights" for these purposes, among them interstate travel, marriage, and above all voting.[180]

The current Court is cool to this line of equal protection cases and, truth be told, has capped it with the decisions already in place.[181] The reason, I dare say, is that the justices now in control are no more enthusiastic about extending the list of "fundamental" interests under this heading than they are about doing so under the more familiar due process banner.[182] For now, though, it is enough to recognize that these equal protection cases exist and to acknowledge that the doctrine they exhibit draws on rational instrumentalism.

SUSPICIOUS CLASSIFICATIONS. The most familiar equal protection cases implicate governmental actions that the Court regards with suspicion not because of the nature of the interests affected but because of the basis of the classifications at work. The paradigm, of course, is a classification on the basis of race. The Court was not always sensitive to the individual harms associated with racial discrimination, far less the societal effects of subordinating whole classes of people on the basis of skin color.[183] Yet in modern times, and certainly since *Brown,* scarcely any proposition is more familiar than this one: Governmental discrimination on the basis of race is "one of the most serious injuries recognized in our legal system."[184] All classifications according to race (including those that ostensibly benefit racial minorities) are subject to a serious brand of means/ends review—as are analogous bases of discrimination.[185] In the case of racial discrimination, government's means must be "narrowly tailored to further compelling governmental interests."[186]

The Court has made it clear that the Equal Protection Clause is addressed only to classifications that are "intentional" or "purposeful."[187] The effect of governmental action alone is immaterial. Yet a policy that is race-neutral on its face may bear disparate consequences for members of racial groups. In that event, the Court engages another variant on the rational instrumentalism theme. The plaintiff must first demonstrate a "discriminatory purpose" by showing that a purpose to discriminate on the basis of race was at least a "motivating factor" behind government's behavior. If the plaintiff carries that burden, the government must demonstrate that the same action would have been taken on some other, race-neutral ground. The Court's language in "discriminatory impact" cases is notoriously confusing.[188] Yet, again, for present purposes it is only important to recognize that the crucial inquiry is whether government has chosen sensible means for achieving public ends. Accordingly, rational instrumentalism is again in play.[189]

Freedom of Expression

Rational instrumentalism also dominates the doctrinal tests the Court has established for First Amendment cases.[190] Of course, the constitutional text ostensibly implicated is largely irrelevant.[191] Occasional attempts to ascribe self-evident meaning to the First Amendment's terms have been roundly rejected as either naive or manipulative. Justice Black insisted that the amendment itself is perfectly clear and protects free speech absolutely,[192] but he almost certainly adopted that view for strategic purposes.[193] Valuable though it is, the freedom of speech is not absolute: "[n]o law" does not mean no law and never has. Justice Scalia once proposed a formal definition of an "abridgement" of expression,[194] but he knows full well that serious analysis cannot proceed as a simple deduction from language. When Scalia pauses to be candid, he, too, acknowledges that the text of the First Amendment is "indeterminate."[195] There are occasional appeals to original understanding, of course,[196] but that cannot be taken seriously, either. As usual, legal historians haggle over the meaning to be attached to surviving materials.[197]

The Court has always taken it upon itself to say what counts as "the freedom of speech" and, in turn, what counts as a law "abridging" that freedom. The Court has likewise specified "an establishment of religion" or "free exercise" and, in turn, elaborated on what constitutes a law "respecting" the one or "prohibiting" the other. As David Strauss has explained, First Amendment law has been "hammered out mostly over the course of the twentieth century . . . [i]n a series of judicial decisions and extrajudicial developments."[198] When the justices create doctrine to organize their consideration of free expression cases, the product is rational instrumentalism. Freedom of speech and religion thus tracks with due process and equal protection. This is not because the First Amendment is applicable exclusively against the Federal Government and must address state authority through the filter provided by Fourteenth Amendment due process.[199] First Amendment doctrine resembles due process (and equal protection) doctrine because it responds to the same considerations that move the Court with respect to substantive rights generally—the developments sketched in chapter 2. Those ideas generate the scheme we have, in which the Court defines the content of free expression on a case-by-case basis with rational instrumentalism as the doctrinal guide.

No one overlooks the crucial role that free expression plays in the very nature and character of American public life.[200] When the justices use instrumentalism to organize the issues in speech cases, they scarcely signal contentment with government's behavior. They proclaim just the opposite—by using rational instrumentalism to identify the special risks that curbs on expression create. I want to be clear about this. To rely on rational instrumentalism here is *not* to permit government to regulate expression much in the way it regulates other forms of human behavior. The same basic doctrine is at work. But the special values attached to free expression (values that rational instrumentalism brings to the fore) allow the Court to hold government's feet considerably closer to the fire. Let me show you wherein instrumentalism figures in free speech analysis in a swath of familiar contexts.

Free Speech

Consider first what may be the oldest theme in free speech lore: the aversion to previous restraints. The Court sometimes makes it sound as though there is an absolute prohibition on prior restraints—as though government can never prevent individuals from speaking without permission in the first instance but must limit itself to punishing speakers after the fact (in limited circumstances, of course).[201] But the Court allows for rare exceptions and (unremarkably) articulates them in the language of rational instrumentalism. When, for example, the justices vacated injunctions against publication of the Pentagon Papers, they explained that the government had not carried its heavy burden of demonstrating a justifying reason for restraining the *Times* and the *Post*—that is, the government had failed to show that its means was genuinely in service of its asserted purpose (to protect national security).[202]

The "clear and present danger" test was an instrumental idea. The point, again, was that government must have a good reason for circumscribing even hot-blooded political diatribe. The stronger the government's interest, the more justifiable its limits on expression. This was true of the original libertarian form of the standard as Holmes announced it and equally true of its republican aspect in Brandeis's hands.[203] In the notorious *Dennis* case,[204] Chief Justice Vinson expressly stated the danger test in instrumental terms. The purpose of the Smith Act, he explained, was to protect the existing government from violent interruption, and the question in the case was whether the act constituted a "means" to that permissible end.[205] The modern reformulation in *Brandenburg*[206] carries forward the instrumental framework, albeit plainly giving it a more powerful speech-protective character: government cannot silence advocates of violence, except in circumstances in which public safety is especially at risk—namely, when the circumstances are such that expression is likely to produce violent action.

The modern idea of overbreadth, illustrated in cases like *Reno v. ACLU,*[207] also partakes of instrumentalism. The idea there is that a regulation of expression that is excessively sweeping in scope may cause potential speakers to change their plans in fear of the consequences, even though, were they to speak and suffer prosecution, they would have a valid First Amendment defense. An overbroad regulation is overinclusive with respect to its purpose, ostensibly imposing costs more widely than can be justified by the public-regarding governmental end in view. True, overbreadth is a readily damning doctrine that dispatches governmental attempts to address expression without investigating any particular application. But the possibility that government might cure overbreadth by rewriting a regulation only demonstrates again that rational instrumentalism fixes the general constitutional framework.[208]

The standard for symbolic expression announced in the draft-card case, *O'Brien*,[209] is explicitly framed as rational instrumentalism. Governmental regulation is valid if it "furthers an important or substantial governmental interest; if the governmental interest is unrelated to the suppression of free expression; and if the incidental restriction on alleged First Amendment freedoms is no greater than is essential to the furtherance of that interest."[210] To be sure, Chief Justice Warren explicitly disclaimed any inquiry into the "purpose" for which Congress enacts statutes. On its face, that part of his opinion was at odds with instrumentalism. Yet Warren sustained the prohibition on mutilating draft cards in *O'Brien* because it was a "narrow means" of protecting the government's "substantial interest" in making draft cards available for administrative purposes. The Court has since made it clear that "purpose" is a legitimate (in point of fact a *crucial*) aspect of the analysis.[211]

The analysis in commercial advertising cases similarly adopts an instrumental structure. Justice Powell offered a summary in *Central Hudson*.[212] Government may regulate or even suppress commercial speech if its means "directly advances" a "substantial" governmental interest.[213] Government is generally entitled to select the kind of regulation it thinks best and need not choose the "least restrictive measure" that promises to achieve its ends.[214] Many people think government should have a good deal of discretion to deal with economically driven expression—more, perhaps, than the Court typically allows.[215] But, again, the only pertinent point here is that the Court's articulated standard is rational instrumentalism: when government curbs commercial expression, the Court marshals the relevant considerations around a baseline means/ends model. The results in actual cases turn on the way the justices deal with those considerations.

The cases on content and viewpoint discrimination obviously draw on instrumentalism. The working premise is that government ordinarily should be indifferent to the content and viewpoint of private expression. Far better that government should confine itself to neutral administrative rules regulating the time, place, and manner of expression, apart from the message conveyed, in order genuinely to further the public interest. In truth, the analysis of content and viewpoint discrimination is indistinguishable from equal protection analysis, where the Court also focuses on classifying lines and the relationship between those lines and some public purpose. Justice Stevens acknowledged as much in *Young v. American Mini-Theaters*,[216] when he explained that Detroit had adopted a content-discriminatory "classification" for "adult" theaters, but one that served well enough the city's interest in preserving the quality of its neighborhoods.[217] The same is true of the "public forum" cases, which largely reproduce the same focus on the basis of classifications when government regulates expression in public places.[218]

The illustrations go on. In cases on speech by government employees, the Court demands that sanctions must constitute "a means of furthering government effectiveness and efficiency."[219] In cases on public subsidies of expression, the Court again asks whether discrimination is sufficiently related to various objectives in the "public interest."[220] In "compelled speech" cases, the Court insists that government cannot require individuals to disclose information (for example, their identity) without demonstrating a connection between its policy and some public "danger sought to be prevented."[221] In cases on the solicitation of funds, the Court insists that regulations must serve a "strong, subordinating interest" that government can safeguard.[222] In cases on associational freedom, the Court explains that regulations must be in service of an "immediate, substantial, and subordinating state interest."[223] In cases on the regulation of political campaigns, the Court insists that limits on expenditures must be narrowly tailored to achieve "compelling" objectives and that curbs on contributions must be "closely drawn to match a sufficiently important interest."[224]

Freedom of Religion

The Court equally employs rational instrumentalism as the fundamental organizing doctrine for addressing questions concerning the Establishment Clause and the Free Exercise Clause. The text of neither provision counts for much, and debatable history is of no more help here than anywhere else.[225] In the Establishment Clause context, instrumentalism takes the form of the much-maligned but resilient *Lemon* test: Government must act with a "secular purpose," and its action must neither "advance nor inhibit" religion nor "foster 'an excessive entanglement with religion.'"[226] That formulation reflects the familiar means/ends framework. It may be hard to predict results in close cases, but the differences among the justices in any given instance largely turn on their evaluation of the considerations that instrumentalism identifies.

Some Free Exercise cases are similarly easy to fit under the rational instrumentalism umbrella. In the *Lukumi* case,[227] for example, the Court listened to the city's argument that a ban on animal sacrifice was instrumentally related to a variety of public purposes, but concluded that the truth was otherwise. The ordinance was not a neutral means of furthering the public interest; it was a deliberate effort to discourage a particular religious practice. Other free exercise decisions are more unruly. Tracking the movement in religious-exemption cases from *Sherbert*,[228] through *Yoder*,[229] to *Smith*[230] requires no small effort. It is clear, though, that the question whether believers are entitled to exemptions from general regulatory laws is all about discrimination—about whether, how, and why government's failure to allow for exemptions should count as an ordinary, sensible means of achieving public ends. The overlap with substantive due process and equal protection analysis may not be perfect in every respect,[231] but the common thread is perfectly clear. Consider, too, that when the justices examine governmental classifications on the basis of religion, they are content to invoke the same instrumental standards they apply to other cases on content and viewpoint discrimination. Writing for the Court in the *Good News Club* case,[232] Justice Thomas expressly invoked familiar "public forum" thinking in a case involving discrimination on the basis of religion.

This is all familiar stuff, of course, and worth sketching only to make the point (by now itself familiar) that the justices invariably employ rational instrumentalism to identify relevant considerations and arrange them for examination. They do this time and again across the range of cases implicating freedom of speech and religion, just as they do in due process and equal protection cases. This is not because the justices are unimaginative and unable to fashion distinct doctrines for ostensibly different contexts. It is because the fundamental means/ends analysis does not vary, but only accommodates the values, interests, and circumstances of each case in which the exercise of governmental power must be appraised and appropriately checked. The justices set about their work, reasonably enough, by organizing each problem in turn against the backdrop of the public law jurisprudence I reviewed in chapter 2. Rational instrumentalism has proved to be the Court's tool for implementing the lessons of that experience in the endless cases demanding attention.

Cruel and Unusual Punishments

The last substantive check on governmental power I want to examine is the Eighth Amendment's prohibition on "cruel and unusual punishments." Here, too, rational instrumentalism is at work. You just have to look for it. Consider, first, cases in which the Court is concerned with *who* may be punished in an especially harsh way. It will not surprise you to learn that these are typically death penalty cases. Writing for the Court in *Roper v. Simmons,*[233] Justice Kennedy started with the usual bow to the pertinent "text" and its "history." Yet in the same breath he said that the Eighth Amendment must be interpreted in light of its "tradition" and "precedent" and "with due regard for its purpose and function in the constitutional design." Kennedy explained that the precedents reserve capital punishment for offenders whose "extreme culpability" makes them "the most deserving of execution." Culpability, in turn, relates to the "social purposes" the Court has attached to the death penalty: retribution and deterrence.[234] It follows that the Eighth Amendment permits government to employ capital punishment only with respect to offenders who are sufficiently blameworthy to warrant execution on retributive grounds and sufficiently cognizant of their actions to justify execution for the utilitarian purpose of discouraging others from committing capital crimes.

The full Eighth Amendment calculus is more complex, of course. The Court relies in part on "evolving standards of decency" to determine whether the imposition of death would be "disproportionate" to the offender's circumstances.[235] And there is no denying that at some basic level the justices make an essentially moral determination. For our purposes, though, it is only important to recognize that they exercise judgment within the familiar framework provided by rational instrumentalism. Insane, mentally disabled, and immature offenders are likely to be less culpable than adults who suffer from no similar impairments. Accordingly, it makes less sense, instrumentally speaking, to punish them with death either to make them atone for moral irresponsibility or to deter others from committing similar crimes in the future.[236]

The Court also employs rational instrumentalism to organize its thinking in cases on what *behavior* can be punished by death. In *Coker v. Georgia,*[237] Justice White acknowledged that executing offenders convicted of rape may serve discernible public objectives (e.g., retribution and deterrence). Nevertheless, the death penalty is an "excessive" punishment for rape cases generally. White explained that a death sentence is out of proportion to the offense: "The murderer kills; the rapist, if no more than that, does not."[238] He might just as easily have said that the policy of making capital punishment an option for rape of any kind imposes the most severe penalty on the individual without sufficient payoff

to the public interest. Or, if you like, such a policy is not tailored to ensure that the death penalty is reserved for cases in which its purposes are
served.[239]

The Court uses a similar proportionality analysis when convicts receive harsh punishments other than death (typically an extended period
of years in confinement). Writing for the Court in *Ewing v. California*,[240]
Justice O'Connor acknowledged that assessments of proportionality are
difficult, but nonetheless insisted that they are necessary. The precedents
identify numerous relevant considerations, and the justices must work
them through in order to determine whether, in any particular instance,
a convict has received a sentence that is disproportionate to his or her
offense.[241] O'Connor did not invoke rational instrumentalism by name,
but the familiar framework we have seen elsewhere was plainly in operation. She explained that outside the death penalty context, states may
pursue additional goals (like incapacitation and rehabilitation). And she
sustained the prisoner's life sentence, imposed under California's notorious "three strikes law," because it was "justified by the State's public-
safety interest in incapacitating and deterring recidivist felons."[242]

I should acknowledge finer points that rational instrumentalism does
not fully explain. Justice Scalia contends that proportionality does not
travel well beyond death penalty cases,[243] and Justice Breyer thinks that
the mix of factors is so rich that case-by-case assessments of proportionality are necessary—providing "guidance through example."[244] Moreover, the Court is almost certainly moved by the hope that, in the case
of harsh sentences, legislatures will ultimately come to their senses. Justice O'Connor explained in *Ewing* that proportionality judgments are
informed by other factors: the "primacy" of legislatures in making decisions about appropriate criminal punishments, the "variety of legitimate
penological schemes," and the "nature of our federal system" (read deference to local judgments regarding criminal law policy).[245] Yet instrumentalism never captures all the details of the analysis, but only erects a
general architecture for identifying relevant considerations and puzzling
them out. That is what is going on in these noncapital cases.[246]

The large body of cases on procedures for administering the death
penalty also illustrates rational instrumentalism in action.[247] In its seminal decisions, the Court has read the Eighth Amendment to mandate
procedural arrangements that ensure two things: "guided discretion" and
"individualized consideration." The sentencing jury may be given discretion about whether to impose capital punishment on a convict who

is legally eligible to receive a death sentence. But to diminish the risk that inexperienced citizens might exercise that discretion arbitrarily, the Court held in *Gregg v. Georgia*[248] that the Eighth Amendment demands procedural mechanisms (separate sentencing hearings, special jury instructions, and other devices) that help jurors do their duty—namely, to separate death-eligible convicts who are sufficiently blameworthy to be put to death from those who are not. You see the generalized means/ ends pattern at the bottom of this. The point is to limit death sentences to cases in which the state's identified interests may be served, and the Eighth Amendment question is whether the sentencing body is given the guidance necessary to decide whether killing a particular convict fits that bill.

Even if a properly guided jury could decide that a death-eligible convict should be put to death, *ceteris paribus,* the jury still might not impose a capital sentence in light of the peculiar circumstances of the case (e.g., the convict's life experiences, past behavior, and current mental state). Accordingly, the Court held in *Lockett v. Ohio*[249] that the jury must be exposed to any information that mitigates against a capital sentence. Here again, rational instrumentalism is plainly visible. The state's objective is to select convicts whose execution may genuinely serve its penal interests: retribution and deterrence. It is not a great stretch for the Court to conclude that the state must allow the jury to consider evidence relevant to its task.

Of course, there are numerous other decisions in this category, most of them ostensibly meant to elaborate and clarify the "guided discretion" and "individualized consideration" elements of the analysis. And, of course, the justices invariably disagree about how Eighth Amendment law should be administered case by case.[250] Those comparative details, albeit important, do not obscure the basic point that the rights ascribed to the Eighth Amendment, too, find their general organizing structure in an assessment of the state's means in relation to its public-regarding ends.

* * *

The rights I have reviewed in this chapter draw their meaning from the Supreme Court's analysis. The Court's analysis, in turn, is guided by the armature that rational instrumentalism supplies. This is not surprising, given that rational instrumentalism is the product of the jurisprudential history I sketched in chapter 2. Instrumentalism has proved to be an effective doctrinal device for realizing the lessons of that history. Then again, to come this far is hardly to get anywhere at all. The really demanding work lies ahead. It is necessary now to probe deeply into the perplexing and relentlessly debatable questions that instrumentalism identifies. That is where we see clearly how much this doctrine asks the justices to decide and, accordingly, how much depends on the judgment of the men and women doing the deciding.

CHAPTER FOUR

Rational Instrumentalism

From the outset, there has been "no very certain standard to guide the Court in drawing its judgments" regarding substantive rights.[1] Instead, the justices have decided case after case and built up a body of precedents in point. The manifest flaws in textualism and originalism demonstrate that the men and women who sit on the Court must go it alone, and the bruising experience with formalism proves that it is futile to pursue prescriptive rules that genuinely cabin their judgment. As Justice Miller put it in *Davidson v. New Orleans*,[2] "there is wisdom" in determining constitutional meaning by "the gradual process of judicial inclusion and exclusion, as the cases presented for decision shall require."[3] I explained in previous chapters that the Court organizes its consideration of substantive rights cases around a means/ends structure informed by four overlapping ideas, born of experience: the rejection of natural rights; the acknowledgment of government's responsibility for private, arms-length arrangements; the recognition of government's authority to regulate private activities in the public interest; and the realization of government's role (and that of the Court) in modern American democracy. Rational instrumentalism thus builds on deeper themes in American public law jurisprudence—themes regarding the pursuit of the public good, or at least the promise of it.

My objective in this chapter is to examine modern illustrations of the work the justices actually perform in cases involving substantive rights. I will identify and (I hope) illuminate the difficult judgments that rational instrumentalism calls on the justices to make. Instrumentalism does not constrain judicial decision making much more than would an entirely *ad hoc* approach. Nor, of course, does rational instrumentalism generate objectively correct results. The justices do not get things right; they do the best they can, no more. Rational instrumentalism only arranges the relevant factors in a systematic way to facilitate serious, informed thinking in hopes of producing sound decisions. There are many features to the analysis and more (much more) than immediately meets the eye. My headings in this chapter overlap one another. Yet by taking them *seriatim,* and occasionally backing and filling, I hope to be rigorous about the many places in the analysis where rational instrumentalism focuses attention on questions over which justices with different ideological perspectives can reasonably disagree.

I begin with the different "standards of review" the Court articulates and purports to apply in substantive rights cases. On the surface, it may appear that the meaning of rational instrumentalism itself shifts with the standard of review the Court invokes, such that the same baseline doctrinal framework does not operate in all instances, after all. On close examination, however, standards of review are not an especially significant part of the story. They have their value as rough indications of the justices' mood, but they don't actually carry much weight—not, anyway, in seriously contested cases. Next, I turn to the elements of rational instrumentalism itself and explore the problems with identifying and characterizing the means government employs to pursue its ends, the individual interests affected, and the public purposes offered to explain government's choice of means.

Standards of Review

While the justices invariably employ rational instrumentalism to orchestrate their thinking about substantive rights, they nonetheless profess to apply different "standards of review" that vary with the subject matter implicated in their cases. This makes a certain amount of sense. The justices cannot very well be rigorously demanding on every occasion, and they cannot always be complacently generous, either. The one polar extreme would routinely frustrate democratically forged policies; the other would abandon any serious inspection of what government is about.[4] Nevertheless, by announcing the applicable standard of review abstractly at the outset of each opinion, the justices make the selection of any particular standard appear more significant than it is. In truth, the different standards of review actually determine very little, mislead very much, and often do more mischief than good. Laurence Tribe argues that the practice of giving them prominence "has not shown itself worthy of being enshrined as a permanent fixture in the armament of constitutional analysis."[5] The standards are all the more troubling inasmuch as they are employed haphazardly. Sometimes the justices are only careless without any attempt to deceive; sometimes they are deliberately vague with the apparent purpose to dissemble; sometimes you can't tell. Michael Dorf describes the standards as a "messy hodgepodge"; Andrew Koppelman complains that they are "thin, fragmentary, and inconsistently followed."[6]

It is fair enough to complain that the Court is sloppy, certainly to charge that it is evasive. Yet it is a mistake to fault the justices for articulating standards of review that do not actually circumscribe judicial judgment and thus seriously predict results. Judicially fashioned standards cannot do that any more than can patches of text plucked from the documentary Constitution. The standard of review the Court purports to apply in a case serves only as a general signal that the justices intend to be more (or less) fussy in appraising the means government has employed to achieve its alleged ends. What counts is the omnipresent doctrinal framework the justices use to organize relevant considerations for serious judgment. Those considerations, in turn, account for the differences in what the justices do (in different contexts) with the monolithic instrumental model on which they lean for methodological structure.

The Court does not typically talk as though this is what it is doing, but occasionally we get explanations that come very close. Justice Marshall famously argued that, in truth, the Court does not choose a standard of review from a short list of candidates but calibrates the appropriate level of scrutiny to the circumstances in the case at bar.[7] The better explanation is that the Court employs the same basic doctrinal framework across the board, but that framework demands attention to the considerations Marshall identifies—and more. Justice Stevens has explained, for example, that the decision whether governmental action is reasonable necessarily entails "elements of legitimacy and neutrality."[8] We may safely add proportionality.[9] Put bluntly, the justices exercise reasoned judgment.[10] That is what differentiates the cases in which the Court formally invokes alternative standards of review—judgment about the character of the governmental action under challenge, about the nature of the individual interests at stake, about the extent of the burdens imposed, and, certainly, about the connection between those regulatory burdens and the achievement of some public-regarding purpose.

The verbal formulations the Court has offered are familiar and take only a little space to recite, though a bit more to evaluate.

The Rational-Basis Test

The standard articulated for most cases has not changed since the late 1930s. Ordinarily, government is "presumed" to act lawfully, and anything government does will be sustained so long as it bears a "rational" relationship to a "legitimate" public interest.[11] The "wisdom" or "desirability" of governmental action is not in issue.[12] If government is merely "improvident," the Court insists that "democratic processes" will "eventually" set things to rights.[13] The means government chooses need not be "logically consistent" with its goals. Nor must there be any genuine factual basis for government's assessment of the interest to be served or the connection between that interest and the particular means the government selects to address it. It is enough if some state of affairs "might" exist to explain government's behavior on a minimally rational basis.[14]

If this standard sounds generous, it is supposed to be. The Court has long since jettisoned primitive ideas that clouded judgment a century ago—natural rights and private markets. In their place, the Court has come to appreciate government's inescapable involvement in all manner of social and economic affairs, its modern responsibility for regulation in the public interest, and its political accountability in the kind of democracy that has developed in this country. Accordingly, the Court acknowledges that, in a society that claims to be democratic, most decisions about social policy, certainly decisions about the distribution of wealth, should be given to politically accountable legislatures rather than politically insulated courts.[15]

This is not to say that when the Court invokes this relaxed "rational-basis" test, it never concludes that governmental action violates some substantive constitutional right. There are modern decisions in which the Court purports to indulge government in this way, but nonetheless takes constitutional arguments quite seriously. There are important cases, too, in which the Court has sided with the individual (or even a corporate party). The leading illustrations are *Cleburne Living Center*[16] (involving the imposition of special regulatory burdens on the mentally retarded), *Romer v. Evans*[17] (involving a prohibition on laws banning discrimination on the basis of sexual orientation), and perhaps *Lawrence v. Texas*[18] (involving sodomy laws, thus again discrimination to the detriment of gays and lesbians). There are not *many* such decisions, but enough to deflect any argument that they are mistakes, mystifying outliers, or exceptions that prove a contrary general rule.

In part, cases of this sort may be explained by institutional arrangements. When potential litigants anticipate that a charitable standard of review will be applied, they either attempt to repackage their claims in a way that invokes a more aggressive standard or drop litigation with so little chance of success.[19] Lower courts, in turn, spare the Court the trouble of addressing the few suits that are initiated. So the Court itself tends to see only cases in which the standard of review is inconclusive. Yet there is a deeper explanation: The articulated standard of review, whatever it may be, is far less important than the basic doctrinal framework supplied by rational instrumentalism, which, in turn, identifies the relevant considerations for hard-minded judgment. In this instance, the rhetoric surrounding the "rational-basis" standard obscures a much richer analysis, sensitive to the facts and values implicated in the case at hand. The cases that reach the Supreme Court demand difficult decisions and thus invite disagreement along the bench. In the crucible of concrete problem-solving, each of the justices works through the analysis, and no case is over until all the votes are in.

Close Scrutiny

In some instances, the Court explains that the presumption runs against the validity of governmental action. When government regulates with respect to "fundamental" interests or "rights," and equally when it classifies individuals along "suspect" lines, the Court engages what it calls "strict scrutiny."[20] Now government must demonstrate that its behavior is "justified" by the public interests sought to be advanced.[21] Typically, the Court explains that government's means must be "necessary" to a "compelling" state interest.[22] These ostensibly common words (*fundamental* individual interests, *suspect* classifications, *necessary* means, and *compelling* governmental interests) have become doctrinal terms of art—buzz words sending rough signals about the rigor of the analysis the Court means to engage. For example, a governmental interest can be "legitimate" in the sense that it is constitutionally acceptable, though not "compelling" in the sense that it is sufficiently weighty to justify governmental actions that trigger close examination.[23] And a means really need not be "necessary" in an absolute sense, but must be "narrowly tailored" to the "compelling" governmental interest said to explain its use.[24] The justices certainly present "strict scrutiny" as challenging; Justice Kennedy once declared it to be "the most demanding test known to constitutional law."[25] But they deny that it is "'strict in theory, but fatal in fact.'"[26] In some cases, governmental action can survive even this exacting standard of review.[27]

Here again, the justices sometimes express themselves loosely—perhaps without intending any particular message, perhaps deliberately to dispel the notion that *any* standard of review can specify a rigid and confining formula for decision making.[28] The result, again, is ambiguity. There are times, for example, when justices confuse the question whether "strict scrutiny" is appropriate with the ultimate question whether the governmental action in question is valid—that is, whether it passes the demanding test. We will see an example of that in the *Davis* case in a minute.[29] And there are times when justices suggest that some other doctrine (itself instrumental in nature) is antecedent to "strict scrutiny." In the *Akron* case,[30] Justice O'Connor initially said that if a court concludes that a statute imposes an "undue burden" on a woman's ability to obtain an abortion, *then* the Court should bring strict scrutiny to bear.[31] Yet in the controlling joint opinion in *Casey,* she said that a regulation that imposes an undue burden on a woman's choice to terminate a pregnancy is on that ground alone unconstitutional—without reference to strict scrutiny.[32]

On some occasions the justices vary the script for the calculated purpose of defining a "heightened" standard of review that is not quite the equivalent of "strict scrutiny" but close enough to make the shortfall inconsequential. In the *VMI* (Virginia Military Institute) case,[33] Justice Ginsburg explained that government must "demonstrate an *exceedingly persuasive* justification" for classifying according to gender.[34] A gender classification must "at least" be "substantially related" to achieving "important governmental objectives." Government's justification must be "genuine, not hypothesized or invented post hoc in response to litigation." And "it must not rely on overbroad generalizations about the different talents, capacities, or preferences of males and females."[35] That

formulation shaves a bit off the standard applicable to race classifications: the governmental objective need not be compelling (only important), and the classifying means need only be substantially related to the
objective (not narrowly tailored).

Now then, it is fair to ask whether ordinary mortals can make anything of the subtle differences in phrasing between the standard of review
appropriate for judging suspect classifications like race and the standard
applicable to gender classifications. Truth is, nobody can. Certainly, the
standard for gender cases is exacting enough to condemn any gender
classification that the "compelling-interest/narrowly-tailored means" test
would reject in a race case. In this instance, of course, the differences in
phraseology are the product of jockeying among the justices over a fairly
short period of years. The story is familiar. The Court took an uncon-
scionably long time to acknowledge that gender classifications are problematic at all. Once the justices let themselves think about it, they divided
over the obvious analogy to race. Justice Brennan and others would have
employed the same standard in both contexts, Chief Justice Rehnquist
and others resisted, Brennan was forced to compromise, the Chief Justice momentarily undercut the deal, and then (after women arrived on
the scene) the Court's majority settled on the standard I just recounted.
Justice Ginsburg describes the current test as "skeptical scrutiny"—
I dare say strict in fact, if not in theory.[36]

If it is fair to ask whether the mild variations between the standards
for gender and race cases make any practical difference, it is also fair to
ask whether similarly modest deviations touching other substantive rights
are any more significant.[37] Take, for example, the formulations articulated in *O'Brien*[38] and *Central Hudson*[39] for symbolic and commercial
expression cases, respectively. In both those instances, the Court plainly
means to drop the bar substantially, even in the free speech context. Yet
in both, the articulated standards partake of the verbiage we associate with "strict scrutiny" or, at least, the "skeptical scrutiny" in gender
cases. In *O'Brien*, Chief Justice Warren explained that governmental action affecting symbolic speech must further an "important" or "substantial" governmental interest unrelated to the suppression of free expression, and any restriction on speech can be "no greater than is essential
to the furtherance of that interest."[40] In *Central Hudson*, Justice Powell
said that government may regulate commercial speech only by means
that are no more intrusive than "necessary" to serve a "substantial" governmental interest.[41] True, the Court has explained (again) that "nec-

essary" doesn't mean logically essential. Government need not choose the "least restrictive measure" that promises to achieve its ends.[42] Even so, a means must be "narrowly tailored" to the stated objective. That requirement, in turn, tracks the Court's explanation of strict scrutiny.

However much the justices try to articulate different iterations of some more aggressive standard of review, the same terms keep coming back. And efforts to infuse them with different meaning come to naught. Consider Justice Scalia's tortured summary of the standard in commercial advertising cases. There must be some "'fit' between the legislature's ends and the means chosen to accomplish those ends, . . . a fit that is not necessarily perfect, but reasonable; that represents not necessarily the single best disposition but one whose scope is 'in proportion to the interest served' . . . [and] that employs not necessarily the least restrictive means but . . . a means narrowly tailored to achieve the desired objective."[43] Within those "bounds," Justice Scalia explained, politically accountable governmental agents (not the courts) get to decide "what manner of regulation may best be employed."[44] You have to wonder what real direction lower courts can take from this kind of back-and-forth ambivalence. Probably not much. So you have to wonder whether manipulating the terms in which the standard of review is stated is worth the candle at all. The justices themselves evidently think it matters whether they choose (at least) between the minimal "rational-basis" standard, on the one hand, and any form of "heightened" or "strict" or "skeptical" scrutiny, on the other. But the announcement of a standard at the outset of an opinion does little more than set the mood for what follows.

Nor is the *failure* to declare the standard especially probative. Consider the tedious academic debate over the standard that Justice Kennedy brought to bear in *Lawrence*. Kennedy himself failed to specify the flavor of the day, at least in so many words.[45] All he said was that Texas offered "no legitimate state interest which can justify its intrusions into the personal and private life of the individual."[46] That statement was ambiguous. Justice Kennedy may have meant that the statute served some constitutionally acceptable, but less than compelling, governmental interest. In that event, it seems he must have been examining the statute on some exacting standard. That is how most observers understand the position. Cass Sunstein infers that Kennedy actually regarded the individual interest at stake to be "fundamental," such that the "rational-basis" standard was inappropriate.[47] Laurence Tribe agrees and insists that the Court need not utter the usual "magic words" in order to signal that it expects a statute to pass some more rigorous test. Other language in an opinion, its tone, and its citations of authority can speak volumes.[48] In the alternative, Kennedy may have meant that no constitutionally legitimate interest appeared at all, in which case the statute was invalid even on the most relaxed of standards. Mary Case thinks this is the better understanding—at least if we assume that Kennedy used "which" (rather than "that") in the way that Dr. Strunk prescribes. The pronoun "which" is not restrictive and thus allows Kennedy's first proposition (that "no legitimate state interest" appeared) to stand alone.[49]

This is lots of fun. But we should not get carried away by it. There is no real mystery about *Lawrence* or any other case in which the Court deliberately overlooks the standard of review in play. The justices continue to believe that creating two (or three) discrete "tiers" of review gives the general rational instrumentalism framework desirable specificity. Yet they also worry that if they once fit some class of cases into the "strict scrutiny" box, they will set in motion developments they will regret or, at least, find difficult to restrain or, certainly, to reverse.[50] Justices on the Right hope to employ standards of review as formalist categories that tend to produce results to their liking: classifications according to sexual identification are *not* "suspect," and government's interest in achieving the benefits of diversity in higher education is *not* "compelling."[51] Justices on the Left use the same tactic in pursuit of results they prefer: classifications according to sexual orientation *are* "suspect," and the interest in obtaining the values associated with diversity *is* "compelling."[52] Justices who occupy the ideological middle ground pick their way through cutting-edge cases, taking no side, mouthing a relaxed standard (or no standard at all). A refusal to articulate and apply a demanding standard of review scarcely escapes judgment regarding the values at stake, but only drives that judgment into the fact-sensitive analysis of particular cases implicating those values. We are left with the familiar framework supplied by rational instrumentalism and a series of judgments by men and women struggling to decide whether governmental regulation is truly explainable as an attempt to serve the public interest.

In the end, then, when the justices are more demanding of government in "fundamental" liberty and "suspect" classification cases, it is not because they employ a different organizing template but because the framework they consistently use identifies and illuminates different relevant considerations and because individual justices value those considerations differently. The justices are hard to please in these cases.

But that is not because they articulate and apply a more exacting standard of review. It is because the relevant considerations raise doubts about whether government is regulating instrumentally in the pursuit of public-regarding objectives. If we once put aside the business of choosing a "standard of review" for a case, we can observe more readily what really divides the justices. That is the mission of this last chapter.

On examination, the justices chiefly fight over the level of generality at which to identify the factors in the instrumentalism mix: governmental means, individual interests, and governmental objectives. It is conventionally understood that the justices focus on the generality question primarily with respect to the individual interests affected by governmental action and that the level of generality at which an interest is captured goes to the standard of review to be applied. The justices define the interest in a case at some level of generality, thus to decide whether (so defined) it is "fundamental," thus to decide whether a regulation of it is subject to "heightened" scrutiny. As it turns out, however, the justices worry about the level-of-generality question not only with respect to individual interests, but also with respect to governmental means and purposes. Moreover, the significance of the generality issue has to do not so much with choosing the appropriate standard of review but, instead, with a careful analysis of the instrumental connection between means and ends. The justices equally appear to quarrel over whether a governmental objective is "compelling" in order to decide whether the means selected to serve that purpose passes a demanding standard of review. In reality, however, the "compelling" label is better understood as a conclusion the Court (sometimes) reaches about government's success in establishing the necessary instrumental relationship between its means and ends.

The justices equally appear to debate whether a regulation serves a "legitimate" governmental objective, thus to decide whether it is valid under any standard of review. There is a way in which that makes sense. Rational instrumentalism does not contemplate merely that government must regulate individual freedom for *some* reason. As Michael Dorf puts it, the whole point of "rights" is to insulate individuals against "*unacceptable* reasons for government action."[53] Yet the justices rarely purport simply to rule governmental objectives constitutionally out of bounds; rather, they insist that government's reasons for behaving as it does must be constitutionally permissible in the sense that benefits are conferred on some individuals and burdens are imposed on others in service of a larger public good. The fight, accordingly, is not over whether government's purpose is by nature constitutionally impermissible, but over whether government's means serves any public purpose at all. As usual, the only doctrinal framework doing any real work is rational instrumentalism. I touched on this in chapter 3. In this chapter, I develop it more fully with the aid of concrete examples.[54]

Means

It is crucial in every case to characterize the means by which government has chosen to regulate. This is true irrespective of the standard of review said to be at work. Even if the articulated standard is extremely deferential to government, the Court can evaluate the connection between the means and possible objectives only if it first identifies the means with the necessary precision. In the common case of a legislative rule, getting the means straight seems easy enough—a simple matter of reading the rule on its face. Yet in many circumstances the task can be more difficult, more subtle.

Consider free speech cases in which the threshold question is whether a regulation classifies according to the content or viewpoint of the speaker's message. A rule classifies according to content if it separates whole topics one from another, according to viewpoint if it separates perspectives regarding a single topic. This distinction sounds straightforward. But its implementation leaves a lot of room for judgment, and the justices constantly quarrel over it. In the *Perry* case,[55] for example, Justice White sustained a collective bargaining agreement that restricted a school mail service to the union currently representing employees and excluded a competing union. White acknowledged that the contract preferred one message to another, but he understood the resulting discrimination to rest on the ensconced union's position, not on the content of its expression. In dissent, Justice Brennan characterized the exclusion of the competing union as viewpoint discrimination, pure and simple. Similar disagreements occur all the time, offering fair arguments over the best characterization to place on government's choice of means.[56] Fair arguments, in turn, demand judgment.

The Level-of-Generality Question

To characterize the nature of a means, the Court must identify it at the proper level of generality. It is hard to generalize about generality, except to say (here again) that the Court's doctrine only presents questions for decision as a matter of judgment. Illustrations are abundant. In *Vincent*,[57] a Los Angeles ordinance prohibited fixed signs (including political campaign placards) on public property. Writing for the Court, Justice Stevens accepted the ordinance as a content-neutral measure furthering the public interest in the elimination of "visual clutter." In dissent, however, Justice Brennan insisted that the ordinance could be fairly understood only in the context of everything the city was doing in service of the same end. If other ordinances prohibited eyesores lacking serious expressive value, the city could plausibly defend the ban on signs as an element of the larger regulatory scheme. But since the city had addressed the clutter problem only by barring expressive signs, Brennan would have demanded a better explanation for that particular policy.[58]

In a free speech case like *Vincent,* at least some of the justices prefer more sweeping prohibitions on expression to tighter, underinclusive rules. On the face of it, this seems odd inasmuch as blanket prohibitions necessarily suppress more speech. Yet if government extends its reach more broadly, drawing more would-be speakers into its net, the risk that government is favoring some messages over others diminishes. Moreover, since the regulatory burden falls on greater numbers of people, one of two things is likely to happen, either of them salutary (with respect to free speech). Opposition to the regulation may increase, perhaps bringing about repeal or adjustment through ordinary political channels without need for judicial action. Or the regulation may survive notwithstanding its more extensive burdens, thus demonstrating that it genuinely serves public-regarding ends and is not a contrivance to play favorites. Recall this same kind of thinking in the due process/equal protection setting.[59]

The challenge of getting the level of generality right constantly reappears, always producing disagreements and, concomitantly, demanding judgment. The *R.A.V.* case offers another illustration.[60] Justice Scalia explained that "fighting words" can be punished *en masse* but not in isolated, content-discriminatory pockets. Then again, government can create discrete classes within the larger category of fighting words generally—so long as the boundaries of those classes parallel the criteria that allow government to outlaw all fighting words together. Having power to reach and prohibit all fighting words, government can choose to address only an especially virulent class of those words, thus checking some fighting words for the same reasons that all such words might be suppressed.

It is easy enough to see Justice Scalia's quandary. On the one hand, he did not want to adopt an all-or-nothing position, allowing government to punish all fighting words or none. After all, government might well conclude that some expression meeting the fighting-words criteria is nonetheless marginally worthwhile and thus might wish to suppress only words located deeper in the fighting words category. On the other hand, Scalia could not very well permit government to classify fighting words any way it likes. An obvious hypothetical explained why: government surely cannot pick out and ban only fighting words that are critical of the government's policies. The occasion called for judgment about the best of the available choices, none of them without flaws and costs. Justice Scalia resolved the dilemma by drawing the best line he could between a kind of content discrimination that should be allowed (i.e., discrimination that tracks the criteria permitting government to suppress all fighting words together) and a kind of content discrimination that should be prohibited (e.g., discrimination that singles out fighting words used to discuss particular topics).

Of course, reasonable minds can differ about whether the discrimination established by a particular statute falls on one side of that line or the other. Writing separately in *R.A.V.*, Justice Stevens insisted that Scalia's attempt to distinguish sharply among different forms of content discrimination would prove difficult to sustain. That prediction was accurate. In *Virginia v. Black*,[61] the justices divided (as well they might) over whether an ordinance can single out cross-burning with an intent to intimidate as an especially heinous form of threat. Justice O'Connor, Justice Scalia, and others in the majority thought so, but Justice Souter and two more dissenters thought not. By Souter's account, an ordinance that selects only cross-burning for punishment does so because of the ugly message associated with that form of symbolic expression. Cross-burning is distinctive not because it is a peculiarly intimidating kind of threat but because it threatens in a content-sensitive way.[62] Accordingly, in Souter's view, a prohibition on cross-burning discriminates in the way Justice Scalia's analysis in *R.A.V.* condemns.[63]

The generality problem can be especially acute in equal protection cases. It is one thing if a statute or regulation explicitly (and thus deliberately) imposes burdens on individuals solely on the basis of race and arguably another if it takes account of race in some other way. The Census Bureau asks race-specific questions; police officers interrogate witnesses about the race of perpetrators and select participants in line-ups accordingly.[64] The Court is inclined to understand all forms governmental action touching race explicitly as racial classifications and to regard them all with suspicion.[65] Still, some considerations of race do serve discernible public goals. The collection of race-sensitive demographic data and the use of racial descriptions to help identify crooks are good illustrations.[66] At the same time, some rules plainly discriminate in a troubling race-conscious way, notwithstanding that they do not draw a simple racial line that treats members of racial groups differently. Remember the "miscegenation" law in *Loving v. Virginia*,[67] which prohibited marriage between people of different racial groups. The state denied any discrimination on the basis of race, because the ban limited the choices of whites as well as blacks. The Court rejected that claim as sophistry.[68]

There is a way, too, that the generality issue is necessarily entailed in the (often controversial) decision whether to examine a classifying rule on its face or only as applied. Consider Justice White's opinion for the Court in *Cleburne Living Center*.[69] At the outset, White explained that the question was whether a city zoning ordinance was invalid as written because it classified according to "mental retardation" (by requiring special permits for group homes housing "feeble minded" residents). By characterizing the issue that way, White concentrated attention on the abstract question whether discrimination on the basis of "mental retardation" was, first, subject to a demanding standard of review and, second, valid when examined under whatever standard of review was appropriate. Further down in his opinion, however, Justice White recast the question as whether the city council had committed unconstitutional discrimination by denying a permit in the circumstances of the instant case. That shift allowed White to consider the city's arguments that the group home in question would be located in a flood plain, that it would add to congestion in the neighborhood, and (most important) that it would provoke abutters who harbored "negative attitudes" about "mentally retarded" persons.[70]

The change in focus was potentially dispositive in *Cleburne*. Justice White was not persuaded that classifications according to "mental retardation" are unlikely to serve public-regarding goals. Nor was he sure (or so it seems) that it is unreasonable to require special permits in cases involving group homes for "retarded" residents. That classification may be defended as merely a means of bringing each individual application before decision makers so that sensitive judgments can be made about the appropriate location of housing for people with special needs. Insofar as *ad hoc* judgments of that kind eschew stereotypes and prejudice, they may constitute a perfectly sensible (even benevolent) means of attending to the "difficulties" involved. By contrast, the city's explanations for denying a permit to the particular group home in *Cleburne* were plainly bogus. Other kinds of multiple-occupancy housing could be established in the same flood plain without a permit, and those group homes would equally exacerbate population density. So, far from justifying the refusal of a permit to a home for the "mentally retarded," the city's explanations proved that the permit had been withheld on the basis of "irrational prejudice."[71]

Disproportionate Impact

Then there are cases in which the rule that government puts on the statute books is not genuinely the rule government acts upon. In *Yick Wo v. Hopkins*,[72] a San Francisco ordinance required a special permit from the Board of Supervisors to operate a laundry in a wooden building. The ordinance itself was unremarkable, but it turned out not to reflect the real law in play. The Board consistently granted permits to Caucasian operators and denied them to Chinese. So the city actually had a covert, racially discriminatory rule hiding behind the overt, race-neutral rule it displayed. The Supreme Court recognized that the former was the operative state action in issue. The cases on jury selection make this same point. When members of minority groups are excluded systematically, the only mathematically possible explanation is race discrimination—notwithstanding that the selection scheme is race-neutral on its face.[73]

Of course, covert rules are hard to spot and harder to demonstrate. More commonly, the Court grapples with genuine (overt) rules that are not especially troubling as written but in operation distribute benefits or burdens in a way that raises serious concerns. The Court insists that the Constitution addresses only "intentional" (sometimes the Court says "purposeful") classifications, not the "effect" that classifications have when they are honestly implemented. Now we come to *Washington v. Davis*,[74] where the District of Columbia selected police officers in part on the basis of their scores on a verbal skills examination. No one argued that *Davis* was another *Yick Wo*. City authorities used the test as prescribed; they did not toss out the results and instead choose candidates on the basis of race,. By contrast, the plaintiffs claimed that the test was culturally biased and thus disqualified African Americans in disproportionate numbers. They contended, accordingly, that the text's discriminatory impact justified treating it as though it were a deliberate means of excluding candidates on the basis of race.

Writing for the Court, Justice White said that a rule can be taken to discriminate on the basis of race only if it "reflects a racially discriminatory purpose."[75] Such a purpose may appear expressly on the face of the rule, or it may be shown by evidence. A disproportionate impact on members of a racial group counts as evidence of that kind, but effects alone are insufficient to carry the day. Later, in the *Arlington Heights* case,[76] Justice Powell explained that plaintiffs are not required to prove that governmental action "rested solely on racially discriminatory purposes," but must show that a "discriminatory purpose has been a motivating factor" in government's behavior.[77] Since it is infeasible actually to retrieve the genuine, sole purpose for which government acts, the Court is satisfied with a second-best alternative: the primary explanation, defined as the "but for" cause of the governmental behavior in question.[78]

Note the confusion this can produce. When the justices insist that a classification must be "intentional" or "purposeful," they are not yet assessing the ends the classification may be said to further. That comes later, or at least independently. At this juncture, they mean that government must have the intention or purpose of classifying in the relevant way: for example, according to race. The task is still the proper characterization of government's means. Then again, the evidence the justices examine to determine the true character of a means is typically the same evidence they explore to determine the end to be served—namely, indications of why the decision to employ the classification in question was made. In *Arlington Heights,* Justice Powell was prepared to consider the sequence of events leading to the vote, departures from ordinary procedures, the minutes of meetings, and public statements by key officials. That kind of evidence is notoriously problematic as a basis for confident judgment about the actual explanation for governmental action—if *actual* explanation there was.[79] All the justices are wary of it; some, most notably Justice Scalia, refuse to consult it at all.[80]

The analysis is confusing in other ways. Justice White explained in *Davis* that disproportionate effects alone do not "trigger the [test] that racial classifications are to be subjected to the strictest scrutiny."[81] That suggests that a plaintiff's threshold demonstration that a "discriminatory purpose" formed a "motivating factor" behind government's action is a prelude to the application of the "narrowly-tailored-means/compelling-interest" standard of review, which then will guide judgment on whether a classification is valid. Yet in *Arlington Heights,* Justice Powell said that "proof of racially discriminatory intent or purpose is required to show a violation of the Equal Protection Clause."[82] That suggests that a plaintiff who carries the burden of demonstrating the necessary "motivating factor" should win outright, unless the government comes forward with rebuttal evidence that it would have done the same thing on alternative grounds. It seems, then, that the familiar "narrowly-tailored-means/compelling-interest" test is inapposite in these cases—superseded by a related standard depending on burden assignment. It is hard to think that if a plaintiff proves that a purpose to impose disproportionate burdens on racial minorities was a motivating factor in government's decision to adopt a classification, and the government fails to demonstrate an alternative race-neutral explanation, the Court will at that late juncture engage the ordinary "strict scrutiny" standard of review it applies to rules that explicitly classify according to race. Then again, perhaps White and Powell were only confusing two things the current Court usually keeps separate: the application of the "strict scrutiny" standard, on the one hand, and the ultimate decision whether a classification genuinely serves the public interest, on the other.

The explanation for *Davis/Arlington Heights* is apparent. The justices take a dim view of governmental actions that explicitly discriminate on the basis of race because they suspect that actions of that kind simply punish the members of racial groups for no public-regarding purpose. They look upon actions having a disproportionate impact on minority groups more favorably, because they tend to believe that government is pursuing the public interest, notwithstanding unfortunate side effects on minorities. Those side effects flow not from what government has done but from the inequities in the socioeconomic system generally (which put members of minority racial groups in a position to be harmed disproportionately by facially race-neutral government policies). Since the 1930s, the Court has recognized the government's role in giving effect to private arrangements. Yet the justices who dominate the modern Court deny that background governmental policies permitting (or even authorizing) individuals and companies to behave as they do transform ostensibly private conduct into governmental action subject to constitutional controls. Government is held to account constitutionally for the regulatory actions it actually takes, but not for *inaction*—not for its failure to regulate in a way that ameliorates injustices worked by private entities.[83] Moreover, if the justices were to equate governmental activities having a disproportionate impact on minorities with explicit race discrimination, they might find themselves policing governmental regulation on a grand scale.[84]

Nevertheless, the *Davis* and *Arlington Heights* cases are intensely controversial and illustrate yet again the judgment that rational instrumentalism calls on the justices to exercise. The floodgates argument proceeds from the sobering premise that lots of governmental activities have the practical effect of cementing the subordination of racial groups. If that is so (and it seems pretty clear that it is), then legislators and executive officers surely must know it. If they do not, they are educated when plaintiffs demonstrate the facts in litigation. Yet they persist in their actions regardless of the foreseeable consequences. In criminal law, knowledge is treated as intent, or at least as culpable reckless disregard. In constitutional law, by contrast, knowledge alone is insufficient to establish the "purpose" necessary to characterize government action that is race-neutral on its face as, instead, racially discriminatory. Accordingly, the people who get hurt typically have no constitutional recourse.

The Court was scarcely obliged to draw a sharp distinction between purpose and impact. Writing separately in *Davis,* Justice Stevens argued that the difference between the two "is not nearly as bright, and perhaps not quite as critical," as the Court seems to assume.[85] It was open, accordingly, to be considerably more flexible in determining the best way to characterize accurately the true governmental policy at work in a case. Preserving deliberate governmental action as the essential element, the Court might have given plaintiffs rather more room in which to establish what government is actually doing. As Justice Stevens put it, the best way to discover "intent" is often to look at "objective evidence of what actually happened."[86]

The analysis in *Davis* and *Arlington Heights* introduces additional judgments into the equation when government adopts policies that are close cousins of classifications on the basis of race. There are old cases, for example, in which states tried to evade the ban on racial discrimination by substituting classifications according to ancestry. The Court quickly saw through the subterfuge and proceeded as though exclusions or exemptions based on genealogy were written explicitly in racial terms.[87] That sounds noncontroversial. Yet in *Rice v. Cayetano,*[88] the justices conducted a perfectly reasonable debate over whether to regard a classification according to Hawaiian lineage in the same way. That classification rested on status, of course, and thus affected people differently because of blood lines they scarcely controlled. Yet there was no real sense that the statute in question was a ruse for subjecting racial groups to burdens that did not correspond to genuine public objectives.

In most modern cases, the justices are inclined to give government the benefit of the doubt. In the *Feeney* case,[89] for example, the Court held that a Massachusetts statute giving hiring preferences to veterans was not a rule subordinating women, notwithstanding that relatively few women enjoyed its benefits. There was no allegation that anyone thought about women when the statute was enacted, nor any evidence that anyone actually hoped to squeeze women out. And in *Hernandez v. New York*,[90] the Court declined to find deliberate racial discrimination in a prosecutor's use of peremptory strikes to eliminate Hispanics from a jury. The prosecutor explained that jurors fluent in Spanish might rely on their own understanding of Spanish-speaking witnesses rather than on the English translations provided by the official interpreter. The trial court accepted that account, and the Supreme Court went along. The criteria government used in *Feeney* and *Hernandez* looked suspiciously like proxies for gender and race. The justices might have worked backward from practical effects and inferred the necessary "purpose" or "intent." They refused—not because rational instrumentalism precluded that course (far less because the Constitution foreclosed it), but because in their judgment it was unwise.[91]

The judgment called for in all these disproportionate impact cases is nowhere clearer than in *Lawrence*.[92] On its face, the Texas sodomy statute made it a crime for persons of the same sex to commit certain sexual acts. It classified, then, according to sexual conduct, not orientation, and the justices might have invoked *Davis/Arlington Heights* to defuse the plaintiffs' assault.[93] They did not. Everyone acknowledged that the statute was as good as a rule demonizing gays and lesbians and thus treated it as classifying on the basis of sexual identification. The matter was sensitive. Sexuality, like race, is a socially constructed concept. It is troubling in the extreme to separate individuals neatly into sexual compartments and concomitantly troubling to do so on the basis of the sexual behavior in which they engage. Sexual orientation can be an affirmative matter of self-identification. Yet it can also be an imposition of law (often for the purpose of oppression). Still, the Court cannot realistically overlook the categories in which individuals find themselves (willingly or not) and the correlation between those categories and sexual conduct. In *Lawrence,* the justices refused to be taken in. They knew a gay-bashing statute when they saw one.[94]

Knowing a Means by Its Purpose

The idea that the nature of a means turns on its purpose can test the boundaries between the task of identifying the true character of a governmental means, on the one hand, and the different task of identifying government's ends, on the other. In *Renton,*[95] for example, Chief Justice Rehnquist insisted that an ordinance singling out adult movie theaters did not discriminate on the basis of content, because its purpose was to discourage the community deterioration that typically accompanies pornographic entertainment. And in *Madsen,*[96] he said that an injunction limited to anti-abortion demonstrators was neither content nor viewpoint discriminatory, because its purpose was to deter further violations of a previous order (whose purpose, in turn, was to keep the peace). Those opinions arguably resist the baseline proposition that there is a difference between government's means and its ends. Justice Kennedy insists, by contrast, that if a statute classifies expression according to content by its explicit terms, it should be treated as content-discriminatory—and should then be sustained or not on the basis of an assessment of its connection to a governmental purpose.[97]

Getting the means straight turns out to be as difficult as it is essential. Fair arguments can often be raised about the proper characterization to press on a statute or other form of governmental action. Nothing in rational instrumentalism offers much guidance to justices who must *decide* what government has done in order to determine whether its conduct is valid. Adversaries understandably package the rules they attack or defend to suit their own positions. And, in the end, the justices can only consult their own best judgment.

Individual Interests

The Court plainly must identify and characterize the individual interests at stake in a case. Since the Progressive Era, the justices have recognized that the freedom individuals enjoy is largely a function of the regulatory scheme that government puts in place. A constitutional challenge to any feature of that scheme can succeed only if government's behavior affects individuals in some untoward way that cannot be justified as an instrumental means of achieving a public end. Most of the time, government regulates individual freedom in market arrangements with a fairly obvious bearing on the public interest. The Court often signals as much by invoking the generous, indulgent, "rational-basis" test as the applicable standard of review.

The position is altered when government adjusts especially personal individual interests or groups individuals into suspicious classifications— this is to say, when government regulates in a way that is unlikely to achieve public-regarding goals. On those occasions, the Court raises the standard of review considerably to "strict scrutiny" or some variant on that theme. This is the stuff of much academic commentary, which attempts to understand why the Court regards some forms of individual freedom and some bases of classification as special—or, perhaps better said, to construct an explanation that both squares with the cases and offers an appealing general account of what is going on. I want to concentrate, instead, on describing how the justices actually set about their work, with the aim of demonstrating, once again, that they create substantive individual rights as a matter of judgment—orchestrated, but not seriously restrained, by the rational instrumentalism they employ as working constitutional doctrine.

Rights (Again)

The best illustrations are cases decided under the heading of substantive due process. Recall that the Court invariably explains that it aggressively superintends governmental regulation of "fundamental" matters and typically refers to those matters as "fundamental rights."[98] I explained in the last chapter that it is not entirely clear why the justices inject "fundamental rights" into the conversation. Maybe they are just careless; maybe they only repeat language borrowed from older cases reflecting the compromise over "incorporation" theory.[99] Yet it is hard to think the justices do not know what they are doing. Moreover, it is perfectly clear that the men and women who now command the Court would never have accepted "incorporation" theory in any of its iterations and certainly would not claim any such textual basis for their "fundamental rights" rhetoric today. The joint opinion in Casey, perhaps the most influential explanation of substantive due process we have, explicitly denied that the Bill of Rights "marks the outer limits of the substantive sphere of liberty" protected by the Fourteenth Amendment.[100] For his part, Justice Scalia would evidently discard the very idea of substantive due process were it not for some precedents he finds so ensconced that they cannot be overturned without unacceptable disruption.[101]

There is a better explanation for all this talk of "fundamental rights." It is a matter of tactics. Justices deliberately say "right" when they ought to say "liberty" or "interest" to promote their notions about what substantive due process should be understood to mean. Recall that in the "assisted suicide" case, *Glucksberg*,[102] Chief Justice Rehnquist explained that due process "provides heightened protection against government interference with certain fundamental *rights* and liberty interests."[103] Justice Souter responded that it is awkward to *begin* a due process analysis by deciding whether some governmental action implicates a "fundamental right" and that it would make more sense to determine whether the "liberty" affected is "fundamental" and then to determine whether the imposition on that liberty is such that a "right" (to due process) is violated.[104]

Souter's way of putting things in substantive due process cases is attractive as a matter of language. The only genuine right in view is the right to due process, and one would have thought that the real question is whether the liberty affected is especially sensitive, such that the Court should be unusually grudging about letting government impose restrictions. Yet it is easy enough to understand why Chief Justice Rehnquist insisted that the first order of business is and should be to decide whether a "fundamental right" is implicated. The "fundamental-rights-based analytical method" is warranted, he said, to "rein in" justices who may be tempted to introduce "subjective elements" into the analysis.[105] In Rehnquist's view, Souter's fluid reliance on due process invites exacting judicial examination of government's actions in all manner of contexts, potentially even a revival of the natural-rights solicitude for liberty in general associated with *Lochner*.[106] For his part, Souter insists that the Court can manage to examine the "reasonableness" of regulation without routinely substituting its own judgment for that of politically accountable decision makers. Therein lies yet another fair basis for debate.

According to Chief Justice Rehnquist, the Court should not engage in a "complex balancing of interests in every case," but should reserve its attention for "fundamental rights found to be deeply rooted in our legal tradition." The idea (again) is to create a formally defined category of cases for serious review and to resist the temptation to second-guess

legislative enactments outside that category. Restricting "fundamental
rights" to the "rights" previously recognized discourages future movement.[107] That strategy does not avoid judgment, of course, but only moves
it to antecedent questions—how to define the specially protected category ("fundamental rights") and how to determine whether a particular
"right" fits into that category as defined. According to Justice Souter,
hard judgments need not be made for all cases at that macro level, but
can be made for individual cases taken one at a time. In *Glucksberg,*
at least, a majority of the justices sided with Chief Justice Rehnquist.[108]
The inference, then, is that most of the justices adopted the position that
the categorization of "fundamental rights" plays a strong, discretion-
limiting role in due process analysis. Justice Scalia, for his part, contended on this ground that *Glucksberg* undermined the joint opinion in
Casey.[109]

This explains the tumult regarding Justice Kennedy's opinion for the
Court in *Lawrence.* Kennedy obviously examined the Texas antisodomy
law with some care. Yet he nowhere stated explicitly that the individual
interest implicated counted as a "fundamental right." Nor did he refer to
Glucksberg, far less to Chief Justice Rehnquist's discussion of the doctrinal significance attaching to the "fundamental rights" label. Observers
on the Right fear that Kennedy discarded *Glucksberg's* "hold-that-line"
position and opened the door to aggressive examination of governmental
programs affecting a wider range of individual freedoms.[110] Observers
on the Left hope that's the case.[111] Randy Barnett, the libertarian, argues that by dropping the dichotomy between "fundamental rights" and
other interests Justice Kennedy opened the door to examining closely *all*
limits on liberty of *all* kinds—including the market activities the Court
has permitted to be regulated heavily since the New Deal.[112]

Justice Kennedy probably meant to say that the interest in *Lawrence*
fit the "fundamental rights" category or, at least, something very close
to it.[113] Yet there is no serious possibility that he took a libertarian turn
back to *Lochner.*[114] If he deliberately side-stepped the "fundamental
rights" rhetoric in cases like *Glucksberg,* it was not to signal a change
in the meaning of substantive due process captured somehow in a manipulation of key terms. He was only feeling his way over new terrain,
wrestling with the considerations in the case at hand, avoiding terms of
art that might carry their own baggage, and exercising his best judgment
within the loose (the very loose) framework that rational instrumentalism
provides. Sodomy statutes are unconstitutional today because Anthony

Kennedy and the justices who voted with him in *Lawrence* (conservative as they are) have come to understand that punitive measures aimed at gays, lesbians, and bisexuals do not serve any genuine public-regarding values. It is that simple (and that complicated).

The Level-of-Generality Question (Again)

Just as the justices must identify governmental action at the proper level of generality, they must also understand the individual interests affected by government's behavior in the same way. Here again, there is plenty of room for judgment. In some instances, fixing an individual interest at a fairly high level of generality may invite a determination that regulation affecting that interest is invalid—particularly if the Court is persuaded that the interest, so defined, is especially personal and sensitive (read "fundamental" in the Court's lexicon). There are no absolutes, of course; even the most sweeping basic freedoms may be adjusted to benefit social welfare. Yet by hypothesis an expansively defined personal interest can be affected by a wide variety of governmental activities. For that very reason, the justices may choose to define the interest in a case at a lower level of generality. A comparatively specific individual interest is typically less likely to be affected by the same array of governmental actions. Then again, if an individual interest is judged to be fundamental at a specific level of generality, it has a very good chance of defeating an attempt by government to regulate (at that level). So, in the final analysis, it is not possible to say that interests are invariably either stronger or weaker according to the level of generality at which they are defined. It depends. And, here again, it depends on judgment.

Consider some common illustrations. The Court understood some *amici* in *Roe v. Wade*[115] to contend for "an unlimited right to do with one's body as one pleases."[116] On that premise, a wide range of governmental actions might have been constitutionally vulnerable—not only limits (and perhaps all limits) on obtaining an abortion, but also restrictions on other medical procedures, personal grooming, sexual conduct, or the use of drugs. Writing for the Court, Justice Blackmun fixed the plaintiff's interest far lower on the generality scale, in fact as far down as he could go and still credit her interest at all—namely, an interest [he actually said a "right"] just "broad enough to encompass a woman's decision whether or not to terminate her pregnancy."[117] Even that understanding of the woman's interest was controversial. And, of course,

Blackmun went on to say that the state could restrict the choice to procure an abortion to achieve certain governmental ends.

Similar judgments are required in every case. They typically bear decisive significance, and thus they invariably excite controversy. In *Cruzan*,[118] for example, it was open to understand the individual's interest as a general "right to die." Instead, Chief Justice Rehnquist chose to state it as an "interest [for once he said "interest"] in refusing unwanted medical treatment."[119] That interest, in turn, included the interest actually implicated by the Missouri statute—the desire to refuse life-sustaining food and water. In *Glucksberg*, Chief Justice Rehnquist explained that the crucial question was whether individuals have a "right [remember that in *Glucksberg* Rehnquist made a point of "fundamental rights"] to commit suicide," which, in turn, would logically include the interest actually at stake in that case: the interest in a physician's assistance.[120] Since most of the justices were not prepared to recognize any such general interest, fundamental or otherwise, the state's ban on assisted suicide was sustained. If, by contrast, they had focused on a less general interest—for example, the interest of a "mentally competent person who is experiencing great suffering"—the case (and perhaps the result) would have been altered.[121]

Justice Scalia has complained that judgments about the level of generality at which to capture individual interests are too free-wheeling. In the *Michael H.* case,[122] he proposed a two-stage solution. First, the Court should determine whether an individual interest is "fundamental" exclusively in a backward-looking way. If the interest is shown to enjoy a historical "tradition" of special respect, it may be entitled to the "fundamental" label. If not, not. In the absence of a sufficient tradition, a liberty is only a liberty—not a "fundamental" liberty with all the pertaining implications. Second, the Court should always start with "the most specific level at which a relevant tradition protecting, or denying protection to, the asserted right [Justice Scalia likes "rights," not interests] can be identified."[123] If, after consulting the historical record, the Court finds no tradition either attaching or denying special significance to an interest, the Court may shift its focus further up the generality ladder. But as soon as the Court locates a tradition "either way," the scope of the interest at that level is controlling. The plaintiff in *Michael H.* was a natural parent who wanted to visit his daughter, but was barred by a state statute designating the mother's husband as the presumptive father. Justice Scalia acknowledged a tradition of respect for the interests of natural parents generally to see their kids. But he insisted that no such tradition existed with respect to the more specifically defined interest in the case at hand—namely, the interest of an adulterous biological father in visiting a child born to a married woman living with her husband.

You begin to see how much rides on the level of generality at which the Court captures the individual's interest and equally how difficult it is to get the level of generality right. I just explained that more general interests need not always fare better than specific interests. Yet if the test of an interest's character turns entirely on tradition, it probably is true that the higher the level of generality, the easier it is to find traditional support for it on Justice Scalia's terms.[124] If you are inclined to side with the individual in *Michael H.*, you describe his interest more generally and thus more easily claim a tradition of respect for it. Dissenting in that case, Justice Brennan insisted that the father asserted the familiar (and traditional) interest "of a parent and child in their relationship with each other."[125] If, by contrast, you are inclined to side with the state, you identify the interest more specifically, perhaps at the dramatically lower level of generality that Justice Scalia selected.

Justice Scalia insists that his methodology is value-neutral. He does not pick the most specific level of generality because he wants plaintiffs to lose, but because doing so disciplines the justices against simply making choices "they think best."[126] So his position is entirely pragmatic. Trouble is, Scalia's proposal cannot deliver on its promise. In fact, Justice Scalia's approach has divided the Court along familiar ideological lines.[127] Consider, first, that an exclusively backward-looking focus is biased against claims that government is regulating individual interests that society values deeply *today*, whatever was true historically.[128] Dissenting in *Michael H.*, Justice Brennan argued that an exclusive focus on history limits the protection of due process to human interests that are already quite secure and thus turns due process into "a redundancy."[129] Writing for the Court in *Lawrence*, Justice Kennedy declared that, whatever older historical tradition may have been, the character of a liberty that has the "most relevance" is the one reflected in society's "emerging awareness," demonstrated by "our laws and traditions in the last half century."[130]

The idea that individual interests should be identified at the most specific level of generality is also controversial. Justice Brennan argued in *Michael H.* that justices can reasonably "disagree about the content of particular traditions" and "even about which traditions are relevant to the definition of 'liberty.'"[131] Laurence Tribe and Michael Dorf contend that any attempt to seize upon the most specific level of generality is both "unworkable" and "incoherent"—unworkable because it only shifts the "problem of abstraction" from "legal precedent to historical precedent," and incoherent because there is no way to locate the most specific level of generality at which the interest can be said to exist.[132] As usual, Justice Scalia makes everything sound simple, as though there is a "single dimension of specificity" and "historical traditions come equipped with instruction manuals explaining how abstractly they are to be described."[133] That is not so.

It was anything but clear in *Michael H.* that the factors on which Justice Scalia focused were any more or less telling than others he overlooked. Scalia took it to be crucial that the father was an adulterer, but he might just as plausibly have emphasized that the father cared for his daughter and had developed a relationship with her. Scalia is surely right that individual interests cannot routinely be understood in the most general terms. It would not do to say that the father in *Michael M.* pressed the broad interest in family relationships or the broader interest in personal relationships of any kind, nor yet the interest, broader still, in "emotional attachments in general."[134] But it won't do, either, to lunge to the other extreme that Scalia himself prefers. The task is not to fix the level of generality at either the top or the bottom of the generality scale, but to fix it where it ought to be—as a matter of serious judgment.

Look again at the sexual conduct cases. One of the key arguments in *Hardwick* and *Lawrence* was over the level of generality at which to identify the individual interests at stake. Justice White's answer in *Hardwick* is notorious: whether "homosexuals" have a "right to engage in sodomy."[135] Justice Kennedy repudiated that idea in *Lawrence*—both because White misstated the interest itself and because he misrepresented the relevant historical materials. There are (at least) two other ways to conceive of the individual interests implicated in *Hardwick* and *Lawrence,* one of them fairly general and the other much more specific. The general understanding is straightforward. Everyone concedes a strong tradition of respect for the interest in choosing one's sexual partner, at least so long as the individuals concerned are not of the same sex. The individuals in *Hardwick* and *Lawrence* merely asserted that gays and lesbians share that same interest. If this is not fully borne out by history, it is supported by a sensible understanding of maturing American values. The specific understanding is that the individuals in those cases advanced concrete interests shaped by the circumstances in which their cases arose. In *Lawrence,* then, it was the interest of "adults" to "engage in a noncommercial, consensual, sexual relationship in private, where their activity involves no injury to a person or harm to an institution [like marriage] the law protects."[136] The choice between these alternatives, or between one or both of them and some additional candidate or candidates, calls for sober judgment—judgment that cannot be escaped in the way Justice Scalia proposes, or anything like it. That judgment is necessarily entailed in the rational instrumentalism that forms the doctrinal structure for the Court's analysis, which (again) only illuminates the difficult questions the justices must resolve and offers no real help toward the answers.

Ends

Rational instrumentalism calls on the justices to consider not only the means government selects, but also the ends those means may serve. By hypothesis, there is a difference between the two. If there were not, the means/ends relation would be tautological. Some justices occasionally resist the distinction between means and ends, but not for long. The statute in *Fritz*[137] eliminated the ability of future federal retirees to draw benefits from two funds (Social Security and a railroad retirement fund), but grandfathered in anyone who had a recent connection to the rail industry. That group included most, but not all, workers who had qualified for double-dipping under prior law. Chief Justice Rehnquist initially declared that the constitutional analysis of the resulting classification could be limited to the text of the classification itself. The only purpose he could fairly ascribe to Congress was a purpose to place that particular classification, reading that way, on the federal books. Justice Brennan insisted on a purposive model of politics, which demands that governmental actions answer to public-regarding goals. Chief Justice Rehnquist protested a bit, but in the end he accepted the purpose the government offered to explain the statute: workers who had worked in the industry recently had a greater "equitable" claim on double-dipping.[138]

Essential as the inquiry into governmental purpose is, it is fraught with difficulty and thus creates ever more occasions for disagreement. In this last section, I want to focus on four problems the justices must face, debate, and resolve. Initially, they must sort through the evidence regarding government's purpose in a particular instance. Second, they must identify the immediate purpose on which to focus the means/ends analysis. Next, they must (sometimes) determine whether the purpose is "compelling." And, finally, they must decide whether the purpose they identify is constitutionally impermissible.

The Search for Purpose

The necessity of identifying some end or ends apart from the means itself creates maddening epistemological puzzles. Consider that the point of the paradigm form of governmental action, legislation, is notoriously elusive, even illusory. Legislative assemblies are not always instrumentally inclined at all—not, at least, in the elevated means/ends sense that rational instrumentalism appears to contemplate. There may *be* no public purpose behind an enacted statute, no objective that government's means can be said to further, and thus no intelligible way in which a means can be judged to be constitutional or not in view of its instrumental relationship to such an objective. We scarcely need Bismarck to tell us that legislatures, including Congress, are often little more than markets in which participants pursue their own desires and the desires of their sponsors. Bills are introduced, investigations are undertaken, and hearings are held for a wide variety of political purposes—without any genuine expectation that they will actually lead to legislation. When bills move, it is only because the necessary political shoulders are behind them. Proposals are disguised, arguments are manufactured, deals are done—and out comes a product whose only real meaning is that a majority of those authorized to vote concluded (on whatever basis) that it was better to answer yea than nay. We are left with the very tautology with which Chief Justice Rehnquist flirted in *Fritz*: a statute having only the meaning and significance of its existence.

Things are actually even more complicated. Even if political bargaining regarding public policy occurred, nothing guarantees that the participants in those discussions settled on statutory language as a means of achieving any particular purpose. Lots of things may have happened. The opposing sides may have aired their differences at the level of overarching policy, without any genuine focus on the specifics of the proposal before them. Or they may have engaged general policy disputes by concentrating on some illustrative feature of the bill, neglecting all the others. In any case, the elected members who voted in the end may not have comprehended the details when they finally closed debate and exercised what political muscle they could. Instead, and this seems most likely, only professional staff and lobbyists may have had any knowledgeable grasp of the specifics. And even they may have long since surrendered any pretense of intellectual integrity in order to produce a draft for their masters.[139] It is a reach to ignore these possibilities and simply to assume that the statute that emerged from the legislative process reflects a finely tuned, negotiated agreement on a means for pursuing any discernible purpose.

If this "market model" of politics is even partly accurate (and it is more accurate than that in many instances), it spells grief for any doctrinal structure that posits the very thing that will not be delivered—genuine, goal-oriented, policymaking in the public interest. Recall that Justice Scalia's methodology for statutory construction assumes that statutes represent compromises over policy but despairs of discovering what those compromises were.[140] Herein, too, lies a link to originalism, which fails (in part) because we cannot confidently recover the meaning that framers or their generation attached to the document at the time. Just as it is impossible for Justice Scalia (or anyone else) to determine the original understanding of the written Constitution, it is at least problematic for the Court to ascertain why a legislature (or an executive officer) took some challenged action. There *is* no original understanding back of the Constitution to find and, if there were, we could not find it. Equally, there may be no confident answer to the question *why* some statute was enacted or some executive action taken.

Rational instrumentalism and originalism thus appear to suffer from the same embarrassment. The point of the exercise is different, of course. Originalism asks the Court to ascertain historical understanding that, in turn, is supposed to specify the Constitution's meaning. Instrumentalism asks the Court to retrieve an explanation for governmental action that, in turn, is supposed to allow the justices to determine as a matter of judgment whether government's behavior counts as a means of achieving a public-regarding end. Still, the conceptual and evidentiary difficulties are similar—and similarly daunting. Rational instrumentalism seems hopelessly naive inasmuch as it depends on a vision of the way government *would* behave if only the men and women who command it were not the frail, self-promoting, devious scrubs they are. These are serious points, and rational instrumentalism suffers for them. But while they are devastating to originalism, they deal instrumentalism more glancing blows.

To begin, it must be said that any analysis of the constitutional validity of governmental action must presuppose a threshold account of that action on its own ground: an understanding of the subject to which constitutional judgment is to be applied. So all the difficulties that attend the search for an explanation of what government has done are necessarily entailed *ex ante,* irrespective of the doctrinal formulation used to organize thinking about the further question whether any particular action is constitutional. Inasmuch as these problems (the market model of politics and the inscrutability of governmental objectives) beset statutory construction generally, it should not make banner headlines that they also attend rational instrumentalism as a doctrinal framework for determining the constitutionality question. After all, any other constitutional account of rights would have to wrestle with these same problems in order to reach whatever questions that alternative analysis makes pertinent.

It is worth saying again that the Court came to rational instrumentalism as its doctrinal framework of choice through hard experience with alternatives that plainly *were* naive, if not corrupt. The justices appreciate the way the American democracy makes public policy. Yet, what is equally important, they understand that there is no better way to do it. If we don't need Bismarck to tell us how legislators behave, we don't need Churchill to tell us how the other guys operate. So there is no use wringing our hands over the sordid political process; it is what it is, and the Court must find a way to deal with it realistically. To put the matter bluntly, the justices recognize that what democracy produces ordinarily must be *treated* as policymaking purportedly in the public interest, whatever they may think of it.

If this analysis is in some way hypothetical, it is not objectionably so in the manner of originalism. Recall that Justice Scalia and others sometimes propose to adopt the understanding of the written Constitution that society at large *would* have had—*if* the people generally had taken up the text and considered it at the time (as they certainly did not).[141] Originalism in that form asks justices to manufacture explanations of the historical document and then to insist that arguments about constitutional meaning are over. We must make do with the historical "facts" alone. Rational instrumentalism also makes room for arguments about governmental purposes that, in turn, can strengthen or weaken a constitutional challenge. Yet the justices honestly engage each other by taking opposing positions regarding the best explanation for what government has done and why. In arguing that way, they take responsibility for judgment; they don't turn palms up and blame James Madison.

To be sure, the Court occasionally disclaims the idea of condemning governmental action on the basis of its purpose alone. In the *O'Brien* draft-card case, for example, Chief Justice Warren declared that Congress's "purpose" in enacting a statute "is not a basis for declaring . . . [it] unconstitutional."[142] Warren did not suggest that governmental purpose is irrelevant only in symbolic speech cases; rather, he disclaimed purpose as an element of the analysis in any context. Other decisions endorse that understanding. Writing for the Court in *Palmer v. Thompson*,[143] Justice Black insisted that purpose should not matter even when it is perfectly clear what was done and why. By his account, the validity of laws must stand or fall on their actual effects and not on what anyone or any body meant to achieve. If a statute can be held unconstitutional solely because the Court rejects the purpose behind it, so this argument goes, then the same law might be valid if it were reenacted for a reason the Court accepts.

Nevertheless, rational instrumentalism plainly makes governmental purpose an essential feature of the content of substantive rights. Chief Justice Warren's treatment of the issue in *O'Brien* has been discredited. In hindsight, it is perfectly clear why he refused to go behind the government's neutral-sounding explanation. If he had, he would have found it inescapable that the ban on mutilating draft cards was, and was meant to be, a brazen means of suppressing dissent regarding the Vietnam War. The evidence was irrefutable, and only willful blindness to the truth offered the Court an escape route.[144] In any event, the single most important element of the doctrine Warren announced (and purported to apply) in *O'Brien* is not at all indifferent to government's purpose. Specifically, government's interest must be "unrelated to the suppression of free expression."[145] It *does* make a difference *why* government behaves as it does; it makes a crucial difference. As Justice Holmes put it, even a dog knows the difference between being stumbled over and being kicked.[146] Trying to understand governmental behavior without taking account of the reasons behind it is like telling the story of King David and Uriah the Hittite without mentioning Bathsheba.

Finally, it is also worth saying that rational instrumentalism delivers what we need—namely, a workable framework for realizing the kind of governmental authority we have developed in this country. This framework works, it works pretty well, and it works better than anything else the Court has tried in the past. Rational instrumentalism ensures that government can regulate arms-length relations in the market without worrying that Supreme Court justices who take a different view of wise social policy will rule such regulations out of constitutional order. At the same time, rational instrumentalism helps identify and worry through cases in which government appears not to be doing the public's business as usual, but rather to be up to no public good.

TECHNIQUES. The justices typically attempt to defuse the difficulties entailed in the search for governmental purpose by limiting their use of the more dangerous sorts of materials. Justice Scalia, for his part, insists that the Court should lay aside anything offered to prove what individual members of an assembly thought, said, or did—matters that go at best to the subjective intentions of those individuals rather than to a more general, objective purpose ascribable to the legislature as a body.[147] Other evidence, like background documents and committee reports, may be equally unreliable, even contrived.[148] Most of the time, the full Court similarly prefers to rely on evidence that is arguably more objective.

The most common technique is to infer the apparent point of a statute from the statute itself. That road doubles back, of course. The Court can draw such an inference only by postulating a purpose the statute might rationally serve. But once that is done, the statute must generally be approved—because the Court is obliged to hold that it can serve the very end or ends the Court just manufactured for it.[149] Fair enough. Then again, that is precisely what the justices typically mean to do. The fact of the matter is that if a plausible public purpose can be inferred from a statute, chances are the statute *should* be counted as a valid means of pursing that purpose and, accordingly, should be sustained. That is how rational instrumentalism works most of the time: *ceteris paribus,* hypothesized explanations are usually sufficient.

But when governmental action resists the understanding that individual freedom is being curbed for public-regarding objectives, the justices look in earnest for actual explanations. They are alerted to the possibility that government is behaving in a manner that does not comport with constitutional government as we know it, that is, as we have fashioned it since the nineteenth century. So it is on those occasions, and only on those occasions, that the inquiry into genuine purpose becomes urgent. The justices probe more deeply, ask hard questions, and attempt to ferret out the truth. In so doing, they search for evidence of governmental ends in all the other likely places—for example, in the determinations of lower courts,[150] in the legislative history behind enactments,[151] and in the arguments advanced by counsel.[152] They entertain explanations that might justify governmental behavior on some instrumental basis. But if they find those arguments unconvincing, they infer that something else is afoot.[153]

Now then, you are to consider what these cases *are*: cases, for example, in which it appears that government is interfering with intimate personal decisions in order to vindicate public morality, distributing benefits and burdens simply to penalize weak or unpopular people, censoring private expression out of disdain for its message, or imposing harsh, mean-spirited punishments for no discernible purpose at all. I present some illustrations in this chapter. If the justices mishandle cases of this kind, it is not because rational instrumentalism sends them off looking for actual explanations that do not exist or cannot be found. The serious problem is not an inability to turn up probative evidence at all, but reaching agreement about the meaning that should be derived from evidence that is plainly there to be considered. The justices can only exercise good judgment, discard any materials or arguments that seem contrived, and work with the rest. Then they must simply decide and explain their decisions as persuasively as possible.

ILLUSTRATIONS.   Consider some illustrations from the cases involving freedom of religion, where governmental purpose is invariably in issue. It was not difficult to conclude in *Edwards*[154] that a statute mandating that "creation science" be taught along with the theory of evolution was meant to advance a religious agenda. Nor was it difficult to hold in *Lukumi*[155] that a city ordinance condemning animal sacrifice was meant to discourage religious practices. There are closer cases, of course—cases, at least, that the justices themselves regard as closer. But those cases generally illustrate only that the inquiry into governmental purpose can be arduous, that it can evoke disagreement, and, as always, that the justices must in the end make judgments as best they can.

In the Kentucky "Ten Commandments" case, *McCreary*,[156] Justice Scalia rehearsed his familiar position that any attempt to recover governmental purpose is unmanageable, a façade behind which judges hide their personal preferences.[157] Writing for the Court, Justice Souter acknowledged the difficulties involved, yet explicitly embraced the practice of making government's purpose an essential, sometimes determinative, aspect of constitutional analysis. Souter pointed out that, *contra* Scalia, the Supreme Court itself and lower courts across the country commonly examine governmental purpose as a "staple" of statutory construction. He insisted that the focus on purpose makes sense there and everywhere else, and that if it did not the "whole notion of purpose in law would have dropped into disrepute long ago."[158]

Justice Souter explained that the investigation of purpose need not be a fruitless attempt to psychoanalyze governmental agents and discover what moved them in their "heart of hearts." The enterprise can be more objective, as the justices infer meaning from "external" signals that support a "commonsense conclusion" about what best explains the action under attack.[159] The text of a legislative measure and the history behind it may be consulted, albeit those sources are admittedly problematic for reasons we have just been through. Above all, the context of governmental action may supply a basis from which to infer what government is attempting to do. It was an apparent difference in context that ultimately condemned the display in *McCreary* but sustained the one in *Van Orden*,[160] the companion case from Texas. Justice Breyer, the only justice to vote with the majority in both cases, was not persuaded that richly controversial exhibits on the walls of court houses in Kentucky were anything but efforts to promote a religious message. But he was convinced that the purpose of an historically noncontroversial, forty-year-old monument on the capitol grounds in Austin was not primarily to advance religion but also to foster secular ideas.[161]

Justice Breyer's position was plausible, but scarcely telling.[162] Every other member of the Court thought the two cases were indistinguishable. The fair debate among the justices demonstrates, once again, that constitutional rights are not precisely articulated prescriptions that ineluctably lead honest judges to the same (correct) results. Men and women with different ideological perspectives simply reach different conclusions—for the necessary and sufficient reason that borderline cases demand judgment that is not captured in any confining framework, drawn either from the written Constitution or from the Court's doctrinal formulations.

A Purpose to Work With

If the distinction between means and ends is granted, as it must be, there is still the problem of isolating the means/ends relationship to be examined. The Court cannot sensibly assess whether the governmental means under attack in a case is reasonably related to the long-term public interest. The gap between a particular action and social welfare generally is too great, the relationship to be tested too attenuated. The justices need something more immediate. They need a near-term end—namely, a discernible state of affairs that the means promises to bring about and that, if established, will serve the long-run public interest.[163] That is a purpose the justices can work with: an immediate purpose, different from a re-statement of the means itself but short of the general public welfare that all governmental action is supposed to serve. The task then becomes manageable. Once they get straight the means whose constitutionality is challenged, and they identify some near-term end (somewhere between the means itself and the long-term public interest), then they can de-termine whether the means is related instrumentally to furthering that purpose.

But the immediate end to be identified can be far from obvious. The governmental means under scrutiny may be said to further some immedi-ate purpose, but that purpose, in turn, can also be understood as itself a means of achieving some other near-term end, which then serves as a means of achieving some further end, which, in turn, is a means of achieving yet another end . . . and so on out to an end that is coextensive with general public welfare broadly conceived.[164] With any imagination at all, it is easy to conceptualize an apparently simple means/ends rela-tionship as a link in a chain of means/ends couplets stretching from an initial governmental activity at one extreme through a host of intermedi-ate positions (call them short-term ends or next-level means, as you like) to the general public interest at the other pole. Accordingly, the task of identifying the *right* immediate purpose with which to work becomes ever so complicated and debatable.

Consider, for example, that legislative schemes typically have gen-eral, overarching objectives that all their features operating together are supposed to achieve. Yet when any particular provision is challenged as unconstitutional, the Court cannot compare that single element to the general ends of the entire scheme, but must look for some more specific explanation for the provision under attack. In *Fritz,* for example, the general point of the legislation enacted by Congress was to eliminate expensive double-dipping. The particular provision under examination, though, was a grandfather clause creating two classes of retirees who had qualified for dual benefits under prior law. Individuals in one class (those who had been in the railroad industry recently) were allowed to continue double-dipping; individuals in the other class were not. It would not do for the government to defend the resulting discrimination on the theory that denying double benefits to the retirees in the disadvantaged group served the general aims of the larger statute, that is, reducing the drain on the federal treasury. Denying double benefits to anyone on any basis would do that. The government needed a more immediate explanation for favoring one class of retirees over the other. The argument that individuals with more recent ties to the railroad business had a better equitable claim was weak. In point of fact, it came very close to restating the means, as though it was enough to say that the classification favored retirees that Congress wanted to favor. As might be expected, the justices divided over whether it was sufficient, but in the economic context of the case, a majority concluded that it was.[165]

The *Moreno* case provides another illustration.[166] The means at issue was a provision of the Food Stamp Act, which denied coupons to households composed of unrelated persons. The government initially argued that depriving unrelated, cohabiting adults of benefits served the objectives Congress had cited for the act generally—namely, improving nutrition among the poor and fortifying the agricultural sector of the economy. Those purposes were too far removed from the challenged provision to make an assessment of its instrumental character intelligible. Any provision that channeled benefits to exceptionally needy people could be defended as a rational means of enhancing nutrition among the impoverished classes, and any provision that restricted benefits (for any reason) could be attacked as an *irrational* diminution of the market for farm products. In *Moreno,* accordingly, the government needed a near-term explanation and came up with the argument that excluding unrelated adults would discourage fraud. That explanation did not amount to a restatement of the provision under challenge, so it did not turn any means/ends analysis into tautology. Yet the legislative history made it perfectly clear that the exclusion was actually a gratuitous penalty aimed at "hippies." Accordingly, the Court found it invalid.[167]

The identification of a purpose to work with was also a key issue in *Grutter,*[168] where the policy under attack was a race-conscious admissions program at the University of Michigan's law school. It was open to argue that taking race into account in admissions decisions furthered the public interest at a fairly high level of generality by, for example, increasing the flow of qualified people of color into responsible positions in government, industry, and the military. Various *amici* made that kind of argument. For its part, however, the state fastened attention on a more immediate purpose—namely, obtaining the benefits of racial diversity in university education. That near-term goal matched up more precisely with the particular admissions scheme used at the law school and thus the steps in the state's argument. Specifically, Michigan contended that it was essential to use race as a factor in admissions to assure that minority students were admitted in nontrivial numbers, thus to obtain a "critical mass" of minority students to make their presence felt and to facilitate their contributions, thus to make racial diversity meaningful, thus to achieve specified educational values. Every link in that chain could be disputed and was. Yet the means/ends relationships the law school advanced were easier to work with and to accept—easier, this is to say, than the comparatively distant relationship between making race a factor in law school admissions, on the one hand, and the diffuse benefits to society at large identified by the *amici,* on the other.

It is not clear that *Grutter* would have been decided the other way if the law school had not argued for and established a tight connection between its admission scheme and an immediate educational objective. Justice O'Connor's opinion for the Court acknowledged the more expansive arguments in the *amici* briefs, and those arguments plainly figured in the majority's thinking. Yet in other cases, the Court has hesitated over claims that race-conscious governmental actions are instrumentally linked to longer term public goals. Writing for the Court in *Croson,* for example, Justice O'Connor herself balked at the argument that the City of Richmond's program setting aside a portion of city contracts for minority-owned businesses could be justified as a means of reducing the lingering effects of past race discrimination in the construction industry nationwide.[169] It does seem clear, in any event, that in *Grutter* the law school's position was much improved by the availability of a closer, near-term end with which its policy could be coupled. The Court was able to credit the academic judgments made by the faculty and the school's administrators and thus to accept the intellectual links in the state's argument. The *Grutter* case thus illustrates a crucial aspect of the analysis that rational instrumentalism brings into play: the justices must identify a purpose they can work with, a purpose that permits them to manage the task of determining whether the governmental action is genuinely instrumental. When they disagree, as they so often do, they must hear each other out and vote.[170]

This feature of instrumental analysis can be conceptualized as yet another problem in getting the level of generality right. Consider the cases implicating sexual behavior. If government identifies its objective in an extremely expansive way—for example, as the general interest in morality—we might expect that most regulatory means will stand on the theory they are instrumentally related to that broadly stated interest. This is not necessarily true. But it is a safe bet that the justices are more inclined to accept the linkage between criminal statutes condemning sexual activity and public morals than they are to accept a similar connection between affirmative action policies and the general public interest.[171] Accordingly, if they are to examine morals legislation seriously, they may decline to let government prevail simply by citing public morality at large and may insist that an immediate working objective be identified at a more specific level of generality.

This is what happened in *Lawrence,*[172] where Justice Kennedy refused to allow Texas to defend an antisodomy law on the strength of a general state interest in promoting moral values. Not to say that Texas would have done better to claim a narrowly defined interest in criminalizing the particular sexual activity in which the defendants engaged in precisely the circumstances in which they acted. That would frustrate means/ends analysis entirely. Remember that making government's ends congruent with its means produces tautology. Rational instrumentalism contemplates that means and ends are different and thus bars government from asserting simplistically that its objective is to do what it is doing. When government manipulates the system that way, adjusting its asserted interests to win every time, the Court is likely to say that no constitutionally legitimate public purpose is served at all. That, indeed, is precisely what Justice Kennedy concluded.[173]

Compelling Objectives

The Court's habit of announcing an especially rigorous standard of review in some cases complicates the inquiry into government's purposes. I have argued that the various "heightened" review standards are a distraction from the Court's genuine analysis. The Court organizes its elaboration of substantive rights around rational instrumentalism, which rests on foundational ideas developed in the last century—including the notion that the political branches largely get to determine what's good for us. It seems troubling, then, for the justices to second-guess legislative notions about the relative importance of policy goals.[174] Still, the justices frequently take it upon themselves not only to identify the purpose that government's action is said to serve, but also to weight that purpose as "compelling" (or "important"). In some minds, the business of evaluating objectives in this way invites the charge that the modern Court behaves in the way the Old Court functioned. The only difference is that in the 1920s the Court invalidated democratically selected regulations of economic liberty, while this Court overrides policies touching sensitive personal interests and classifications on the basis of race or analogous criteria.[175] The law journals are filled with articles trying valiantly either to sustain or to repudiate that claim.

It is necessary, then, to account for the Court's occasional demand for "compelling" governmental goals or something close. Consider two possibilities. The first explains many cases, even if it fights the justices' own descriptions of what they are doing: the justices do not determine in the abstract whether a governmental purpose is important enough to warrant interfering with a fundamental interest or classifying people on sensitive grounds. Instead, they assess government's arguments in defense of its actions and stamp those arguments compelling (or not) as a conclusion. The second explanation covers most other cases in the way the Court itself describes its work: the point of insisting that the end must be compelling is, instead, to force the different question whether the purpose government offers for its action genuinely explains it at all.

It is true that the Court portrays its more rigorous standards of review as though they require governmental objectives to meet a prescribed measure of importance. If no compelling governmental interest appears, it is unnecessary to go further. Even if the means government chooses to pursue some less vital goal is "narrowly tailored" to achieve that end, the means is nonetheless unconstitutional. In her opinion for the Court in *Grutter,* for example, Justice O'Connor conducted an abstract inquiry into whether achieving the beneficial effects of racial diversity in university-level education is a compelling governmental objective.[176] Only after she established that a compelling purpose was in view did she pass on to an assessment of whether the admissions scheme the law school had established was sufficiently related to that purpose. Nevertheless, Justice O'Connor might have said (and perhaps should have said) that she was convinced there was no race-neutral way to integrate the student body and, accordingly, that the argument for using race as a factor in admissions was compelling. She did not have to *begin* her analysis by asking whether the law school's *objective* was sufficiently important to justify taking race into account to achieve it; she might have *concluded* her assessment by finding that the law school's *argument* for using race to obtain its objective was sufficiently persuasive.

This understanding accounts for *Grutter* fairly well. The law school persuaded Justice O'Connor that racial diversity contributes mightily to the quality of legal education and that it is essential to make race a factor in admissions to achieve that diversity. To say that diversity cannot be attained in some other way is arguably to say, or to conclude, that there is a truly compelling reason for a race-conscious admissions system of some order. Recall the elements of the law school's means/ends case in *Grutter* itself,[177] and run the chain backward. The goal in view was to obtain the educational advantages of racial diversity. To realize that objective, it was essential to achieve racial diversity in the viable form of a critical mass of minority students. And to accomplish *that,* it was essential to take race into account in the limited manner the law school did. Justice O'Connor accepted that means/ends chain, concluded that the law school really could not achieve its purpose in any other way, and thus found the argument for using race to be persuasive, convincing, or, one might say, compelling.

You begin to see how the compelling character of a governmental interest is related to the means the state adopts to pursue it. The end and the means for achieving it are different. They have to be; we've been through that. Yet the justices do not necessarily treat them in isolation from each other, but keep both in mind as they size up a case. Look again at *Croson*.[178] Writing for the Court, Justice O'Connor allowed that a governmental purpose to redress the current effects of historical discrimination can count as a compelling interest, but only if the state demonstrates "a strong basis in evidence for its conclusion that remedial action [is] necessary."[179] The evidence the state adduces regarding past mistreatment of minorities will clarify the form that mistreatment took, its scope, and its duration. There is, then, some specification of what happened and, in turn, some measure of the lingering consequences that the state's current race-conscious action is supposed to address. The Court is then in a position to determine whether the scheme under challenge is narrowly tailored to its target.

I hasten to say that Justice O'Connor made this analysis sound much more precise than it can ever be in practice. The state's evidence of discrimination in the past is not likely to quantify the damage done very well, nor yet the current effects of that damage. Even if existing conditions warranting remedial action are proved up in some measurable way, it is not obvious how the elements of a race-sensitive program should be calibrated—as though a rough account of the target conditions necessarily justifies setting some particular percentage of city contracts aside for minority firms over some specific period of time. Here again, the justices can only exercise their best judgment and decide whether a state's means corresponds closely enough to the conditions to be addressed. Even Justice Scalia concedes that the determination whether government's means is narrowly tailored to its ends entails "value judgment."[180]

The second explanation for demanding compelling purposes is more familiar. By this account, the justices do not assert authority simply to determine whether politically accountable bodies have chosen especially important public objectives to pursue. Instead, following John Ely,[181] they ask whether purposes are compelling (and equally whether means are narrowly tailored) as a way to ascertain the best explanation for what government has done without straightforwardly examining the available evidence and thus engaging all the difficulties a more direct inquiry into purpose would entail.[182] The idea is to "smoke out" *illegitimate* ends.[183] When the justices come upon regulations touching fundamental personal interests or classifications according to race or a cousin of race, they are suspicious that government is up to no constitutional good. Whatever explanation government's lawyers may offer for what is being done, something else is likely at the bottom of things.[184] So the justices test government's behavior against an exacting standard of review. If it survives "heightened scrutiny," they set their preliminary doubts aside and accept the powerful explanation they have been given. If, however, government's action fails the rigorous test either for want of a compelling purpose or a narrowly tailored means, the justices are confirmed in the view that the real explanation is the one they suspected all along. This indirect approach allows the justices to decide only that a policy flunks the stringent standard and leave it at that—without expressly declaring the conclusion that the real explanation for government's behavior is constitutionally impermissible.[185] Then again, they do sometimes acknowledge that conclusion.[186]

By this second account, the justices do not really make the validity of a governmental means turn on whether it serves an interest they regard as insufficiently grave. The compelling character of a governmental end is only a tool for getting at the actual explanation for what government is about. This becomes clear in cases in which the Court does not (explicitly) apply an exacting standard of review and thus does not worry over whether government's goal is compelling, but nonetheless rejects all the ends offered to explain government's behavior and deduces that the truth lies elsewhere. In the *Moreno* case, no genuine public-regarding purpose (compelling or otherwise) explained denying food stamps to unrelated adults living together, but an illegitimate explanation (the desire to penalize "hippie communes") fit "like a glove."[187] There are other familiar illustrations—*Cleburne Living Center* (where the Court concluded that only "irrational prejudice against the mentally retarded" could explain a zoning board's failure to permit a group home);[188] *Romer* (where a prohibition on anti-discrimination ordinances could be explained only by "animus" toward gays and lesbians);[189] and (maybe) *Lawrence* (where the Texas antisodomy law also rested on homophobia).[190]

Impermissible Explanations

The idea that means/ends scrutiny can uncover illegitimate explanations for governmental action presupposes that some regulatory goals *are* constitutionally impermissible. Government may find excellent means of pursuing them, means that would unquestionably be successful if employed, yet still those means are unconstitutional because the ends themselves are constitutionally out of bounds. The Court has always maintained that governmental action must further a purpose "which it is competent for government to effect."[191] But precisely what government is *not* entitled to "effect" is elusive.[192]

The Court is wont to describe some objectives as illegitimate in the abstract, as though they are by nature constitutionally unacceptable—the polar opposites of governmental purposes that are not only permissible but compelling. In freedom of religion cases, for example, the Court explains that it is "illegitimate" for government to select as its purpose either to advance or inhibit any particular religion or, for that matter, religion in general as against secular ideologies.[193] In free speech cases, the Court has it that it is equally impermissible for government to act out of "hostility" to the speaker's point of view.[194] And in equal protection cases, the Court insists that it is "illegitimate" for government to be "motivated" by "notions of racial superiority or simple racial politics."[195] These statements may seem unremarkable, but they are problematic if they are meant to dismiss some explanations for governmental behavior because they offend values attached to particular substantive rights.

Rational instrumentalism can accommodate the idea of intrinsically impermissible objectives; it is just a matter of adding another judgment to the mix—namely, a judgment about whether government's goals are constitutionally acceptable. Yet if the Court genuinely proposes to rule out some objectives on the ground they conflict with values linked to discrete constitutional rights, obvious difficulties arise. The Court has never been able to derive constitutional meaning from substantive rights as they are articulated in the text of particular provisions of the Constitution. Any attempt to revive those futile efforts in order to disclaim some governmental goals as illegitimate ignores the reasons (the many reasons) why the Court has employed rational instrumentalism as its doctrinal framework across the board. In this final section, I want to suggest that when the Court refers to an explanation for governmental action as illegitimate, it does not mean (or at least does not have to mean) that the explanation is inconsistent with some special value associated with the substantive right in issue. Instead, the Court means (or can mean) one of two related things: either that the explanation offered for governmental action amounts to a restatement of government's means and thus defies the maxim that means and ends are necessarily distinct, or that the asserted explanation entails no public-regarding benefits at all.

TAUTOLOGICAL ENDS.   Consider, first, the Court's common warning that it is "illegitimate" for government to explain its behavior on the basis of a "bare desire to harm" the members of some group.[196] That idea decided *Cleburne Living Center,* as well as *Romer* and probably *Lawrence*.[197] There is a rich theoretical literature on why the Constitution does not allow government simply to hurt people, without more. But there is also a very simple account: If the only reason for imposing burdens on individuals is the desire to inflict harm, then government's purpose is not distinguishable from its means. The two are synonymous: government hurts people because that is what government chooses to do. Of course, if a tautological purpose were sufficient to justify governmental action, then government would win every case. That won't do. Accordingly, a tautological purpose is constitutionally insufficient.

Lots of important cases can be understood on this ground. Consider *VMI,* for example.[198] The state argued in that case that excluding women from the Virginia Military Institute *en masse* was sensible, because the "adversative" method of instruction employed there was unsuitable for women. That argument did not work, because it couldn't—not without allowing the state to define the purpose it wanted to achieve as congruent with the means it selected to pursue that purpose, so that the state must always act constitutionally for the necessary and sufficient reason that it always does what it wants to do.[199] There are more vivid illustrations. In the Court's decisions ostensibly elaborating the meaning of cruel and unusual punishments, the very point of the exercise is that government cannot punish wantonly, senselessly, for its own sake. There must be some public-regarding end in sight, some reason for causing human suffering. Thus in *Ford v. Wainwright*,[200] Justice Marshall explained that capital punishment cannot be visited on the insane: "We may seriously question the retributive value of executing a person who has no comprehension of why he has been singled out and stripped of his fundamental right to life."[201]

OF CONDUCT AND STATUS. Consider, next, the Court's equally familiar declaration that racially discriminatory statutes are "seldom relevant to the achievement of any *legitimate* state interest."[202] Doubtless the justices are moved in part by the knowledge that members of minority racial groups may lack the capacity to obtain relief through ordinary political channels. And, of course, the academic literature offers hosts of other explanations of varying persuasive power. Here again, however, there is a comparatively simple and straightforward account, which fits comfortably into the rational instrumentalism the Court employs to organize its thinking about substantive rights generally. Burdens imposed on the basis of race rarely operate as instruments for achieving public interest goals of *any* kind. They simply hurt the individuals on whom they fall, without any justifying public payoff. It is in that sense that race discrimination is "seldom" relevant to any "legitimate" end.

The point here is obvious enough. The core idea in rational instrumentalism, drawn from the intellectual developments traced in chapter 2, is that government is charged to make policy for public-regarding ends, that is, public purposes whose value to the collective whole explains and justifies the impositions suffered by its regulated members. Government typically does that by creating incentives to act in the way government identifies with the public interest or by creating disincentives to behave in a way government thinks is not for the public good. Those who find themselves in a disadvantageous category can improve their condition by changing their behavior and thus moving themselves to another category whose members receive better treatment. The public interest is served instrumentally as socially desirable behavior is rewarded and undesirable conduct punished. This works, of course, only if the categories the law creates depend on performance rather than status—only if individuals can extricate themselves from one category and join another by altering their conduct. If, by contrast, categories are drawn according to fixed characteristics that individuals cannot change, the semblance of rational instrumentalism is lost. Individuals suffer not for what they do, but rather for who they are.[203] Accordingly, government is not taking action as a sensible means of achieving any public purpose, but only harming people needlessly.

Gender classifications are similarly troubling if they are meant to exclude or protect women on the basis of stereotypical assumptions about the talents and interests of women as a group. The reason is not (entirely) that gender classifications are grossly under or overinclusive with respect to some valid public objective, but (more important) that the "objective itself is illegitimate."[204] The near-term end in view, rarely articulated but routinely acted upon, is that government wishes to perpetuate arrangements under which women as a class perform duties associated with procreation and the home. Put bluntly, government wants women to bear children, to superintend them during their tender years, and, into the bargain, to keep house for their bread-winning husbands. Now then, *someone* needs to perform child-care and household duties (in one way or another). Accordingly, government can validly adopt instrumental means of encouraging willing individuals to take up that line of work—that is, policies that create incentives to do what needs doing. But it is another thing entirely for government simply to assign familial responsibilities to women as a cost of *being* female. That is the imposition of burdens without any legitimating instrumental justification in the public interest.

The distinction between classifications according to conduct and status also explains most cases involving penalties on the basis of religious faith or unpopular views. You may say those cases are different. A Catholic can become a Buddhist, and a dissenter can become an apparatchik. But that is not how the world works most of the time. Basic religious and ideological commitments are not volitional in the ordinary sense; they are not like choices about what health and safety precautions to take at industrial plants or what pay scale to set for factory workers. When government attaches advantages or disadvantages to *being* Christian (or engaging in Christian practices) or to *being* a Republican (or voicing support for the party ticket), the idea is not seriously to channel behavior into socially desirable activities. Here again, rational instrumentalism helps the justices decide whether government is acting rationally in the pursuit of public ends. When government dishes out benefits and burdens on the basis of personal beliefs, the only consequence is that affected individuals are helped or hurt for what they think or say. Government is not, then, making policy in the public interest, and it is in that sense that government's ends are constitutionally illegitimate.

Academicians reaching back at least to John Ely have argued that the conduct/status distinction offers an important, though partial, answer to the legitimacy puzzle.[205] But understood in light of rational instrumentalism in the background, this distinction explains much more than is popularly understood.[206] By this second account, the identification of a purpose as illegitimate is actually a conclusion that government's means serves no public-regarding purpose at all. Put the other way, a governmental objective is legitimate only if it is *public*—in the sense that the general social-welfare benefits to be achieved warrant the costs imposed on affected individuals. Of course, even if this is what the inquiry into the acceptability of objectives typically comes to, the justices still must exercise judgment. There is no escaping that.

Conclusion

I have tried in these pages to bring a little realism into the assessment of the Constitution and the substantive rights with which it is associated. This society is wedded, I know, to the idea that a single ancient text is our Constitution and, into the bargain, that if the justices of the Supreme Court must interpret it at all, they can and should conform their interpretations to the text as it was originally understood. But that won't do. The text we call "the" Constitution is not doing any work in the resolution of constitutional questions. It is a pretense to suggest that it is and equally a pretense to think that it could. As Wittgenstein explained, "A wheel that can be turned though nothing else moves with it, is not part of the mechanism."[1] The real Constitution is unfolding every day in Supreme Court decisions and explanatory opinions. Academics know this, have known it for years, routinely own up to it among themselves, and really ought to be more candid with the public. The truth may take some of the starch out of legal theory, but we do not have a Constitution to allow law professors to sound like scholars.

I have tried to show that the only guidance the Supreme Court has in constitutional cases touching substantive rights lies in the doctrine the Court itself has established. Over the last century, as the justices have labored to lay the foundations of modern public law, they have found that rational instrumentalism captures the crux of the issues most of the time. Unsurprisingly, instrumentalism appears again and again across familiar borders between substantive rights conventionally understood to be distinct from one another. The lesson is not that instrumentalism is simply a common tool the justices use to make it appear that their exercise of judgment is restricted in some formal way. Instead, we ought to understand that rational instrumentalism reflects underlying ideas that have shaped the system now in place.

Finally, I have tried to describe the numerous problems that rational instrumentalism brings to the fore and, concomitantly, the expansive room this doctrinal formulation allows for judgment. Instrumentalism does not determine results and, in fact, scarcely limits the justices at all. It only (though importantly) helps to identify the issues and considerations and to organize them for attention. It is daunting, not to say frightening, that my account of substantive rights leaves them pretty much up to the men and women who reach the Supreme Court (though—and this is crucial—I hope that those who get there arrive with a genuine sense of responsibility). But it could not be otherwise.

The justices themselves appreciate the nature of their task. To be sure, they often parade textualism and originalism before us. And, to be sure, they often explain their judgments as though they are deductions from doctrinal rules that genuinely cabin judicial discretion. Yet they also candidly acknowledge the inevitable truth. Listen to the joint opinion in *Casey*: "The inescapable fact is that adjudication of substantive due process claims may call upon the Court to exercise . . . *reasoned judgment*."[2] Listen to Justice Breyer in *Van Orden,* the Establishment Clause case: "[I]n [borderline] cases, I see no test-related substitute for the exercise of legal *judgment*."[3] And listen to Justice Kennedy in the capital punishment case, *Roper*: "The Constitution contemplates that in the end our own *judgment* will be brought to bear on the question of the acceptability of the death penalty."[4]

In the final analysis, all we can do is be careful—careful to select good and wise people in the first instance and careful to critique their work once they are there. For my own part, I will say again that I am far from satisfied with many of the Court's decisions, though I am quite pleased with some. I have offered no critique of the Court's efforts in particular cases, but tried, instead, only to situate those efforts in the larger framework. Maybe this is the easy part. Now that we know how to free ourselves, the "arduous" thing is to know "what to do with [our] freedom."[5]

Notes

Introduction

1. See Laurence H. Tribe, *Taking Text and Structure Seriously: Reflections on Free-Form Method in Constitutional Interpretation,* 108 Harv. L. Rev. 1221, 1246 (1995). I do not mean to say, of course, that those provisions have self-evident meaning and cannot engender disagreements. Compare Tribe, *supra,* with Bruce Ackerman & David Golove, *Is NAFTA Constitutional?* 108 Harv. L. Rev. 799 (1995).

2. See Frederick Schauer, *Judicial Supremacy and the Modest Constitution,* 92 Calif. L. Rev. 1045, 1065 (2004); Evan H. Caminker, *Appropriate Means-Ends Constraints on Section 5 Powers,* 53 Stan. L. Rev. 1127 (2001). The same or similar thinking pervades administrative law, as well. In that context, rational instrumentalism has to do with ensuring that federal agencies genuinely implement the policies embedded in the statutes they are given to enforce. See Edward Rubin, *It's Time to Make the Administrative Procedure Act Administrative,* 89 Cornell L. Rev. 95 (2003).

3. H. Jefferson Powell, A Community Built on Words 6, 211 (2002).

4. This is not to say that we could not improve on the justices' performance by adopting mechanisms for introducing the insights of modern philosophy, science, and technology into constitutional analysis more effectively. Morton Horwitz and Michael Dorf, among others, argue that the Court's conventional (common-law, backward-looking) adjudicative method ill-suits the challenge of keeping pace with fast-moving aspects of the larger culture. Morton J. Horwitz, *Foreword: The Constitution of Change: Legal Fundamentality without Fundamentalism,* 107 Harv. L. Rev. 32 (1993); Michael C. Dorf, *Foreword: The Limits of Socratic Deliberation,* 112 Harv. L. Rev. 4 (1998). I'm sure they are right, but I leave those (monumentally difficult) problems aside in this study.

5. See, e.g., Stephen M. Feldman, American Legal Thought from Premodernism to Postmodernism: An Intellectual Voyage 137–87 (2000).

6. Mark V. Tushnet, The New Constitutional Order (2003).

7. *Id.* at 3.

8. See also Timothy Conlan, From New Federalism to Devolution: Twenty-Five Years of Intergovernmental Reform (1998).

9. For accounts of these decisions generally (and competing explanations), see Richard H. Fallon Jr., *The "Conservative" Paths of the Rehnquist Court's Federalism Decisions,* 69 U. Chi. L. Rev. 429 (2002); John O. McGinnis, *Reviving Tocqueville's America: The Rehnquist Court's Jurisprudence of Social Discovery,* 90 Calif. L. Rev. 485 (2002); Thomas W. Merrill, *The Making of the Second Rehnquist Court: A Preliminary Analysis,* 47 St. Louis L. J. 569 (2003).

10. Tushnet himself distinguishes between the "thick" Constitution, concerned largely with the details of governmental structure, and the "thin" Constitution, reflecting great visionary ideas (like due process, equal protection, and free speech). He proposes that the American people should liberate the thin Constitution from the judiciary and establish a "populist" constitutional law "oriented to realizing the principles of the Declaration of Independence and the Constitution's Preamble." See Mark V. Tushnet, Taking the Constitution Away from the Courts 181 (1999); cf. James E. Fleming, *The Constitution Outside the Courts,* 86 Cornell L. Rev. 215 (2000) (reviewing the relevant literature). Larry Kramer contends that our system is already primarily a "popular constitutionalism" drawing its strength and direction from nonjudicial sources. Larry D. Kramer, The People Themselves: Popular Constitutionalism and Judicial Review (2004). See also Robert A. Burt, The Constitution in Conflict (1992); Neal Devins & Louis Fisher, The Democratic Constitution (2004); V. F. Nourse, *Toward a New Constitutional Anatomy,* 56 Stan. L. Rev. 835 (2004). Scholarship in this vein can be as surprising as it is provocative. Reva Siegel has shown, for example, that impressive arguments from the text of the Constitution have been developed in political debates and even in the streets. Reva B. Siegel, *Text in Contest: Gender and the Constitution from a Social Movement Perspective,* 150 U. Pa. L. Rev. 297 (2001).

11. Frank H. Easterbrook, *The Influence of Judicial Review on Constitutional Theory,* in A Workable Government? 170, 175 (B. Marshall ed. 1987).

12. Theorists who advance these arguments take their lead from Justice Antonin Scalia and (to some lesser extent) from Judge Frank Easterbrook and Robert Bork. Antonin Scalia, A Matter of Interpretation: Federal Courts and the Law (A. Gutmann ed. 1997); Frank H. Easterbrook, *Textualism and the Dead Hand,* 66 Geo. Wash. L. Rev. 1119 (1998); Robert H. Bork, The Tempting of America: The Political Seduction of the Law (1990). They include, among others, Randy Barnett, Steven Calabresi, Gary Lawson, John Manning, Michael Paulsen, and Keith Whittington. Randy Barnett, *An Originalism for Nonoriginalists,* 45 Loy. L. Rev. 611 (1999); Steven G. Calabresi, *Textualism and the Countermajoritarian Difficulty,* 66 Geo. Wash. L. Rev. 1373 (1998); Gary Lawson, *On Read-*

ing Recipes . . . and Constitutions, 85 Gtn. L. J. 1823 (1997); John F. Manning, *The Eleventh Amendment and the Reading of Precise Constitutional Texts,* 113 Yale L. J. 1663 (2004); Vasan Kesavan & Michael S. Paulsen, *The Interpretive Force of the Constitution's Secret Drafting History,* 91 Gtn. L. J. 1113 (2003); Keith E. Whittington, Constitutional Interpretation: Textual Meaning, Original Intent and Judicial Review (1999). Professor Amar also fits in this group, I think, though his "intratextualist" approach to the text and its history presents a special case. See Akhil R. Amar, The Bill of Rights (1998).

13. Here I think of academics who hope to accommodate change even as they, too, hold fast to textualist and originalist methodology of a kinder, gentler nature. Jed Rubenfeld contends, for example, that the document is binding only insofar as it reflects basic commitments that settle "paradigm" cases. And Bruce Ackerman famously argues that we can amend the text without employing the machinery specified in Article V. Jed Rubenfeld, Freedom and Time: A Theory of Constitutional Self-Government (2001); Bruce Ackerman, We the People: Foundations (1996); see also Akhil R. Amar, *The Consent of the Governed: Constitutional Amendment Outside Article V,* 94 Colum. L. Rev. 457 (1994).

14. I count in this group Ronald Dworkin, Lawrence Sager, and Christopher Eisgruber. All three begin with the document. But none of the three sticks with it very long or, more important, for any really serious purpose. Dworkin constructs an interpretive strategy that links constitutional meaning in hard cases to principles of "political morality." Ronald Dworkin, Freedom's Law: The Moral Reading of the American Constitution 7–15 (1996). See also Frank I. Michelman, *Constancy to an Ideal Object,* 56 N.Y.U. L. Rev. 406 (1981). Sager and Eisgruber contend that the Constitution leaves matters of "principle" to the Court, which has the capacity to refine long-term values (by which they mean values touching personal liberty). Sager proposes a "justice-seeking account" of "constitutional practice," which gives an important (though not exclusive) role to adjudication in the Court. Eisgruber argues that open-ended constitutional provisions like the Due Process Clauses and the Equal Protection Clause invite the Court to fashion modern ideas about those basic principles. Lawrence G. Sager, Justice in Plainclothes: A Theory of American Constitutional Practice (2004), hereafter cited as Justice; Christopher L. Eisgruber, Constitutional Self-Government (2001). Others advance their own systems for wedging the Court's decisions, if not the Court's articulated analysis, into some larger picture with its own internal logic. See, for example, James E. Fleming, *Securing Deliberative Autonomy,* 48 Stan. L. Rev. 1 (1995).

15. I have in mind, in particular, Richard Fallon's argument that the Court creates and applies doctrine as a way of implementing (rather than interpreting) the Constitution; Anthony Amsterdam's contention that the rights associated with the Fourth Amendment are "regulatory" in nature; Richard Pildes's argument that individual rights in general are "structural" rather than "atomistic";

Steven Smith's claim that the Constitution embodies the general idea that government must conform its activities to reason; David Beatty's argument that constitutional courts around the world make proportionality the crucial element in substantive rights; and Cass Sunstein's argument that the Court employs means/ends analysis to unmask governmental action in behalf of private (rather than public) interests. Richard H. Fallon Jr., Implementing the Constitution (2001); Anthony Amsterdam, *Perspectives on the Fourth Amendment*, 58 Minn. L. Rev. 349 (1974); Richard H. Pildes, *Why Rights Are Not Trumps: Social Meanings, Expressive Harms, and Constitutionalism*, 27 J. Legal Stud. 725 (1998); Steven D. Smith, The Constitution and the Pride of Reason (1998); David M. Beatty, The Ultimate Rule of Law (2004); Cass R. Sunstein, *Naked Preferences and the Constitution*, 84 Colum. L. Rev. 1689 (1984). See chapter 1, notes 12–15 and accompanying text; chapter 3, notes 16–41 and accompanying text. I should also note Laurence Tribe's general approach to doctrinal questions and Judge Posner's thesis that American law generally is best understood as pragmatism. Laurence H. Tribe, Constitutional Choices (1988); Richard A. Posner, Law, Pragmatism, and Democracy (2003). See also Richard A. Posner, Overcoming Law 387–405 (1995). On the one hand, I'm inclined to think that the doctrinal work I want to describe comes close to judicial decisions marked by what Posner calls "everyday pragmatism." Posner, Pragmatism, *supra* at 49–56. Certainly, I agree that sound constitutional decision making depends on reliable information about the way the world works. Cf. Richard A. Posner, *Against Constitutional Theory*, 73 N.Y.U. L. Rev. 1 (1998) (explaining that constitutional judgment demands attention to available data). Nevertheless, I would not necessarily reach the results that Posner thinks the evidence entails. On the other hand, Judge Posner has criticized Professor Tribe for proposing that the Court must exercise the very kind of judgment that I, too, think is necessary. It is hard to think that Posner and Tribe are compatible if they are at each other's throats.

I'm going to duck Professor Sager's argument that judicial decisions systematically under-enforce constitutional norms and that a fraction of the Constitution's rightful "domain" is left to decisions by other political institutions. Sager, Justice, *supra* note 14, at 84–160. That argument is attractive; it accounts for occasions when judges consciously limit their substantive decisions or remedial orders out of deference to the supposed knowledge and democratic credentials of others. Professor Fallon builds on it in defending his thesis that the Court's doctrinal implementation of the Constitution often falls short of the Constitution's true meaning. Yet the significance of an extrajudicial constitutional field of operations is questionable. And Sager's description of the content of such a residual segment of constitutional practice is contestable (as either too capacious or too confined). When I say that Supreme Court decisions regarding substantive rights *are* the Constitution, I mean the part of constitutional practice that Sager, too, ascribes to the Court and (in his view) other courts, as well. But

I doubt the proposition, shared by Fallon and Sager, that there is a meaningful distinction between the Constitution and what the Court says about it. Realistically speaking, the Court's own doctrine is all we have, and we had best make our peace with it. Then again, the justices invariably avoid deciding constitutional questions they can bypass for the moment and thus at least postpone confrontations with other power centers. See Cass R. Sunstein, One Case at a Time (1999) (systematically exploring the practice of judicial "minimalism").

16. Arthur A. Leff, *Unspeakable Ethics, Unnatural Law,* 1979 Duke L. J. 1229, 1248.

Chapter One

1. David A. Strauss, *Common Law, Common Ground, and Jefferson's Principle,* 112 Yale L. J. 1717, 1719 (2003); hereafter cited as *Jefferson's Principle.*

2. Daniel Farber & Suzanna Sherry, Seeking Certainty: The Misguided Quest for Constitutional Foundations 2–3 (2002).

3. Ronald Dworkin, *The Arduous Virtue of Fidelity: Originalism, Scalia, Tribe, and Nerve,* 65 Fordham L. Rev. 1249, 1251 (1997).

4. Michael S. Moore, *Do We Have an Unwritten Constitution?,* 63 S. Calif. L. Rev. 107, 115 (1989).

5. William F. Harris II, The Interpretable Constitution 1 (1992).

6. Mark V. Tushnet, *Marbury v. Madison Around the World,* 71 Tenn. L. Rev. 251 (2004).

7. Alec S. Sweet, *Why Europe Rejected American Judicial Review and Why It May Not Matter,* 101 Mich. L. Rev. 2744 (2003).

8. See Henry P. Monaghan, *Stare Decisis and Constitutional Adjudication,* 88 Colum. L. Rev. 723, 768–69 (1988) (collecting authorities distinguishing between the Constitution and judicial "interpretations" of it); hereafter cited as *Stare Decisis.*

9. There are many variations on this theme. Larry Kramer contends that "[c]onstitutional law is best understood as a species of customary law refracted through a text" and that "the 'law' we apply at any given time is the end product of historically evolving understandings of the text." Larry D. Kramer, *When Lawyers Do History,* 72 Geo. Wash. L. Rev. 387, 388 (2003); hereafter cited as *History.* Frank Michelman recognizes a difference between the Constitution and constitutional law but finds the distinction "annoying" and acknowledges that protests against it may have some "logic and common sense" on their side. Frank I. Michelman, *Living with Judicial Supremacy,* 38 Wake Forest L. Rev. 579, 606 (2003).

10. See, for example, Keith E. Whittington, Constitutional Interpretation: Textual Meaning, Original Intent and Judicial Review 1–2, 47–109 (1999); here-

after cited as Interpretation. David Strauss acknowledges that the document is peripheral, at best. Yet he thinks that an approach to the Constitution that rejects the "significance" of the text cannot "gain widespread acceptance in the legal culture." David A. Strauss, *What Is Constitutional Theory?* 87 Calif. L. Rev. 581, 586 (1999); hereafter cited as *Theory*. Richard Kay insists that setting the text aside entirely would be "unthinkable." Richard Kay, *The Illegality of the Constitution*, 4 Const. Commentary 57, 57 (1987).

11. Cf. Max Lerner, *Constitution and Court as Symbols*, 46 Yale L. J. 1290, 1294 (1937) (describing the Constitution as a tribal "totem"), quoted in Henry P. Monaghan, *The Constitution of the United States and American Constitutional Law*, in Constitutional Justice under Old Constitutions 175, 180 (Smith ed. 1995); Arthur S. Miller, *Toward a Definition of "the" Constitution*, 8 U. Dayton L. Rev. 633, 646 (1983) (arguing that "Americans today are tied to the Document of 1787 only symbolically or metaphorically"); hereafter cited as *Definition;* Gene R. Nichol, *Toward a People's Constitution*, 91 Calif. L. Rev. 621 (2003) (relating the symbolism associated with the Constitution and the flag). See also H. Jefferson Powell, A Community Built on Words 203 (2002) (arguing that the use of constitutional terms to debate public issues helps to perpetuate "political community across time"); hereafter cited as Community.

12. Richard H. Fallon Jr., Implementing the Constitution 37–38 (2001); hereafter cited as Implementing; see also Richard H. Fallon Jr., *Judicially Manageable Standards and Constitutional Meaning*, 119 Harv. L. Rev. 1274 (2006); hereafter cited as *Manageable*. See Lawrence G. Sager, *Fair Measure: The Legal Status of Underenforced Constitutional Norms*, 91 Harv. L. Rev. 1212 (1978); see also Lawrence G. Sager, Justice in Plainclothes: A Theory of American Constitutional Practice (2004). For a similar account, see Kermit Roosevelt III, The Myth of Judicial Activism: Making Sense of Supreme Court Decisions 19–23 (2006), hereafter cited as Myth.

13. Robert F. Nagel, *The Formulaic Constitution*, 84 Mich. L. Rev. 165, 177, 182 (1985). Nagel offers this assessment as a descriptive lament. Nevertheless, he acknowledges a dilemma. The Court can maintain some distance between itself and the authoritative Constitution by simply announcing decisions and citing some provision of the document in justification. But that classical, formalist style of decision making is unattractive today and, in most academic circles, has been "discredited" (*id.* at 182). At the same time, "[w]hen a court claims something more ambitious—when it seeks to demonstrate rather than to announce—there is correspondingly less reason to distinguish the external authority [i.e., the text of the Constitution] from the court's opinion" (*id.* at 183).

14. Professor Levinson makes this point in connection with his Holmsean assault on the conventional distinction between rights and remedies. See Daryl J. Levinson, *Right Essentialism and Remedial Equilibration*, 99 Colum. L. Rev. 857, 924 (1999). Fallon responds that if the Court's doctrinal accounts are "close

enough" to true constitutional meaning, there is no need actually to spell out the latter, and it is just as well if the Court does not. Fallon, *Manageable, supra* note 12, at 1316. Moreover, by Fallon's account, aspirations ascribed to actual constitutional meaning are valuable, even if we cannot "agree on what those aspirations are" (*id.* at 1326–27). See also Mitchell N. Berman, *Constitutional Decision Rules,* 90 Va. L. Rev. 1 (2004) (distinguishing between "constitutional operative propositions" that specify true constitutional "meaning" and doctrinal "constitutional decision rules" that guide judicial decision making). This same debate is carried on with respect to rules of law the Court itself explains as non-constitutional devices for protecting constitutional rights prophylactically—for example, the rule that evidence seized in violation of the Fourth Amendment must (sometimes) be excluded from criminal trials. David Strauss argues that lots of rules the Court presents as constitutional might, instead, be regarded as prophylactics. David A. Strauss, *The Ubiquity of Prophylactic Rules,* 55 U. Chi. L. Rev. 190, 195 (1988). Michael Dorf agrees and then concedes that with so many non-constitutional prophylactic rules in play, we end up with such a "small core of *real*" constitutional norms that it is hard to defend the difference between the two at all. Michael C. Dorf, *Foreword: The Limits of Socratic Deliberation,* 112 Harv. L. Rev. 4, 71–72 (1998), emphasis in original; hereafter cited as *Foreword.* Accord Levinson, *supra* at 900. Nevertheless, Dorf contends that conceiving of some rules as functionally prophylactic (apart from whether they are equally conceived to be non-constitutional in nature) may facilitate valuable experimentation. Michael C. Dorf & Charles F. Sabel, *A Constitution of Democratic Experimentalism,* 98 Colum. L. Rev. 267, 444–69 (1998).

15. Fallon, Implementing, *supra* note 12, at 111–26.

16. Edward S. Corwin, Liberty Against Government: The Rise, Flowering and Decline of a Famous Juridical Concept 42 (1948); emphasis in original.

17. Thomas Paine, The Rights of Man 309 (Dolphin ed. 1961); emphasis added.

18. *Id.* at 422–23.

19. See Charles H. McIlwain, Constitutionalism: Ancient & Modern 2–15 (1947). Accord Mary S. Bilder, The Transatlantic Constitution: Colonial Legal Culture and the Empire 2 (2004); Jed Rubenfeld, Freedom and Time: A Theory of Constitutional Self-Government 164 (2001); hereafter cited as Freedom.

20. Burke thus linked his idea of a constitution with an elitist regime we would scarcely want to reproduce today. Our body of judicial decisions establishing constitutional meaning can be considerably more progressive than his conservative brand of incrementalism would allow. See Bruce Ackerman, We the People: Foundations 17–18 (1991) (explaining the excessively backward-looking character of Burke's thinking). But see Ernest Young, *Rediscovering Conservatism: Burkean Political Theory and Constitutional Interpretation,* 72 N. Car. L. Rev.

619 (1994) (arguing that Burkean traditionalism might be reconciled with modern evolutionary constitutional law-making by the Supreme Court).

21. Paine, Rights, *supra* note 17, at 309.

22. English courts are entitled, even obligated, to give statutes a reasonable reading. And if a statute lends itself to alternative constructions, the one inequitable and the other sensible, a court is duty-bound to adopt the latter interpretation. Still, according to classic theory, Parliament has authority "to make or unmake any law whatever." English judges "do not claim or exercise any power to repeal a Statute, whilst Acts of Parliament may override and constantly do override the law of the judges." A. Dicey, Introduction to the Study of the Law of the Constitution 39–40, 60 (1885). When Chief Justice Coke proclaimed that an act of Parliament might fall victim to the "common law," he may have meant only that English courts would construe Parliament's enactments carefully to ensure that they were accurately enforced—not that courts might override valid statutes in the name of some higher form of law. Compare Larry D. Kramer, *Foreword: We the Court,* 115 Harv. L. Rev. 4, 24 (2001) (taking this view in reliance on Blackstone and Holdsworth), with Barbara A. Black, *The Constitution of Empire: The Case for the Colonists,* 124 U. Pa. L. Rev. 1157, 1207–10 (1976) (tending to the view that Coke meant to endorse judicial review of some ilk); accord Allen D. Boyer, Sir Edward Coke and the Elizabethan Age 84–85 (2003) (crediting Coke with laying the groundwork for *Marbury v. Madison*).

23. William E. Gladstone, *Kin Beyond Sea,* North Am. Rev. (Sept. 1878) 127, 185, quoted in Michael Kammen, A Machine That Would Go of Itself: The Constitution in American Culture 162 (Vintage ed. 1987).

24. *Marbury v. Madison,* 5 U.S. (1 Cranch) 137, 177–78 (1803).

25. See John Hart Ely, Democracy and Distrust 51–52 (1980).

26. Rubenfeld, Freedom, *supra* note 19, at 165–66.

27. Whittington, Interpretation, *supra* note 10, at 6.

28. Kammen, Machine, *supra* note 23, at 162 (noting that Johnson had used very similar language a quarter century earlier).

29. Thomas C. Grey, *The Constitution as Scripture,* 37 Stan. L. Rev. 1 (1984); Sanford Levinson, Constitutional Faith (1988).

30. Paine, Rights, *supra* note 17, at 422.

31. Barbara Jordan, *Opening Statement, House Judiciary Committee Proceedings on the Impeachment of Richard Nixon,* 93rd. Cong., 2d. sess. 111 (July 25, 1974). See Miller, *Definition, supra* note 11, at 669 (also recalling Jordan's speech to make something of this same point).

32. McIlwain, Constitutionalism, *supra* note 19, at 15.

33. See David E. Bernstein, *Lochner Era Revisionism, Revised: Lochner and the Origins of Fundamental Rights Constitutionalism,* 92 Gtn. L. J. 1, 31 (2003) (documenting a body of opinion to the effect that this country had "an unwritten constitution" that "complemented and supplemented the written document").

Accord Suzanna Sherry, *The Founders' Unwritten Constitution,* 54 U. Chi. L. Rev. 1127, 1155–67 (1987).

34. Lawrence Lessig, *What Drives Derivability: Responses to Responding to Imperfection,* 74 Tex. L. Rev. 839, 874 (1996); hereafter cited as *Derivability.*

35. Akhil Reed Amar, America's Constitution: A Biography 319 (2005); hereafter cited as America's Constitution.

36. Sherry, *Unwritten Constitution, supra* note 33, at 1162–67.

37. Kammen, Machine, *supra* note 23, at 162–66.

38. *Olmstead v. United States,* 277 U.S. 438, 472 (1928) (Brandeis, J., dissenting).

39. Benjamin Cardozo, The Nature of the Judicial Process 17 (1921). See Morton J. Horwitz, *Foreword: The Constitution of Change: Legal Fundamentality without Fundamentalism,* 107 Harv. L. Rev. 30, 51–54 (1993); hereafter cited as *Foreword.*

40. In *Georgia v. Randolph,* 126 S.Ct. 1515 (2006), for example, Justice Scalia insisted that while the property rights protected by the Fourth Amendment may change, the measure of the Fourth Amendment's protection of whatever property rights exist does not. *Id.* at 1540 (Scalia, J., dissenting).

41. See, for example, Christopher G. Tiedeman, The Unwritten Constitution of the United States (1890) (Mersky & Jacobstein eds. 1974).

42. Miller, *Definition, supra* note 11, at 645–46. See Arthur S. Miller, Toward Increased Judicial Activism: The Political Role of the Supreme Court (1982).

43. Arthur E. Wilmarth Jr., *Elusive Foundation: John Marshall, James Wilson, and the Problem of Reconciling Popular Sovereignty and Natural Law Jurisprudence in the New Federal Republic,* 72 Geo. Wash. L. Rev. 113, 170–72 (2003). Madison agreed, but changed his mind when it proved necessary to win a seat in the House.

44. See chapter 3, notes 98–102 and accompanying text.

45. Anyone who doubts this should read Dan Farber's colorful account of the ways we might have manufactured a wide variety of familiar individual rights even if the Bill of Rights had never come to the House floor. See Daniel A. Farber, *Terminator 2 1/2: The Constitution in an Alternate World,* 9 Const. Commentary 59 (1992). Professor Strauss has argued (more soberly) that other formal amendments were largely unnecessary and that we would have achieved the same purposes without them, albeit Strauss makes an exception for the Bill of Rights. David A. Strauss, *The Irrelevance of Constitutional Amendments,* 114 Harv. L. Rev. 1457 (2001).

46. Frederick Schauer, *An Essay on Constitutional Language,* 29 UCLA L. Rev. 797, 831–32 (1982); hereafter cited as *Constitutional Language.*

47. Dorf, *Foreword, supra* note 14, at 11–12.

48. Mark V. Tushnet, Red, White, and Blue: A Critical Analysis of Constitutional Law 68 (1988). In this vein, Professor Seidman contends that the great

value of the Constitution is that it nurtures a sense of community by giving opposing sides a basis for carrying arguments on even after (temporary) political solutions have been reached. Louis Michael Seidman, Our Unsettled Constitution (2001).

49. Judge Easterbrook so argues. Frank H. Easterbrook, *Textualism and the Dead Hand*, 66 Geo. Wash. L. Rev. 1119, 1121 (1998); hereafter cited as *Textualism*. For commentaries, see Michael C. Dorf, *Integrating Normative and Descriptive Constitutional Theory: The Case of Original Meaning*, 85 Gtn. L. J. 1765, 1766 (1997); hereafter cited as *Integrating;* Paul W. Kahn, *Reason and Will in the Origins of American Constitutionalism*, 98 Yale L. J. 449, 453 (1989).

50. Edward S. Corwin, *The Progress of Constitutional Theory between the Declaration of Independence and the Meeting of the Philadelphia Convention*, 30 Am. Hist. Rev. 511, 522 (1925), reprinted in The Formation and Ratification of the Constitution 113, 124 (Hall ed. 1987).

51. See, for example, Ackerman, We the People, *supra* note 20; Akhil R. Amar, *A Few Thoughts on Constitutionalism, Textualism, and Populism*, 65 Fordham L. Rev. 1657 (1997); hereafter cited as *Thoughts*.

52. Randy Barnett, *An Originalism for Nonoriginalists*, 45 Loy. L. Rev. 611, 621 (1999); hereafter cited as *Originalism*.

53. See, for example, Amar, America's Constitution, *supra* note 35, at 5.

54. *Id.* at 7–19, 64–98, 151–73, 274–81.

55. Gordon S. Wood, The Creation of the American Republic, 1776–1787, 73–76 (1969).

56. Alexander Keyssar, The Right to Vote: The Contested History of Democracy in the United States 5 (2000); see also Chilton Williamson, American Suffrage: From Property to Democracy, 1760–1860 (1960).

57. Keyssar, Right to Vote, *supra* note 56, at 5–9 (making this and preceding points).

58. Jack N. Rakove, Original Meanings: Politics and Ideas in the Making of the Constitution 106 (1997); hereafter cited as Original Meanings. Professor Sherry argues that the idea of constitution-writing at the time did not necessarily contemplate the creation of a higher form of law insulated from majoritarian control. She recalls, for example, that most state constitutions were enacted by state legislatures and not by any supermajoritarian process connoting higher-law significance. Sherry, *Unwritten Constitution, supra* note 33, at 1131. Rakove counters that the Philadelphia Convention deliberately chose the minority approach in Massachusetts, where the state constitution had been adopted by state convention.

59. Rakove, Original Meanings, *supra* note 58, at 106.

60. See generally Ratifying the Constitution (Gillespie & Lienesch eds. 1989) (describing individual ratifying conventions).

61. Amar, America's Constitution, *supra* note 35, at 7 (emphasis added) and 17.

62. I rely here on Professor Simon's summary. Larry G. Simon, *The Authority of the Framers of the Constitution: Can Originalist Interpretation Be Justified?* 73 Calif. L. Rev. 1482, 1498 n. 44 (1985). Simon relies, in turn, on Robert E. Brown, Charles Beard and the Constitution: A Critical Analysis of "An Economic Interpretation of the Constitution" 69 (1956); and Forrest McDonald, We the People: The Economic Origins of the Constitution 14 and n. 11 (1958). Brown argued that modern commentators assume incorrectly that most adult males failed either to qualify or, if qualified, to vote. He contended, for example, that men in Massachusetts usually had enough property to make them eligible. Yet Brown, now relying on J. Franklin Jameson, *Did the Fathers Vote?* N. E. Mag., n.s. I, 484–90 (Jan., 1890), reported that adult white men accounted for only about 20 percent of the general population. Beard estimated that about 160,000 men were eligible to vote in the elections for delegates to the ratifying conventions and that only about 100,000 of those favored ratification. McDonald surveyed surviving voting records and came away convinced that Beard's estimates were "remarkably accurate." McDonald, Economic Origins, *supra*, at 14 n. 11. For Amar's criticisms, see Amar, America's Constitution, *supra* note 35, at 503–5.

63. See also Charles W. Roll Jr., *We, Some of the People: Apportionment in the Thirteen State Conventions Ratifying the Constitution*, 56 J. Am. Hist. 21 (1969), reported in Hall, Formation and Ratification, *supra* note 50, at 521.

64. Or, as Robert Dahl puts it, "Why should we feel bound today by a document produced more than two centuries ago by a group of fifty-five mortal men, actually signed by only thirty-nine, a fair number of whom were slaveholders, and adopted in only thirteen states by the votes of fewer than two thousand men, all of whom are long since dead and mainly forgotten?" Robert A. Dahl, How Democratic Is the American Constitution? 2 (2003).

65. Michael W. McConnell, *Textualism and the Dead Hand of the Past*, 66 Geo. Wash. L. Rev. 1127, 1128 (1998), hereafter cited as *Dead Hand;* Dorf, *Integrating, supra* note 49, at 1776.

66. See Michael J. Klarman, *What's So Great About Constitutionalism?* 93 Nw. U. L. Rev. 145 (1998) (sketching a host of arguments and finding them all inadequate).

67. Henry P. Monaghan, *Our Perfect Constitution,* 56 N.Y.U. L. Rev. 353, 384 (1981) (actually contending that the authoritative written Constitution is anything but ideal). See H. L. A. Hart, The Concept of Law 97 (1961) (supplying the "rule of recognition" concept on which Monaghan relies).

68. Rubenfeld, Freedom, *supra* note 19.

69. *Id.* at 11, 167–68.

70. Jed Rubenfeld, Revolution by Judiciary 13–14 (2005); hereafter cited as Revolution.

71. Many academicians have spun theories of constitutional justification from Ulysees's gambit: for example, Jon Elster, Ulysees and the Sirens: Studies in

Rationality and Irrationality (1979); Cass R. Sunstein, After the Rights Revolution: Reconceiving the Regulatory State 58 (1990); Michael J. Klarman, *Constitutional Fact/Constitutional Fiction: A Critique of Ackerman's Theory of Constitutional Moments*, 44 Stan. L. Rev. 759, 795 (1992); hereafter cited as *Ackerman's Theory*. See generally Stephen Holmes, *Precommitment and the Paradox of Democracy*, in Constitutionalism and Democracy 195–240 (Elster & Slagstad eds. 1988) (offering a good discussion of the "precommitment" defense of constitutional legitimacy).

72. See Klarman, *Ackerman's Theory, supra* note 71, at 796 (arguing that "majoritarian precommitments" can legitimately be enforced only "*intra*generationally"); emphasis in original.

73. Rubenfeld, Freedom, *supra* note 19, at 158.

74. Michael J. Klarman, *Antifidelity*, 70 S. Calif. L. Rev. 381, 383 (1997). Professor Rubenfeld acknowledges that Jon Elster, who pioneered the "precommitment" justification for the Constitution, has now qualified his approach considerably. Jon Elster, Ulysses Unbound: Studies in Rationality, Precommitment, and Restraints 92–96 (2000), cited in Rubenfeld, Revolution, *supra* note 70, at 80. Rubenfeld himself recognizes that the American "people" began as "white, propertied, Christian males" and that "individuals kept as slaves" had "no part" in the Constitution the "people" created and "are not bound by it." Rubenfeld, Freedom, *supra* note 19, at 158.

75. Paul W. Kahn, Legitimacy and History: Self-Government in American Constitutional Theory 63–64 (1992); hereafter cited as Legitimacy.

76. Alexander M. Bickel, The Least Dangerous Branch: The Supreme Court at the Bar of Politics 16 (1962).

77. See Philip Bobbitt, Constitutional Interpretation 9 (1991); hereafter cited as Interpretation; Philip Bobbitt, Constitutional Fate 5 (1982); Rebecca L. Brown, *Accountability, Liberty, and the Constitution*, 98 Colum. L. Rev. 531, 556 (1998); Erwin Chemerinsky, *Foreword: The Vanishing Constitution*, 103 Harv. L. Rev. 43, 74–77, 102 (1989); Frank H. Easterbrook, *The Influence of Judicial Review on Constitutional Theory*, in A Workable Government? 170, 179–80 (Marshall ed. 1987).

78. See, for example, Earl M. Maltz, *Murder in the Cathedral—The Supreme Court as Moral Prophet*, 8 U. Dayton L. Rev. 623, 631 (1983).

79. Barry Friedman, *The Birth of an Academic Obsession: The History of the Countermajoritarian Difficulty, Part Five*, 112 Yale L. J. 153, 159–60 (2002).

80. Christopher L. Eisgruber, Constitutional Self-Government 10–14 (2001); James E. Fleming, *Constructing the Substantive Constitution*, 72 Tex. L. Rev. 211, 292–97 (1993); James E. Fleming, *We the Unconventional American People*, 65 U. Chi. L. Rev. 1513, 1516 (1998).

81. Robert Post & Reva Siegel, *Popular Constitutionalism, Departmentalism, and Judicial Supremacy*, 92 Calif. L. Rev. 1027, 1042 (2004).

82. See Barry Friedman, *Mediating Popular Constitutionalism*, 101 Mich. L. Rev. 2596 (2003) (reviewing the literature in point).

83. See Keith E. Whittington, *Congress Before the Lochner Court*, 85 B. U. L. Rev. 821, 825–27 (2005) (surveying the literature in point).

84. *Id.* at 829–55 (arguing that decisions in the early part of the twentieth century followed this pattern).

85. See Larry A. Alexander, *Painting Without the Numbers: Noninterpretive Judicial Review*, 8 U. Dayton L. Rev. 447, 463 (1983).

86. Dorf, *Integrating, supra* note 49, at 1772.

87. Richard H. Fallon Jr., *How to Choose a Constitutional Theory*, 87 Calif. L. Rev. 535, 547 (1999); hereafter cited as *How to Choose*.

88. See Easterbrook, *Textualism, supra* note 49; Laurence H. Tribe & Michael C. Dorf, On Reading the Constitution 11 (1991).

89. *Fletcher v. Peck*, 10 U.S. (6 Cranch) 87, 137–38 (1980), cited in Wilmarth, *Elusive Foundation, supra* note 43, at 128.

90. See Thomas C. Grey, *Do We Have an Unwritten Constitution?* 27 Stan. L. Rev. 703, 706 (1975).

91. Thomas C. Grey, *The Uses of an Unwritten Constitution*, 64 Chi-Kent L. Rev. 211, 220 (1988). Michael Perry once accepted the "noninterpretivist" label. Michael J. Perry, *Noninterpretive Review in Human Rights Cases: A Functional Justification*, 56 N. Y. U. L. Rev. 278 (1981). He, too, has discarded it. Michael J. Perry, We the People: The Fourteenth Amendment and the Supreme Court 23–35 (1999).

92. See, for example, Ronald Dworkin, *The Forum of Principle*, 56 N. Y. U. L. Rev. 469, 471–76 (1981); Fallon, *How to Choose, supra* note 87, at 544–45.

93. See, for example, Barnett, *Originalism, supra* note 52.

94. John F. Manning, *What Divides Textualists from Purposivists?* 106 Colum. L. Rev. 70, 78 (2006); hereafter cited as *What Divides?*

95. Antonin Scalia, *Common-Law Courts in a Civil-Law System: The Role of United States Federal Courts in Interpreting the Constitution and Laws*, in A Matter of Interpretation: Federal Courts and the Law 3, 22 (Gutmann ed. 1997); hereafter cited as *Common-Law Courts.*

96. Whittington, *Interpretation, supra* note 10, at 175–77; Dorf, *Integrating, supra* note 49, at 1769; Larry A. Alexander, *Modern Equal Protection Theories: A Metatheoretical Taxonomy and Critique*, 42 Ohio St. L. J. 3, 5 (1981). Professor Lessig has explained that getting the context right demands an account of the "background understandings" that gave the framers' words significance at the time and promise, in turn, to make them intelligible to us today. Lessig, *Derivability, supra* note 34, at 854.

97. See Easterbrook, *Textualism, supra* note 49, at 1120; McConnell, *Dead Hand, supra* note 65, at 1132.

98. See Fallon, *How to Choose, supra* note 87, at 541 (treating "originalism"

as an example of "text-based" theories of interpretation). Cf. Vasan Kesavan & Michael S. Paulsen, *The Interpretive Force of the Constitution's Secret Drafting History,* 91 Gtn. L. J. 1113, 1127–29, 1131 (2003) (arguing that the Supremacy Clause makes textualism the only legitimate approach to constitutional interpretation and that originalism is the best way to ascribe meaning to the text when it is not conclusive by its very terms).

99. See Richard S. Kay, *Adherence to the Original Intentions in Constitutional Adjudication: Three Objections and Responses,* 82 Nw. U. L. Rev. 226 (1988). Sai Prakash contends that originalism is merely a methodology for interpreting a text (any text) and thus does not presuppose that this particular text is the authoritative American Constitution. He maintains, accordingly, that originalism cannot be blamed for enforcing the meaning the framers assigned to this document. Saikrishna B. Prakash, *Overcoming the Constitution,* 91 Gtn. L. J. 407, 427–32 (2003). I am not sure what to make of that. Prakash quickly concedes that "[m]ost" originalists think this writing "as originally understood by the Founders" is the "legitimate Constitution" (*id.* at 427). And he names no originalist who takes a different view. Moreover, he freely concedes that he has always assumed that this document counts as the legitimate Constitution "because of who originally enacted it (the Founders), how it was ratified (by supermajority), and subsequently how it was amended" (*id.* at 417). All that agreed to, it is hard to see any space between originalism as an abstracted methodology and originalism as part and parcel of the Constitution itself—as understood by an originalist.

100. *Marbury v. Madison,* 5 U.S. (1 Cranch) 137 (1803).

101. Antonin Scalia, *Originalism: The Lesser Evil,* 57 U. Cin. L. Rev. 849, 854 (1989); hereafter cited as *Lesser Evil.* Some commentators dispute this view of the matter, to be sure. See, for example, John Harrison, *The Constitutional Origins and Implications of Judicial Review,* 84 Va. L. Rev. 333 (1998); Saikrishna B. Prakash & John C. Yoo, *Questions for the Critics of Judicial Review,* 72 Geo. Wash. L. Rev. 354 (2003); Saikrishna B. Prakash & John C. Yoo, *The Origins of Judicial Review,* 70 U. Chi. L. Rev. 887 (2003).

102. Michael Gerhardt has critiqued Jed Rubenfeld along these lines. Rubenfeld insists that we need the Court to preserve our commitments grounded in the document and must think, accordingly, that judicial review has to exist whether or not the text provides for it. See Michael J. Gerhardt, *The End of Theory,* 96 Nw. U. L. Rev. 283, 305 (2001).

103. Strauss, *Jefferson's Principle, supra* note 1.

104. U.S. Const., art. II. § 1, cl. 6; U.S. Const., art. III, § 3, cl. 1.

105. Akhil Amar suggests that the age requirement was meant to prevent presidents from grooming their young sons as successors and that the two-witness rule derived from the English Treason Trials Act of 1696. Amar, America's Constitution, *supra* note 35, at 160, 244.

106. See The Rights Retained by the People: The History and Meaning of the Ninth Amendment (Barnett ed. 1989); Calvin R. Massey, Silent Rights: The Ninth Amendment and the Constitution's Unenumerated Rights (1995); Bennett B. Patterson, The Forgotten Ninth Amendment (1955); Kurt T. Lash, *The Lost Original Meaning of the Ninth Amendment*, 83 Tex. L. Rev. 331 (2004).

107. *Hearings before the Senate Committee on the Judiciary*, 100th Cong., 1st sess. 249 (1987). It is argued on occasion that the Ninth Amendment might have supplied a textual basis for Supreme Court decisions purporting to elaborate substantive due process. See, for example, Mark C. Niles, *Ninth Amendment Adjudication: An Alternative to Substantive Due process Analysis of Personal Autonomy Rights*, 48 UCLA L. Rev. 85 (2000). But since the Ninth Amendment offers no genuine account of "unenumerated" rights, it obviously provides no more textual guidance than does due process, perhaps less. Cf. *Troxel v. Granville*, 530 U.S. 57, 91 (2000) (Scalia, J., dissenting) (insisting that "the Constitution's refusal to 'deny or disparage' other rights is far removed from affirming any one of them"). In any event, it is hard to take seriously any argument that the Court would have developed "unenumerated" rights into protections for individuals that it has not generated by other means. See chapter 3, notes 86–88 and accompanying notes.

108. See Powell, Community, *supra* note 11 (contending that the Constitution's chief purpose has been to supply language in which to debate public issues). See also Stephen R. Munzer & James W. Nickel, *Does the Constitution Mean What It Always Meant?* 77 Colum. L. Rev. 1029, 1059 (1977); Frederick Schauer, *Constitutional Language, supra* note 46, at 831–32.

109. See Frederick Schauer, *Formalism*, 97 Yale L. J. 509, 523–24 (1988) (arguing that it is "possible" for a text to restrict a decision maker in a way that he or she would not be constrained in its absence).

110. Louis Michael Seidman & Mark V. Tushnet, Remnants of Belief 4–9 (1996); Tribe & Dorf, Reading, *supra* note 88, at 15; Roosevelt, Myth, *supra* note 12, at 18. Let me be clear. I do not argue that since the terms by which the written Constitution refers to individual rights defy noncontroversial interpretation, we should abandon judicial enforcement of rights. See Adrian Vermeule, Judging Under Uncertainty: An Institutional Theory of Legal Interpretation 233 (2006) (taking that position). I argue that since judicial enforcement is vital, we should abandon the futile attempt to derive the meaning of rights from elusive constitutional terms.

111. Thomas Merrill advocates something along these lines, dubbing his approach a "conventionalist" kind of textualism to distinguish it from the more common "originalist" brand. Thomas W. Merrill, *Bork v. Burke,* 19 Harv. J. L. Pub. Pol. 509 (1995).

112. See, for example, *NEA v. Finley,* 524 U.S. 569, 595 (1998) (Scalia, J., concurring in the judgment) (giving the term *abridging* in the First Amendment the definition provided by a 1791 dictionary). See Randy Barnett, *The Original*

Meaning of the Commerce Clause, 68 U. Chi. L. Rev. 101, 112–25 (2001); John Harrison, *Forms of Originalism and the Study of History,* 26 Harv. J. Law & Pub. Pol. 83, 90 (2003).

113. Lawrence Lessig, *Understanding Changed Readings: Fidelity and Theory,* 47 Stan. L. Rev. 395 (1995).

114. The justices insisted that *commerce* had a settled, self-evident definition that differentiated it from other activities, most particularly manufacturing, mining, and agriculture. Commerce was "'intercourse for the purposes of trade.'" *Carter v. Carter Coal Co.,* 298 U.S. 238, 298 (1936). Manufacturing, by contrast, was "transformation—the fashioning of raw materials into a form for use." *Kidd v. Pearson,* 128 U.S. 1, 20 (1888). Commerce thus "succeed[ed] to manufacture, and [was] not a part of it." *United States v. E. C. Knight Co.,* 156 U.S. 1, 12 (1895). When the justices found the simple definition of *commerce* insufficient, they turned to additional terms of their own creation. They did not insist that Congress was limited to the regulation of matters that themselves fit the tight definition of *commerce,* but rather allowed that Congress could reach activities having a direct effect on commerce. Yet the Court then made everything turn on a categorical definition of effects that were "direct" as opposed to "indirect." Distinguishing between "direct" or "indirect" effects was not a matter of appraising the actual, real-world consequences of an activity for "intercourse for the purposes of trade." *Carter Coal,* 298 U.S. at 303. It was an exercise in logic. An activity either was or was not directly related to interstate commerce, and therein lay the proper result in any given instance.

115. See chapter 2, notes 152–68 and accompanying text.

116. *United States v. Lopez,* 514 U.S. 549, 566 (1995). You know the drill: possessing a gun near a school is *not* commercial behavior, *Lopez,* 514 U.S. at 560; *declining* to purchase wheat at the market *is* commercial, *Wickard v. Filburn,* 317 U.S. 111, 127–28 (1942); and it is anybody's guess where nicking a purse at Park Street Station falls. Compare *United States v. Morrison,* 529 U.S. 598, 613 (1995) (declaring that assaulting women is not economic activity), with *Gonzales v. Raich,* 545 U.S. 1, 25 (2005) (asserting that possessing drugs is "quintessentially economic").

117. See Scalia, *Common-Law Courts, supra* note 95, at 38 (explaining that the task is to identify "the original meaning" of either kind of text). But see Kevin M. Stack, *The Divergence of Constitutional and Statutory Interpretation,* 75 U. Colo. L. Rev. 1 (2004) (contending that there are sound reasons for taking divergent approaches to statutes and the Constitution).

118. See John F. Manning, *Textualism and the Equity of the Statute,* 101 Colum. L. Rev. 1, 18–21 (2001); hereafter cited as *Equity of the Statute.*

119. See *Artuz v. Bennett,* 531 U.S. 4, 10 (2000) (opinion for the Court); cf. *Edwards v. Aguillard,* 482 U.S. 578, 636–39 (Scalia, J., dissenting) (making similar points in the context of constitutional interpretation).

120. See Manning, *Equity of the Statute, supra* note 118, at 7, 18–20. This account is necessarily overgeneralized. See John F. Manning, *Justice Scalia and the Legislative Process,* 62 N. Y. U. Annual Survey of Am. L. 33 (2006) (providing a more searching account of Justice Scalia's position). Specialists in statutory construction argue at length about whether textualism is all so different, in the end, from other methodologies—including the "purposivism" associated with the Legal Process School. Jonathan Molot contends that any divide between textualism and purposivism has closed. Jonathan T. Molot, *The Rise and Fall of Textualism,* 106 Colum. L. Rev. 1 (2006). John Manning largely agrees, albeit he identifies certain distinctions remaining. Manning, *What Divides? supra* note 94.

121. John Manning has developed this argument. See John F. Manning, *The Eleventh Amendment and the Reading of Precise Constitutional Texts,* 113 Yale L. J. 1663 (2004) (allowing an exception for cases in which literalism would lead to an absurd result).

122. See chapter 4, notes 137–90 and accompanying text.

123. See William N. Eskridge Jr., *The New Textualism,* 37 UCLA L. Rev. 621 (1990); William N. Eskridge Jr., *All About Words: Early Understandings of the "Judicial Power" in Statutory Interpretation,* 1776–1806, 101 Colum. L. Rev. 990 (2001).

124. For a recent examination of the Constitutional Convention from this point of view, see David B. Robertson, The Constitution and America's Destiny (2005).

125. See Stack, *Divergence, supra* note 117, at 58; Trevor W. Morrison, *Lamenting Lochner's Loss: Randy Barnett's Case for a Libertarian Constitution,* 90 Cornell L. Rev. 839, 850 (2005).

126. 17 U.S. (4 Wheat.) 316 (1819).

127. Charles Black, Structure and Relationship in Constitutional Law (1969).

128. Bobbitt, Interpretation, *supra* note 77, at 15–16, 133–35; Richard H. Fallon Jr., *A Constructivist Coherence Theory of Constitutional Interpretation,* 100 Harv. L. Rev. 1189, 1195–1207 (1987). See also Stephen L. Carter, *Constitutional Adjudication and the Indeterminate Text: A Preliminary Defense of an Imperfect Muddle,* 94 Yale L. J. 821, 847–48 (1985).

129. 478 U.S. 833 (1986).

130. *Id.* at 847.

131. 521 U.S. 898 (1997).

132. *Id.* at 905. See Gene R. Nichol, *Justice Scalia and the Printz Case: The Trials of an Occasional Originalist,* 70 U. Colo. L. Rev. 953 (1999).

133. *Seminole Tribe v. Florida,* 517 U.S. 44 (1996).

134. 527 U.S. 706 (1999).

135. *Seminole Tribe,* 517 U.S. at 69.

136. Amar, *Thoughts, supra* note 51, at 1659.

137. See Easterbrook, *Textualism, supra* note 49, at 1125 (arguing that the framers "did not share a single vision but reached a complex compromise").

138. Raoul Berger, *Ely's Theory of Judicial Review,* 42 Ohio St. L. J. 87, 123 (1981).

139. See Alain Levasseur, *Civilian Methodology: On the Structure of a Civil Code,* 44 Tulane L. Rev. 693, 703 (1970) (explaining that a French court's responsibility is to "gather the pieces together and reconcile the code articles in order to achieve the systematization that was the goal of the drafters").

140. *McCulloch v. Maryland,* 17 U.S. 316 (1819).

141. *Id.* at 414.

142. Ely, Democracy and Distrust, *supra* note 25.

143. Akhil R. Amar, *Intratextualism,* 112 Harv. L. Rev. 747 (1999). Charles Black was not primarily concerned with interpreting particular provisions of the document in context. See Michael C. Dorf, *Interpretive Holism and the Structural Method, or How Charles Black Might Have Thought About Campaign Finance Reform and Congressional Timidity,* 92 Gtn. L. J. 833 (2004).

144. Adrian Vermeule & Ernest A. Young, *Hercules, Herbert, and Amar: The Trouble with Intratextualism,* 113 Harv. L. Rev. 730, 739 (2000).

145. See Tribe & Dorf, Reading, *supra* note 88, at 24 (criticizing "hyperintegration").

146. Jack N. Rakove, *Confessions of an Ambivalent Originalist,* 78 N. Y. U. L. Rev. 1346, 1353 (2003).

147. Mitchel de S.-O.-I'E. Lasser, *Judicial (Self-)Portraits: Judicial Discourse in the French Legal System,* 104 Yale L. J. 1325, 1344–55 (1995).

148. See David A. Strauss, *The New Textualism in Constitutional Law,* 66 Geo. Wash. L. Rev. 1154 (1998) (describing Amar's "heroic view" of the drafters); cf. Cass R. Sunstein & Adrian Vermeule, *Interpretation and Institutions,* 101 Mich. L. Rev. 885, 940–41 (2003) (contending that Amar also overestimates the capacity of judges to command the entire board).

149. Peter J. Smith, *Commas, Constitutional Grammar, and the Straight-Face Test: What If Conan the Grammarian Were a Strict Textualist,* 16 Const. Commentary 7 (1990).

150. Amar, *Thoughts, supra* note 51, at 1659.

151. See Vermeule & Young, *Hercules, supra* note 144, at 749; accord Tribe & Dorf, Reading, *supra* note 88, at 20–24.

152. Akhil R. Amar, *The Second Amendment: A Case Study in Constitutional Interpretation,* 2001 Utah L. Rev. 889, 913.

153. 483 U.S.635 (1987).

154. *Id.* at 643.

155. *Id.* at 643–44 (emphasis added).

156. 494 U.S. 259 (1990).

157. *Id.* at 265.

158. *Id.* at 276 (Kennedy, J., concurring).

159. Justice Brennan suggested, for example, that the Fourth Amendment uses the term *people* rather than *person* merely to avoid saying (awkwardly): "'The right of persons to be secure in their persons.'" *Id.* at 287 n. 9 (Brennan, J., dissenting).

160. *Id.* at 275 (opinion of the Chief Justice). See *id.* at 278 (Kennedy, J., concurring) (making practical points about applying the Fourth Amendment overseas); *id.* at 279 (Stevens, J., concurring in the judgment) (noting that federal magistrates have no express authority to issue warrants for searches outside the United States).

161. 540 U.S. 551 (2004).

162. *Id.* at 557; emphasis in original.

163. The ultimate question in *Groh* was whether the officer was immune from liability on the theory that he acted reasonably—the same issue the Court faced in *Anderson*. Thomas and Scalia would have allowed immunity even if the search was invalid. But it is likely that their antecedent account of the Fourth Amendment issue itself was colored by the implications of finding a constitutional violation.

164. 126 S.Ct. 1494 (2006).

165. *Id.* at 1503 (Souter, J., concurring in part and concurring in the judgment) (joined by Stevens & Ginsburg, J. J.).

166. 126 S.Ct. 2557 (2006).

167. See *id.* at 2561.

168. As might be expected, Justice Scalia went on to explain why, as a matter of policy, it is a good idea to let paying clients select their own champions (*id.* at 2564). Other illustrations are plentiful. The question in *Iowa v. Tovar*, 541 U.S. 77 (2004), was whether a defendant had acted voluntarily in pleading guilty. The Iowa Supreme Court thought not, because he had not been told that by waiving his Sixth Amendment right to counsel he risked overlooking defenses that a lawyer might identify. Writing for a unanimous Court, Justice Ginsburg plowed through the Court's closest precedents, explained that those precedents established that a waiver of counsel is valid if the defendant "fully understands the nature of the right [to counsel] and how it would likely apply in general in the circumstances" of his case, and concluded that the warning required by the Iowa Supreme Court would not enlighten the decision whether to waive counsel. *Id.* at 91–92, quoting *United States v. Ruiz*, 536 U.S. 622, 629 (2002). That was straightforward judgment about what the Constitution should sensibly mean. The text of the Sixth Amendment played no role, apart from supplying the formal starting point for the Court's discussion. There are times, of course, when the justices are fiercely divided over the meaning to be attached to precedents. Writing for the Court in *Georgia v. Randolph*, 126 S.Ct. 1515 (2006), Justice Souter massaged prior Fourth Amendment decisions into line behind a

holding he found sensible in the case at hand (*id.* at 1527). The dissenters, Chief Justice Roberts and Justice Scalia, did not quarrel with Souter's use of earlier cases to establish his point, but argued that he had misread those precedents (*id.* at 1533).

169. 126 S.Ct. 1727 (2006).

170. *Id.* at 1732, citing *Crane v. Kentucky,* 476 U.S. 683, 690 (1986).

171. Paul Brest, *The Misconceived Quest for the Original Understanding,* 60 B. U. L. Rev. 204, 234 (1980).

172. See, for example, Roosevelt, Myth, *supra* note 12, at 47–58; Terrence Sandalow, *Constitutional Interpretation,* 79 Mich. L. Rev. 1033 (1981); Schauer, *Constitutional Language, supra* note 46.

173. Barry Friedman & Scott B. Smith, *The Sedimentary Constitution,* 147 U. Pa. L. Rev. 1 (1998).

174. Horwitz, *Foreword, supra* note 39, at 44.

175. See Wilmarth, *supra* note 43, at 128–29.

176. See text accompanying notes 98–99.

177. See, for example, *Missouri v. Holland,* 252 U.S. 416, 434 (1920) (explaining that the Court must consider "what this country has become"); *Home Bldg. & Loan Ass'n v. Blaisdell,* 290 U.S. 398, 443 (1934) (explaining that "the great clauses of the Constitution" cannot "be confined to the interpretation which the framers... would have placed upon them").

178. Johnathan O'Neill, Originalism in American Law and Politics: A Constitutional History 101–60 (2005); Horwitz, *Foreword, supra* note 39, at 35.

179. Scalia, *Lesser Evil, supra* note 101, at 862–63.

180. See, for example, Amar, America's Constitution, *supra* note 35. See Larry D. Kramer, *Madison's Audience,* 112 Harv. L. Rev. 611, 677 (1999) (insisting that many academicians purport to endorse originalism of some stripe); accord Dorf, *Integrating, supra* note 49, at 1766 (naming Ackerman, Lessig, and Bobbit as illustrations).

181. I rely primarily on seminal articles by Paul Brest, Ronald Dworkin, and Michael Dorf, splicing in references to contributions by others. See Brest, *Quest, supra* note 171; Dworkin, *Forum, supra* note 92; Dorf, *Integrating, supra* note 49.

182. See William H. Rehnquist, *The Notion of a Living Constitution,* 54 Tex. L. Rev. 693 (1976), cited for this point in Kesavan & Paulsen, *Drafting History, supra* note 98, at 1135 n. 74. Akhil Amar adopts this approach in the main. Amar, America's Constitution, *supra* note 35.

183. Kesavan & Paulsen, *Drafting History, supra* note 98, at 1125.

184. Michael Perry has his own idiosyncratic position. He insists that originalism is the appropriate approach to the task of "interpreting" the Constitution where it supplies a text to work with, but he offers a different approach for "specifying" constitutional meaning where we are given only "indeterminate constitutional norms or directives *represented* by the constitutional text."

Michael J. Perry, The Constitution in the Courts: Law or Politics? 28 (1994); emphasis added.

185. Mark V. Tushnet, *Following the Rules Laid Down: A Critique of Interpretivism and Neutral Principles,* 96 Harv. L. Rev. 781, 798 (1983); hereafter cited as *Following the Rules.*

186. See Stack, *Divergence, supra* note 117, at 10 (explaining that this approach is textualist in that it hopes to identify the objective meaning of words and also originalist in that it seeks that meaning at the time the text was adopted). One can imagine an argument that we should search for constitutional meaning exclusively in the intentions of those who wrote and ratified the Constitution. Thus what we want to get at (and to be governed by) is not so much *what* the framers did, but *why.* This on the theory that the text is not the Constitution, but only evidence of the thinking behind the text—which *is.* Larry Simon calls this approach "classical originalism." Simon, *Authority of the Framers, supra* note 62, at 1483 & n.10. Serious people sometimes talk as though this is what they think. Cf. Ely, Democracy and Distrust, *supra* note 25, at 16 (noting the argument that the text of the Constitution is the best evidence of the framers' thinking). But originalists typically regard the document as the Constitution, whose proper interpretation is informed by historical materials.

187. See, for example, *Saenz v. Roe,* 526 U.S. 489, 528 (1999) (Thomas, J., dissenting) (complaining that the majority's interpretation of the Privileges or Immunities Clause had departed from what the "framers" of that clause "thought that it meant" in circumstances with which they were familiar). See also Raoul Berger, Government by Judiciary: The Transformation of the Fourteenth Amendment 4, 18–23 (2d ed. 1997).

188. Critics dismiss the idea of recovering the results that the authors of a text would have reached in particular cases on the conventional ground that a rule of law must have some broader field of operation, else it would not be a rule at all. See Schauer, *Constitutional Language, supra* note 46, at 806.

189. 541 U.S. 36 (2004).

190. *Id.* at 61–62.

191. *Id.* at 69–76 (Rehnquist, C. J., concurring in the judgment; joined by O'Connor, J.).

192. See notes 49–75 and accompanying text.

193. Cf. Jaroslav Pelikan, Interpreting the Bible and the Constitution (2004) (connecting biblical exegesis and constitutional interpretation).

194. John P. Roche, *The Founding Fathers: A Reform Caucus in Action,* 55 Am. Pol. Sci. Rev. 799, 816 (1961), reprinted in Hall, *supra* note 50, at 490, 507.

195. See Dworkin, *Forum, supra* note 92, at 482–83.

196. See Brest, *Quest, supra* note 171, at 214.

197. See, for example, Whittington, Interpretation, *supra* note 10, at 35–36. Robert Bork, too, originally took this view, but has since abandoned it. Robert H. Bork, The Tempting of America 144 (1990).

198. This is true of Akhil Amar in the main. See Amar, America's Constitution, *supra* note 35.

199. See Brest, *Quest, supra* note 171, at 214–15.

200. Dorf, *Integrating, supra* note 49, at 1801; emphasis in original.

201. Kesavan & Paulsen, *Drafting History, supra* note 98, at 1118–19.

202. See notes 117–20 and accompanying text.

203. Dworkin, *Forum, supra* note 92, at 480, 483–85.

204. Tushnet, *Following, supra* note 185, at 800.

205. Professor Whittington acknowledges the difficulties in sorting intentions (which he thinks should count in the originalist analysis) from motivations and expectations (which he thinks should not). Whittington, Interpretation, *supra* note 10, at 178. The arguments in this and surrounding paragraphs are really pretty simple, drawing very little from sophisticated modern theories of language. Whittington contends that the insights of structuralism, poststructuralism, and hermeneutics do not demolish originalism (*id.* at 47–109). His argument is careful but ultimately dissatisfying. Originalism's beef is not with fancy theory, but with common sense.

206. Dworkin, *Forum, supra* note 92, at 480–81.

207. Rakove, Original Meanings, *supra* note 58, at 6.

208. Roche, *Founding Fathers, supra* note 194, at 815; emphasis in original.

209. *Id.* It is hard to finesse these problems by proposing that when the evidence is insufficient, the Court can uphold whatever governmental action is under attack for want of any justifiable (i.e., originalist) basis for reading the Constitution to bar it. See Whittington, Interpretation, *supra* note 10, at 89. That is not what happens. Justices who are among the Court's most committed originalists may vote to uphold statutes restricting individual liberty on the ground that the Constitution as originally understood supplies no warrant for upsetting modern legislative judgments. Yet they are perfectly prepared, in the next breath, to invalidate social welfare legislation without benefit of any serious originalist justification.

210. Martin S. Flaherty, *History "Lite" in Modern American Constitutionalism,* 95 Colum. L. Rev. 523, 526 (1995).

211. See Alfred H. Kelly, *Clio and the Court: An Illicit Love Affair,* 1965 Sup. Ct. Rev. 119, 155–58; Laura Kalman, *Border Patrol: Reflections on the Turn to History in Legal Scholarship,* 66 Fordham L. Rev. 87, 114–15 (1997) (citing many others on the same point).

212. The Records of the Federal Convention of 1787 (Farrand ed. 1987); see Kesavan & Paulsen, *Drafting History, supra* note 98, at 1121–24, 1191–96.

213. James Madison to William Eustis, July 6, 1819, vol. 3, Letters and Other Writings of James Madison (Philadelphia, 1865) 140, quoted in Rakove, Original Meanings, *supra* note 58, at 3. Accord Dorf, *Integrating, supra* note 49, at 1800 (questioning whether Madison's notes are in any way "authoritative").

214. Others contend that Madison would have had no occasion to make serious changes. See Kesavan & Pauslen, *Drafting History, supra* note 98, at 1116–17 (reporting commentators' views on the value of Madison's notes); *id.* at 1191–96 (describing the work done by Crosskey, Farrand, and James Hutson).

215. Arnold A. Rogow, *The Federal Convention: Madison and Yates,* 60 Am. Hist. Rev. 323–35 (Jan. 1955), reprinted in Hall, *supra* note 50, at 508.

216. Rakove, Original Meanings, *supra* note 58, at 4–7.

217. See Kesavan & Paulsen, *Drafting History, supra* note 98, at 1114.

218. For helpful accounts, see Ratifying the Constitution (Gillespie & Lienesch eds. 1989).

219. See, for example, Amar, America's Constitution, *supra* note 35, at 42–53; Kesavan & Paulsen, *Drafting History, supra* note 98, at 1150–59. See also Ackerman, We the People, *supra* note 20, at 165–99.

220. See, for example, *Printz v. United States,* 521 U.S. 898, 971 (1997) (Souter, J., dissenting) (reporting that he rested his vote on what he regarded as the best reading of Hamilton's No. 27). See Melvyn R. Durchslag, *The Supreme Court and the Federalist Papers: Is There Less Here Than Meets the Eye?* 14 Wm. & Mary Bill Rts. J. 243 (2005) (counting and organizing the Court's citations to the Federalist Papers).

221. William N. Eskridge, *Should the Supreme Court Read "The Federalist" but Not Statutory Legislative History?* 66 Geo. Wash. L. Rev. 1301, 1309 (1998); hereafter cited as *"Federalist."* Cf. Kesavan & Paulsen, *Drafting History, supra* note 98, at 1158 (taking this point). See generally Kramer, *Madison's Audience, supra* note 180.

222. Ira C. Lupu, *Time, the Supreme Court, and the Federalist,* 66 Geo. Wash. L. Rev. 1324, 1327 (1998).

223. John F. Manning, *Textualism and the Role of "The Federalist" in Constitutional Adjudication,* 66 Geo. Wash. L. Rev. 1337, 1348 (1998); hereafter cited as *Role of "The Federalist."*

224. Roche, *Founding Fathers, supra* note 194, at 804. Cf. John J. Gibbons, *The Eleventh Amendment and State Sovereign Immunity: A Reinterpretation,* 83 Colum. L. Rev. 1889, 1910–12 (1983) (contending that Hamilton used "Federalist No. 81" to *obfuscate* the effect of Article III on state sovereign immunity).

225. See Eskridge, *"Federalist," supra* note 221, at 1309 (describing what would be required to study the Federalist Papers in their historical context).

226. See Kramer, *History, supra* note 9, at 390–91 (arguing that legal historians should read more secondary materials than they do in order to gain context and perspective). John Manning, a strong proponent of originalism, argues only that the Federalist Papers can fairly be considered part of a much richer mix of probative materials. Manning, *Role of "The Federalist," supra* note 223, at 1360.

227. *Crawford,* 541 U.S. at 43 (arguing that English common law supplied the "founding generation's immediate source of the [confrontation] concept"); cf. text

accompanying notes 33–34. See also *Apprendi v. New Jersey*, 530 U.S. 466 (2000) (relying on common law practice to fill in the meaning of the right to trial by jury).

228. 494 U.S. 259, 266–67 (1990).

229. See *Printz*, 521 U.S. at 907–8.

230. Jack N. Rakove, *Once More into the Judicial Breach*, 72 Geo. Wash. L. Rev. 381, 381–82 (2003).

231. Brest, *Quest, supra* note 171, at 215–17.

232. H. Jefferson Powell, *The Original Understanding of Original Intent*, 98 Harv. L. Rev. 885 (1985). Peter Smith argues that proponents of the Constitution expected that questions about the new federal structure would be resolved through adjudication in the Supreme Court. Smith critiques the modern Court's failure to take early decisions by the Marshall Court as evidence of the original understanding of federal legislative power. Peter J. Smith, *The Marshall Court and the Originalist's Dilemma*, 90 Minn. L. Rev. 612 (2006).

233. Whittington, Interpretation, *supra* note 10, at 181–82.

234. Brest, *Quest, supra* note 171, at 222.

235. Dworkin, *Forum, supra* note 92, at 477 (explaining that we cannot "discover" the "intention of the Framers" as a matter of historical fact and can only "invent" an intention to satisfy modern needs and desires).

236. Rakove, Original Meanings, *supra* note 58, at 6.

237. Bork, Tempting, *supra* note 197, at 144. In his initial article, Bork insisted on identifying (whenever possible) the meaning the "framers" actually "intended." Robert H. Bork, *Neutral Principles and Some First Amendment Problems*, 47 Ind. L. J. 1, 17 (1971). See O'Neill, Originalism, *supra* note 178, at 161–70 (describing the evolution of Bork's thinking).

238. Gary Lawson and Guy Seidman date this form of originalism from a speech Scalia gave a few months before he joined the Supreme Court. Gary Lawson & Guy Seidman, *Originalism as a Legal Enterprise*, 23 Const. Commentary 47, 48 n.10 (2006). See also Cass R. Sunstein, *Justice Scalia's Democratic Formalism*, 107 Yale L. J. 529, 537 (1997), hereafter cited as *Democratic Formalism;* Mark D. Greenberg & Harry Litman, *The Meaning of Original Meaning*, 86 Gtn. L. J. 569, 583 (1998). Thus, by Scalia's account, any practice generally accepted at the time of adoption must necessarily be constitutional (*id.* at 572). See chapter 3, note 144 and accompanying text.

239. See Barnett, *Originalism, supra* note 52, at 105; Gary Lawson, *On Reading Recipes . . . and Constitutions*, 85 Gtn. L. J. 1823, 1826–35 (1997); Kesavan & Paulsen, *Drafting History, supra* note 98, at 1118, 1132–33. Michael Perry also takes this approach in the context in which he employs originalism at all, though he adds bells and whistles that others would not necessarily include in the analysis. Perry, Law or Politics? *supra* note 184, at 32–38.

240. Jed Rubenfeld, *The Moment and the Millennium*, 66 Geo. Wash. L. Rev. 1085, 1103 (1998). But see Kesavan & Paulsen, *Drafting History, supra* note 98

(arguing that the "secret" drafting history of the Constitution and even entirely private communications can help identify this kind of original meaning); Whittington, Interpretation, *supra* note 10, at 35 (insisting that interpretation must rest on understandings "made public" at the time).

241. *Crawford*, 541 U.S. at 5. See note 189 and accompanying text. But cf. Aviam Soifer, *Courting Anarchy*, 82 B. U. L. Rev. 699, 727 (2002) (recalling that the editors of Black's caution that their work should be at most a point of departure).

242. See Kesavan & Paulsen, *Drafting History, supra* note 98, at 1162.

243. Kramer, *History, supra* note 9, at 407. See also Rubenfeld, Freedom, *supra* note 19, at 52–54 (critiquing Robert Bork for failing to acknowledge that this version of originalism does not explain why choices made by a majority in 1787 are entitled to our loyalty today).

244. See, for example, Roche, *Founding Fathers, supra* note 194, providing this summary: Political theorists from Aristotle to Montesquieu had recognized that government performed three functions: making law in the first instance, interpreting that law, and administering it. Most of the early state constitutions specified in the most general way that those functions should be kept separate from each other. Yet the idea that different functions should be performed by different arms of government was another thing entirely, not well developed at all. In England, Coke insisted that the king was subject (at least on occasion) to the judgments of the courts staffed by royal judges. But Coke explained that the chief court, in turn, was the High "Court" of Parliament, which had evolved from the ancient *curia regis* and now doubled as an emergent legislature. Blackstone took a similar view. Borrowing from Locke, he regarded law as generally prospective in nature, making policy for the future. Judges, he explained, operated retrospectively—resolving disputes arising under preexisting legal standards. Nevertheless, both Coke and Blackstone assumed that since judges were charged only to bring the law made by Parliament to bear in individual cases, they could be by-passed. Parliament was free to impose its will more directly by deciding cases itself. In the American states, too, early local assemblies went under the label "courts" and routinely disposed of disputes via legislative bills, without resort to separately designated judicial tribunals. Accordingly, when the delegates began their work, they had no tangible tradition of the separation of powers on which to draw. In addition to Blackstone, they had John Adams's recently published treatise entitled "Defense of the Constitution." That work elaborated on Montesquieu and pressed the separation of powers as an important element of effective government. Still, the content of the idea remained vague and scarcely laid the groundwork for the adoption of any particular distribution of authority among the branches of the new national government.

245. See Philip Hamburger, *Law and Judicial Duty,* 72 Geo. Wash. L. Rev. 1 (2003).

246. See Steven G. Calabresi, *A Government of Limited and Enumerated Powers: In Defense of United States v. Lopez*, 94 Mich. L. Rev. 752 (1995).

247. As Frank Strong once put it, "Nothing is clearer than that it was a federalism the Founders devised, midway between confederation and nationalism." Frank R. Strong, Judicial Function in Constitutional Limitation of Governmental Power 41 (1997).

248. Madison proposed a substitute system that would have centralized power in what Professor Roche described as "breathtaking" proportions: the new Congress should be given authority to veto legislation enacted by state assemblies. Roche, *Founding Fathers, supra* note 194, at 804.

249. *Id.* at 814. Peter Smith argues that the Court's ideas about federalism actually comport with the views of the antifederalist opponents of the Constitution. Peter J. Smith, *Sources of Federalism: An Empirical Analysis of the Court's Quest for Original Meaning*, 52 UCLA L. Rev. 217 (2004).

250. 527 U.S. 706 (1999).

251. *United States v. Verdugo-Urquidez*, 494 U.S. 259, 266 (1990); see text accompanying notes 156–60.

252. *Verdugo-Urquidez*, 494 U.S. at 266.

253. *Crawford v. Washington*, 541 U.S. 36 (2004); see text accompanying notes 189–91.

254. See Stephanos Bibas, *Originalism and Formalism in Criminal Procedure: The Triumph of Justice Scalia, the Unlikely Friend of Criminal Defendants*, 94 Gtn. L. J. 183 (2005).

255. 126 S.Ct. 1515 (2006).

256. *Id.* at 1539 (Roberts, C. J., dissenting). See generally Tracey Maclin, *Let Sleeping Dogs Lie: Why the Supreme Court Should Leave Fourth Amendment History Unabridged*, 82 B. U. L. Rev. 895 (2002) (offering a thoroughgoing critique of the Court's references to original understanding in Fourth Amendment cases).

257. 539 U.S. 558 (2003).

258. *Id.* at 579.

259. See Thomas W. Merrill, *Bork v. Burke*, 19 Harv. J. L. & Pub. Policy 509, 518 (1995).

260. See Brest, *Quest, supra* note 171; Fallon, Implementing, *supra* note 12; Friedman & Smith, *Sedimentary Constitution, supra* note 173; Monaghan, *Stare Decisis, supra* note 8; Sandalow, *Constitutional Interpretation, supra* note 172.

261. Sylvia Snowiss, *The Marbury of 1803 and the Modern Marbury*, 20 Const. Commentary 231, 250–51 (2003); see text accompanying notes 100–101.

262. 347 U.S. 483 (1954).

263. Robert Bork and Michael McConnell have tried to supply one. Bork, Tempting, *supra* note 197, at 75–84; Michael M. McConnell, *Originalism and the Desegregation Decisions*, 81 Va. L. Rev. 947 (1995). But they manage the exercise only by fixing the supposed intentions or purposes of the framers at such

a lofty level of generality as to attenuate any genuine link between the framers and the Court's result. Rubenfeld, Freedom, *supra* note 19, at 179.

264. Scalia, *Common-Law Courts, supra* note 95, at 138–39. In this, Justice Scalia implicitly acknowledges the circularity of his own position. Originalism is supposed to produce consistency over time, but it must be modified occasionally to accommodate stare decisis, which, in turn, is supposed to produce consistency. See Daniel A. Farber, *The Rule of Law and the Law of Precedents*, 90 Minn. L. Rev. 1173 (2006). Cf. Thomas W. Merrill, *Originalism, Stare Decisis and the Promotion of Judicial Restraint*, 22 Const. Commentary 271 (2005) (ticking off the ways that adhering to precedent fosters judicial restraint).

265. Sunstein, *Democratic Formalism, supra* note 238, at 560.

266. Monaghan, *Stare Decisis, supra* note 8, at 723–24; Strauss, *Theory, supra* note 10, at 584. Some academics do insist that originalism must prevail over precedent. See, for example, Randy Barnett, *Trumping Precedent With Original Meaning: Not as Radical as It Sounds*, 22 Const. Commentary 257 (2005); *Gary Lawson, The Constitutional Case Against Precedent*, 17 Harv. J. L. & Pub. Pol. 23 (1994).

Chapter Two

1. See, for example, David A. Strauss, *Common Law, Common Ground, and Jefferson's Principle*, 112 Yale L. J. 1716, 1716 (2003). On the general acceptance of judicial decisions and doctrine as the primary content of constitutional law, see Daniel A. Farber & Suzanna Sherry, Seeking Certainty: The Misguided Quest for Constitutional Foundations 154 (2002); Charles Fried, Saying What the Law Is: The Constitution in the Supreme Court 187 (2004), hereafter cited as Saying; Cass R. Sunstein, One Case at a Time 1–45 (1999); Harry H. Wellington, Interpreting the Constitution: The Supreme Court and the Process of Adjudication 77–95 (1990); Frank I. Michelman, *Constancy to an Ideal Object*, 56 N. Y. U. L. Rev. 406, 410 (1981); Suzanna Sherry, *Hard Cases Make Good Judges*, 99 Nw. U. L. Rev. 3 (2004); David A. Strauss, *Common Law Constitutional Interpretation*, 63 U. Chi. L. Rev. 877 (1996).

2. See Henry P. Monaghan, *The Constitution of the United States and American Constitutional Law*, in Constitutional Justice under Old Constitutions 175 (Smith ed. 1995); cf. John Hart Ely, *Another Such Victory: Constitutional Theory and Practice in a World Where Courts Are No Different from Legislatures*, 77 Va. L. Rev. 833 (1991) (charging "liberal" academics with failing to acknowledge any difference between judges and elected officials); hereafter cited as *Another Victory*.

3. Morton Horwitz has explained that, before the Revolution, judges and legislatures were understood to be responsible for two different forms of law, but that the distinction broke down in the nineteenth century when courts came

to understand that they, too, forge general legal rules in service of the public interest. Morton J. Horwitz, *The Emergence of an Instrumental Conception of American Law, 1780–1820,* in vol. 5 of Perspectives in American History 309 (Fleming & Bailyn eds. 1971); hereafter cited as *Emergence.*

4. See chapter 4, notes 137–206 and accompanying text.

5. "Federalist No. 78" (declaring that the judiciary has "neither Force nor Will, but merely judgment"). Justice Scalia was dead wrong when he said, "Laws promulgated by the Legislative Branch can be inconsistent, illogical, and ad hoc; law pronounced by the courts must be principled, rational, and based on reasoned distinctions." *Vieth v. Jubelirer,* 541 U.S. 267, 278 (2004).

6. Roscoe Pound, *Courts and Legislation,* 7 Am. Pol. Sci. Rev. 361, 382 (1913); hereafter cited as *Courts.*

7. Fried, Saying, *supra* note 1, at 117 (specifically addressing governmental restrictions on free expression).

8. Literary theorists actively debate the character and nuances of interpretive conventions in a sophisticated literature that reaches beyond my purposes here. For analogues in legal academic commentaries, see, for example, Owen M. Fiss, *Objectivity and Interpretation,* 34 Stan. L. Rev. 739 (1982); Stanley Fish, *Fish v. Fiss,* 36 Stan. L. Rev. 1325 (1984); see also Owen M. Fiss, *Conventionalism,* 58 So. Calif. L. Rev. 177 (1985). For more complete accounts of the institutional practices that influence decision making in the Supreme Court, see Forrest Maltzman, James F. Spriggs Jr. & Paul J. Wahlbeck, Crafting Law on the Supreme Court: The Collegial Game (2000); Barry Friedman, *The Politics of Judicial Review,* 84 Tex. L. Rev. 257 (2005).

9. Of course, when the Court's analysis is controversial, its detractors are inclined to say that the justices have not analyzed at all but have given vent to their own views or the views of peculiarly influential groups. Then there are instances in which the Court attracts similar charges by departing dramatically from ordinary conventions of practice. The Court's extraordinary treatment of *Bush v. Gore,* 531 U.S. 98 (2000), may be the chief example of this last. Cf. Ward Farnsworth, *"To Do a Great Right, Do a Little Wrong": A User's Guide to Judicial Lawlessness,* 86 Minn. L. Rev. 227 (2001) (critiquing the argument that the Court may have been justified in acting as it did even assuming that its decision was lawless).

10. See Henry P. Monaghan, *Stare Decisis and Constitutional Adjudication,* 88 Colum. L. Rev. 723 (1988). For an empirical study of the Court's practice of reshaping precedents to conform to current preferences, see Thomas G. Hansford & James F. Spriggs II, The Politics of Precedent on the U.S. Supreme Court (2006).

11. See Charles Fried, *Constitutional Doctrine,* 107 Harv. L. Rev. 1140, 1141–42 (1994). My jump from abstract principles to doctrine is crude by serious philosophical standards. See Frederick Schauer, Playing by the Rules: A

Philosophical Examination of Rule-Based Decision-Making in Law and in Life 12–16 (1991) (describing these common terms while contending that they are insufficiently rigorous). Professor Roosevelt articulates the conventional understanding that the point of doctrine is to "mediate" between "the words of the Constitution and specified judicial decisions." Kermit Roosevelt III, The Myth of Judicial Activism: Making Sense of Supreme Court Decisions 19 (2006). Professor Lupu identifies three layers—"first premises" operating at the highest level of abstraction, "intermediate premises" connecting "basic building-block assumptions" to "adjudicative standards," and then "doctrines, standards, and constitutional rules from which constitutional decisions can be made and defended." Ira C. Lupu, *Constitutional Theory and the Search for the Workable Premise,* 8 U. Dayton L. Rev. 579, 618–20 (1983). Professor Goldstein has explained that, because the Constitution itself is imprecise, the Court is obliged to supply more concrete rules in the form of doctrine. Joseph Goldstein, The Intelligible Constitution: The Supreme Court's Obligation to Maintain the Constitution as Something We the People Can Understand 14–16 (1992). Professor Nagel contends that the Court uses doctrine to bridge the gap between "conceptualism" and "fact-responsivness" and thus to occupy a "middle ground" between the extreme forms of formalism and realism, neither of which is attractive. Robert F. Nagel, *The Formulaic Constitution,* 84 Mich. L. Rev. 165, 203 (1985); hereafter cited as *Formulaic Constitution.* The nature of doctrine figures significantly in ongoing debates about the difference, if any, between true constitutional meaning and judicial decisions about the Constitution. See Mitchell N. Berman, *Constitutional Decision Rules,* 90 Va. L. Rev. 1 (2004); chapter 1, notes 13–14 and accompanying text.

12. See, for example, Nagel, *Formulaic Constitution, supra* note 11, at 196–97.

13. Richard H. Fallon Jr., Implementing the Constitution 77–79 (2001); see also Nagel, *Formulaic Constitution, supra* note 11, at 166–69.

14. See William W. Fisher III, *Texts and Contexts: The Application to American Legal History of the Methodologies of Intellectual History,* 49 Stan. L. Rev. 1065 (1997).

15. 198 U.S. 45 (1905).

16. See Lloyd L. Weinreb, Oedipus at Fenway Park: What Rights Are and Why There Are Any 1, 162 (1994) (explaining that a claim that the handicapped have rights is actually a claim that "there *ought* to be a law establishing the legal right in question"; emphasis in original).

17. Lloyd L. Weinreb, *A Secular Theory of Natural Law,* 72 Fordham L. Rev. 2287, 2290 (2004), hereafter cited as *Secular Theory;* see also Lloyd L. Weinreb, Natural Law and Justice 2 (1987) (explaining that "the terrain of natural law is much reduced" apart from Catholic dogma and a branch of jurisprudence).

18. Stephen M. Feldman, American Legal Thought from Premodernism to Postmodernism 49 (2000); emphasis added.

19. Weinreb, *Secular Theory, supra* note 17, at 2288. Professor Weinreb concedes that "[f]ull-blown secular natural law has had little staying power and for the present has little influence" (*id.* at 2288). Yet he argues that there is a place for natural-rights thinking in modern philosophy and, by means of a sophisticated analysis, develops a short list of "human rights" that people have simply because they are responsible human beings. There is surely something to that. Few of us would be bold (or reckless) enough flatly to deny *any* floor beneath which the treatment of human beings cannot dip. And many of us hope that the world will one day recognize basic dignities that differentiate human beings from stones, plants, and animals.

20. See chapter 1, notes 26–27, 49–87 and accompanying text.

21. Randy Barnett, Restoring the Lost Constitution: The Presumption of Liberty 58 (2004); hereafter cited as Restoring.

22. See William M. Wiecek, The Lost World of Classical Legal Thought: Law and Ideology in America, 1886–1937 (1998); Suzanna Sherry, *The Founders' Unwritten Constitution,* 54 U. Chi. L. Rev. 1127 (1987); Thomas C. Grey, *Do We Have an Unwritten Constitution?* 27 Stan. L. Rev. 703 (1975); cf. Philip A. Hamburger, *Natural Rights, Natural Law, and American Constitutionalism,* 102 Yale L. J. 907 (1993) (ranging more broadly through various sources to identify and characterize the natural rights/natural law ideas abroad in the eighteenth century). Historians attribute some of the explanation to Blackstone's influence, particularly with regard to the "right of property." William Blackstone, Commentaries 2 (1765). It also seems likely that early Americans were driven to the idea of a higher law in order to challenge Parliament's assertion of absolute power to decide what rights the colonists would have. Joyce Appleby, *The Americans' Higher-Law Thinking behind Higher Lawmaking,* 108 Yale L. J. 1995, 1996 (1996).

23. Professor Appleby argues that Jefferson may have meant to flag Lockean natural rights in this passage, but speculates that his audience may have taken a variety of meanings from it. Appleby, *Higher Lawmaking, supra* note 22, at 1997.

24. *Ogden v. Saunders,* 25 U.S. 213, 345 (1827) (dissenting opinion), cited in James W. Ely Jr., *The Protection of Contractual Rights: A Tale of Two Constitutional Provisions,* 1 N. Y. U. J. L. & Liberty 370, 383 (2005).

25. 3 U.S. (3 Dall.) 386 (1798).

26. This is the conventional reading, but it has been questioned. By some accounts, Chase only meant that precursor sources should be consulted when the Court interpreted the Constitution. See, for example, Paul W. Kahn, *Reason and Will in the Origins of American Constitutionalism,* 98 Yale L. J. 449, 477–79 (1989). Of course, Justice Iredell's opinion in *Calder* contradicted the idea that the Court could enforce "natural justice" apart from the Constitution itself. *Calder,* 3 U.S. at 398 (Iredell, J.).

27. Richard A. Epstein, Bargaining With the State 25–38 (1993), hereafter cited as Bargaining; Richard A. Epstein, Takings: Private Property and the

Power of Eminent Domain 9 (1985), hereafter cited as Takings. In cases of conflicting claims, the "first possessor" prevailed. Epstein, Takings, *supra*, at 10. Epstein ascribes this understanding to the common law, but he also defends it on independent economic policy grounds. See also Richard A. Epstein, Principles for a Free Society: Reconciling Individual Liberty with the Common Good (1998). But see Myrl L. Duncan, *Property as a Public Conversation, Not a Lockean Soliloquy: A Role for Intellectual and Legal History in Takings Analysis*, 26 Envt'l L. 1095 (1996) (contending that Locke allowed for considerably more governmental regulation of property in the interest of the broader society).

    28. See Edward S. Corwin, *The Doctrine of Due Process of Law before the Civil War*, 24 Harv. L. Rev. 366, 373–74 (1910). This is the understanding generally ascribed to the New York Court of Appeals in *Wynehamer v. People*, 13 N.Y. 378 (1856). See Bernard H. Siegan, Economic Liberties and the Constitution 96 (2d ed. 2006). Most cases on substantive due process have to do with governmental action said to interfere with liberty rather than property. The early Court may not have distinguished much between the two (see note 39). Professor Merrill has suggested that the definition of property has always been and should continue to be expansive, such that it is unnecessary now to separate property from liberty for these purposes. See Thomas W. Merrill, *The Landscape of Constitutional Property*, 86 Va. L. Rev. 885, 958–59 (2000).

    29. See, for example, Wiecek, Law and Ideology, *supra* note 22, at 44–49; Edward A. Purcell Jr., The Crisis of Democratic Theory: Scientific Naturalism and the Problem of Value 74 (1973); hereafter cited as Crisis.

    30. *Commonwealth v. Alger*, 7 Cushing 53, 85 (Mass. 1851); emphasis added. Professor Levy's great book examines *Alger* and other decisions by Shaw. See Leonard Levy, The Law of the Commonwealth and Chief Justice Shaw 229–65 (1957). Professor Novak contends that Shaw's work was important but not unprecedented—given the many similar decisions by other courts at the time. William J. Novak, The People's Welfare: Law and Regulation in Nineteenth Century America 21 (1996); hereafter cited as People's Welfare.

    31. *Losee v. Buchanan*, 51 N.Y. 476, 485 (1873), quoted in Wiecek, Law and Ideology, *supra* note 22, at 45.

    32. *Louis Pizitz Dry Goods Co. v. Yeldell*, 274 U.S. 112 (1927).

    33. *Id.* at 116. See also *Noble State Bank v. Haskell*, 291 U.S. 104, 111 (1911) (Holmes, J.) (explaining that legislatures were free to prohibit activities that had been permitted at common law). See David E. Bernstein, *Lochner's Legacy's Legacy*, 82 Tex. L. Rev. 1, 29–30 (2003) (citing *Yeldell*); hereafter cited as *Legacy*. The more familiar authority on this point is Charles Warren, vol. 2 of Supreme Court in United States History 741 (1926).

    34. See note 76 and accompanying text.

    35. 83 U.S. 36, 83 (1883) (Field, J., dissenting).

    36. *Id.* at 111.

37. 165 U.S. 578 (1897).

38. *Id.* at 589.

39. In *Slaughterhouse* and *Allgeyer,* Field and Peckham focused on liberty rather than property, even with respect to economic affairs. *Slaughterhouse,* 83 U.S. at 110–11 (Field, J., dissenting) (referring both to "liberty" and to "property"). See Herbert Hovenkamp, *The Political Economy of Substantive Due Process,* 40 Stan. L. Rev. 379, 400–401 (1988); C. Edwin Baker, *Property and Its Relation to Constitutionally Protected Liberty,* 134 U. Pa. L. Rev. 741 (1986). Barbara Fried explains that they thought property had to do with the "vertical relationships" between individuals and land or other "things" they owned, while liberty contemplated "horizontal relationships" between one individual and another. Barbara H. Fried, The Progressive Assault on Laissez Faire: Robert Hale and the First Law and Economics Movement 50 (1998). The prevailing syntax, then, placed general economic freedom under the heading of liberty, specifically "liberty of contract." To the extent that liberty of contract was thought to be prior to the Constitution, it could constitute a "right" independent of the Due Process Clauses. The convergence of liberty with independent, pre-constitutional rights remains a common theme among libertarians. Randy Barnett contends, for example, that the term *liberty* used in the Constitution was meant to be coextensive with preexisting natural rights; he himself thinks the better formulation is "liberty rights." Barnett, Restoring, *supra* note 21, at 4, 57.

40. Pound, *Courts, supra* note 6, at 374.

41. Historians debate whether the Court's attitude took a sharp turn in this direction at the outset of the Formalist Era and, if so, why. Compare Robert E. Cushman, *The Social and Economic Interpretation of the Fourteenth Amendment,* 20 Mich. L. Rev. 737 (1921) (arguing that the Court did alter its thinking and suggesting that a change in membership had something to do with it), with Stephen Griffin, American Constitutionalism (1998) (contending that the Court elaborated on ideas reflected in prior decisions). Cf. *Lincoln Fed. Labor Union v. Northwestern Iron & Metal Co.,* 335 U.S. 525, 529 (1949) (depicting decisions in the early 1900s as a departure from the past and post-1934 decisions as a return to an older wisdom). Professor Collins has shown that, at least in part, the Court identified a constitutional basis for limits previously articulated as features of federal "general" common law. If shift there was, in his view, it was largely a shift from a nonconstitutional to a constitutional basis for judicial decisions. Michael G. Collins, *October Term, 1896—Embracing Due Process,* 45 Am. J. Legal Hist. 71 (2001).

42. *Frisbie v. United States,* 157 U.S. 160, 165 (1895), quoted in David E. Bernstein, *Lochner Era Revisionism, Revised: Lochner and the Origins of Fundamental Rights Constitutionalism,* 92 Gtn. L. J. 1, 43 (2003); hereafter cited as *Revisionism.*

43. 262 U.S. 390 (1923).

44. 268 U.S. 510 (1925).

45. Bernstein, *Revisionism, supra* note 42, at 45.

46. See Thomas C. Grey, *Judicial Review and Legal Pragmatism,* 38 Wake Forest L. Rev. 473 (2003); hereafter cited as *Pragmatism.* Judge Posner defines *formalism* as "the use of deductive logic to derive the outcome of a case from premises accepted as authoritative." Richard A. Posner, *Legal Formalism, Legal Realism, and the Interpretation of Statutes and the Constitution,* 37 Case W. Res. L. Rev. 179, 180 (1987). Professor Schaur does not disagree fundamentally, but emphasizes a preference for rules rather than principles. See Frederick Schauer, *Formalism,* 97 Yale L. J. 509, 511 (1988); hereafter cited as *Formalism.* There is much more to the system of beliefs ascribed to classical legal thought. For rich accounts, see Morton J. Horwitz, The Transformation of American Law, 1870–1960: The Crisis of Legal Orthodoxy 9–31 (1992), hereafter cited as Transformation; Purcell, Crisis, *supra* note 29, at 15–73; Wiecek, Law and Ideology, *supra* note 22, at 3–174.

47. 198 U.S. 45 (1905).

48. Descriptions of the litigation in *Lochner* are plentiful. I rely chiefly on Wiecek, Law and Ideology, *supra* note 22, at 152–54; Owen M. Fiss, Troubled Beginnings of the Modern State, 1888–1910, 46–49 (1993); Cass R. Sunstein, *Lochner's Legacy,* 87 Colum. L. Rev. 873 (1987), hereafter cited as *Legacy;* and David E. Bernstein, *The Story of Lochner v. New York: Impediment to the Growth of the Regulatory State,* in Constitutional Law Stories 325–57 (Dorf ed. 2004); hereafter cited as *Story.*

49. *Lochner,* 198 U.S. at 48. The argument was not only that the work-hour provision applied to bakeries but not to other businesses. It was that the ten-hour limit chiefly affected comparatively large, unionized bakeries situated in factories (and typically employing German immigrants) but not small non-unionized and family businesses operating in tenement buildings (and employing workers from other ethnic groups, particularly the French). Bernstein, *Story, supra* note 48, at 326–31.

50. *Lochner,* 198 U.S. at 48–49 (referring to the arguments made by Lochner's attorneys).

51. *Id.* at 53, 56.

52. Fred Schauer contends that the formalism we associate with Peckham's opinion lies in his equation of "liberty" with "unrestricted contracting." Schauer, *Formalism, supra* note 46, at 511–12. Cf. David A. Strauss, *Why Was Lochner Wrong?* 70 U. Chi. L. Rev. 373, 386 (2003) (arguing that the Court's mistake in *Lochner* was its attempt to vindicate "freedom of contract" without confronting competing values that a legislature might sensibly identify).

53. O. W. Holmes, *Natural Law,* 32 Harv. L. Rev. 40, 41 (1918).

54. *Lochner,* 198 U.S. at 76 (Holmes, J., dissenting).

55. Roscoe Pound, *Mechanical Jurisprudence,* 8 Colum. L. Rev. 605 (1908).

56. Fried, Progressive Assault, *supra* note 39, at 33.

57. Cass R. Sunstein, After the Rights Revolution: Reconceiving the Regulatory State 18 (1990); hereafter cited as Rights Revolution.

58. See generally Fried, Progressive Assault, *supra* note 39 (focusing on Robert Hale); Horwitz, Transformation, *supra* note 46, at 145–67 (crediting in particular Wesley Hohfeld, John R. Commons, and Morris Cohen, as well as Hale); Cass R. Sunstein, The Second Bill of Rights: FDR's Unfinished Revolution and Why We Need It More Than Ever 20–28 (2004).

59. *West Coast Hotel v. Parrish,* 300 U.S. 379 (1937).

60. See chapter 3, notes 75–96 and accompanying text; chapter 4, notes 98–114 and accompanying text.

61. *Hearings before the Senate Judiciary Committee,* 100th Cong., 1st sess. 101 (1987), cited in Ely, *Another Victory, supra* note 2, at 847–48.

62. *Hearings before the Senate Judiciary Committee,* 102nd Cong., 1st sess. 1229–33 (1991). Senator Biden was at pains to distinguish his views on natural law from the position he understood Judge Thomas to adopt. Cf. Joseph R. Biden Jr., *Law and Natural Law: Questions for Judge Thomas,* Wash. Post, Sept. 8, 1991, C1.

63. *Gompers v. United States,* 233 U.S. 604, 610 (1914).

64. See, for example, chapter 1, note 254 and accompanying text. Professor Vermeule propounds this strategic use of formalism in a wide variety of circumstances, including the elaboration of individual constitutional rights. See Adrian Vermeule, Judging Under Uncertainty: An Institutional Theory of Legal Interpretation 72–73 (2006).

65. See chapter 4, notes 102–9 and accompanying text.

66. Epstein, Takings, *supra* note 27, at 11, 118; Epstein, Bargaining, *supra* note 27, at 29.

67. See Amy Dru Stanley, From Bondage to Contract: Wage Labor, Marriage, and the Market in the Age of Slave Emancipation 13–16 (1998) (explaining that the Blackstonian conception of contract insisted that mutual agreement existed and defused any argument that contracts were unfair).

68. Sunstein, *Legacy, supra* note 48, at 874; Fiss, Modern State, *supra* note 48, at 6–49.

69. See notes 47–50 and accompanying text.

70. Justice Peckham accepted the state's argument that the statute barred employers from *permitting* bakers to work long hours only to prevent unscrupulous managers from bullying them into remaining on the line beyond ten hours and then claiming that they acted voluntarily.

71. Peckham acknowledged that in some circumstances workers might be "constrained by the rules laid down by proprietors in regard to labor." *Lochner,* 198 U.S. at 54. In a previous case, *Holden v. Hardy,* 169 U.S. 366 (1898), the Court had sustained a statute limiting the hours that coal miners could be employed. Yet Peckham insisted that the workers in *Holden* were subjected to the "peculiar conditions" of underground mining and, evidently for that reason, were not in a position to choose for themselves whether to work longer hours.

72. Sunstein, *Legacy, supra* note 48, at 873–83.

73. See Sunstein, Rights Revolution, *supra* note 57, at 20 (noting that the New Dealers who followed understood the Court in this way—and rejected the analysis).

74. See notes 32–33 and accompanying text.

75. Wiecek, Law and Ideology, *supra* note 22, at 158.

76. Horwitz, Transformation, *supra* note 46; Fried, Progressive Assault, *supra* note 39. Professor Pope has described the attempts of trade unions to establish the validity of this economic analysis both by litigation and by direct action. James Gray Pope, *Labor's Constitution of Freedom,* 106 Yale L. J. 941 (1997).

77. See Cass R. Sunstein, Free Markets and Social Justice 5 (1997).

78. Of course, this does not mean that government is responsible for all private activities in the different sense that those activities count as action by the government itself. It is easy enough to see how some progressive academicians reached that conclusion. Professor Fried notes that Robert Hale, one of the principal players in these events, later helped with the winning brief in *Shelley v. Kraemer,* 334 U.S. 1 (1948). Fried, Progressive Assault, *supra* note 39, at 88. See Horwitz, Transformation, *supra* note 46, at 207 (noting that the critique of classical thought mounted by Legal Realists could not be squared with the public/private distinction); Gary Peller & Mark Tushnet, *State Action and a New Birth of Freedom,* 92 Gtn. L. J. 779, 806–7 (2004) (suggesting that the Realists themselves may not have appreciated the tension between their assault on *Lochner* and the conventional state action doctrine). But that is not the way it works. If it were, private behavior would be subject to the restrictions the Constitution imposes on government. Race discrimination practiced by a private person, company, or organization would be ascribed to government and thus would very likely be unconstitutional. Government is implicated in private activities in very important and practical ways. But that governmental involvement alone does not transform private behavior into public action. Nor does government's responsibility for the social and economic status quo establish an affirmative constitutional duty to take action to correct injustice. See Robin West, *Response to State Action and a New Birth of Freedom,* 92 Gtn. L. J. 819 (2004). Constitutional law still recognizes the public/private distinction, reserving constitutional restraints for conduct that can be attributed to government in a much more graphic sense. See, for example, *Jackson v. Metropolitan Edison Co.,* 419 U.S. 345, 351–58 (1974) (explaining that a practice fashioned by a "governmentally protected monopoly" will be ascribed to the state only if state authorities put the state's "weight on the side of the . . . practice by ordering it").

79. Professor Wiecek has traced the movement away from classical legal thinking along numerous parallel tracks—economic, political, and academic. See Wiecek, Law and Ideology, *supra* note 22, at 175–217.

80. See Fried, Progressive Assault, *supra* note 39, at 109.

81. See Roscoe Pound, *Liberty of Contract,* 18 Yale L. J. 454 (1909).

82. 290 U.S. 398 (1934).

83. *Id.* at 442.

84. 300 U.S. 379 (1937); see text accompanying note 59.

85. Locke, Two Treatises 406, quoted in Barnett, Restoring, *supra* note 21, at 71.

86. See Epstein, Takings, *supra* note 27, at 7–16. See also Sunstein, Rights Revolution, *supra* note 57, at 19 (describing this line of argument). Randy Barnett has argued that the emergence of legislative authority to enact regulatory statutes improved on the common law administered by courts only inasmuch as legislatures could safeguard natural rights earlier, by preventing violations in the first place. Barnett, Restoring, *supra* note 21, at 328–33. In both instances, the end in view had to be the maintenance of preexisting, natural, individual rights. They and they alone provided the justification for governmental regulation.

87. Jennifer Nedelesky, Private Property and the Limits of American Constitutionalism: The Madisonian Framework and Its Legacy 19 (1990); hereafter cited as Private Property.

88. *Calder,* 3 U.S. at 388 (Chase, J.); emphasis in original.

89. *Id.* at 394. Professor Harris has argued that Chase cast his position as an interpretation of the 1789 document. He did not mean that the Constitution could not override the natural rights that formed its *raison d'etre* but that the document could not sensibly be interpreted that way. William F. Harris II, The Interpretable Constitution 135–38 (1992). But see William R. Casto, *James Iredell and the American Origins of Judicial Review,* 27 Conn. L. Rev. 329, 355 (1995) (arguing that Chase regarded the state of nature as a fiction and actually believed that the principles he discussed in *Calder* "had no standing as law until they were adopted by an appropriate human lawmaking institution").

90. Gordon S. Wood, The Creation of the American Republic, 1776–1787, 58 (1969). But see William P. Adams, The First American Constitutions: Republican Ideology and the Making of the State Constitutions in the Revolutionary Era 218–29 (1973) (describing the early struggle to develop an understanding of the public good that *did* transcend individual interests in the aggregate).

91. Horwitz, *Emergence, supra* note 3. Professor Novak cites numerous decisions to the same effect. Novak, People's Welfare, *supra* note 30, at 19–234. Novak contends that the nineteenth century saw "a deeply rooted American tradition of police and regulatory governance vital to social and economic development" (*id.* at 235). Yet he warns that it would be a mistake to regard that tradition as an early version of the New Deal (*id.* at 236–37). Stephen Feldman concurs that mid-nineteenth-century jurists were coming to think that law was not merely a means of perpetuating natural rights but could also be an instrument of social progress. Feldman, Legal Thought, *supra* note 18, at 76.

92. *Commonwealth v. Alger,* 7 Cushing 53, 85 (Mass. 1851).

93. *Id.* See note 30 and accompanying text.

94. See, for example, *Coppage v. Kansas,* 236 U.S. 1, 16 (1915); Thomas M. Cooley, A Treatise on the Constitutional Limitations Which Rest Upon the Legislative Power of the States of the American Union 1223 *et seq.* (Carrington ed. 1927); Westel W. Willoughby, The Constitutional Law of the United States 1765 *et seq.* (2d ed. 1929).

95. See D. Benjamin Barros, *The Police Power and the Takings Clause,* 58 U. Miami L. Rev. 471, 481–89 (2004). Cf. Stephen A. Siegel, *Historicism in Late Nineteenth-Century Constitutional Thought,* 1990 Wis. L. Rev. 1431 (arguing that Cooley, Tiedeman, and other prominent treatise writers thought that history revealed basic social values from which legislatures were not free to stray). Before the advent of regulatory legislation, the common law recognized that individual interests could be sacrificed to the larger societal welfare—but, perhaps, only in exigent circumstances. According to Chancellor Kent, it was a maxim of the common law that a "private mischief" should be "endured" rather than a "public inconvenience" suffered. James Kent, vol. 2 of Commentaries on American Law 523 (Gould ed. 1896). On this theory, Kent explained, a person who found that a public roadway was blocked could lawfully step on private land at the side of the road in order to avoid the obstruction. Apart from the emergency, the slightest invasion of the landowner's property would have been a trespass. Yet when no other course was available, the pilgrim's intrusion was not unlawful, and the landowner could not recover damages. In cases of "necessity," private property must "yield to the general interest" (*id.* at 524). On a parity of reasoning, government officials could take affirmative steps to protect the public. It was lawful, according to Kent, to "raze houses to the ground to prevent the spreading of a conflagration" (*id.*)

96. See, for example, *Barling v. West,* 29 Wis. 307 (1871) (invalidating an ordinance forbidding the operation of a lemonade stand without a license), cited in Norton T. Horr & Alton A. Bemis, A Treatise on the Power to Enact, Passage, Validity and Enforcement of Municipal Police Ordinances 98 (1887).

97. Kent, Commentaries, *supra* note 95, at 528.

98. See Ernst Freund, The Police Power: Public Policy and Constitutional Rights (1904).

99. Horr & Bemis, Treatise, *supra* note 96, at 92, 164. For an updated assessment, see David A. Thomas, *Finding More Pieces for the Takings Puzzle: How Correcting History Can Clarify Doctrine,* 75 U. Colo. L. Rev. 497 (2004).

100. Kent, Commentaries, *supra* note 95, at 526–27. For a treatment of early efforts to reconcile classical conceptions of property with the police and eminent domain powers, see Harry N. Scheiber, *The Road to Munn: Eminent Domain and the Concept of Public Purpose in the State Courts,* in Perspectives in American History 329 (Fleming & Bailyn eds. 1971).

101. See chapter 3, note 6 and accompanying text.

102. Sunstein, Rights Revolution, *supra* note 57, at 13.

103. 236 U.S. 1 (1915).

104. *Id.* at 16.

105. 261 U.S. 525, 560–61 (1923).

106. *Id.* at 546.

107. *Lochner,* 198 U.S. at 57.

108. Fiss, Modern State, *supra* note 48, at 159–60; Paul W. Kahn, Legitimacy and History: Self-Government in American Constitutional Theory 109–10 (1992); hereafter cited as Legitimacy.

109. *Lochner,* 198 U.S. at 60, 62–63. See Kahn, Legitimacy, *supra* note 108, at 112–13.

110. 219 U.S. 104, 111 (1911).

111. 348 U.S. 26 (1954).

112. *Id.* at 32.

113. 467 U.S. 229 (1984).

114. *Midkiff v. Tom,* 702 F.2d 788, 798 (9th Cir. 1983).

115. *Kelo v. City of New London,* 125 S.Ct. 2655 (2005).

116. *Id.* at 2671 (O'Connor, J., dissenting).

117. *Id.* at 2664 (opinion for the Court). If the Court were to insist that property must be kept in public hands or under an arrangement that allows for public access, there would be no satisfying way to explain other dispositions the Court has long sustained—for example, takings to promote the mining and agriculture industries (carried on by private entities but serving larger societal welfare). *Id.* at 2665.

118. *Id.* at 2661. Justice Stevens set aside the question whether it is permissible for government to transfer ownership of private property to another private party on the sole ground that the receiving party will put it to a more productive use and thus pay more taxes into the public treasury (*id.* at 2666–67). That, no doubt, would be a close case in which the public benefit is comparatively remote. Remember, though, that takings cases are about things of tangible economic value, and persons who are deprived of their property receive compensation.

119. *Id.* at 2669 (Kennedy, J., concurring).

120. I mean here to compare only the "public interest" and "public use" ideas. Of course, we should not lose sight of an important difference between police power and eminent domain power cases. When the Court sustains police power action that diminishes an individual's assets, the implication is that the affected person must suffer the consequences unless there is a plausible due process or equal protection argument that government's behavior is not instrumentally rational in the necessary sense. I explain in the next chapter that claims of that sort rarely succeed, because the Court is typically content that

government's means are rational. It would not do to hold government even to that generous test regarding what counts as a taking for purposes of eminent domain cases. The reason is clear enough. If governmental action constitutes a taking, the implication is that the individual is not obliged to accept his or her lot but is rather entitled to just compensation. See *Lingle v. Chevron*, 544 U.S. 528 (2005).

121. See Paul Kens, Judicial Power and Reform Politics: The Anatomy of *Lochner v. New York* 128–37 (1990).

122. See Kahn, Legitimacy, *supra* note 108, at 116; Purcell, Crisis, *supra* note 29, at 9–10; Wiecek, Law and Ideology, *supra* note 22, at 82–84. See generally Richard Hofstadter, Social Darwinism in American Thought (1959).

123. *Lochner*, 198 U.S. at 75 (dissenting opinion).

124. Edward A. Purcell Jr., Brandeis and the Progressive Constitution: Erie, the Judicial Power, and the Politics of the Federal Courts in Twentieth-Century America 20 (2000); hereafter cited as Brandeis. See Arnold M. Paul, *Legal Progressivism, the Courts, and the Crisis of the 1890's*, 83 Bus. Hist. Rev. 497 (1959); see also Max Lerner, Nine Scorpions in a Bottle: Great Judges and Cases of the Supreme Court 116 (1994) (contending that Holmes's dissent struck at "the whole dark and intolerant judicial tradition that Peckham was expressing").

125. Learned Hand, *Due Process of Law and the Eight-Hour Day*, 21 Harv. L. Rev. 495, 502 (1908), cited in Purcell, Brandeis, *supra* note 124, at 20.

126. As illustrations only, I will cite Charles A. Beard, An Economic Interpretation of the Constitution of the United States (1913); Sidney Fine, Laissez-Faire and the General-Welfare State (1956); Frank R. Strong, Substantive Due Process of Law: A Dichotomy of Sense and Nonsense (1986); Benjamin R. Twiss, Lawyers and the Constitution: How Laissez Faire Came to the Supreme Court (1942). For discussions, see William J. Novak, *The Legal Origins of the Modern American State*, in Looking Back at Law's Century (Sarat, Garth & Kagan eds. 2002), hereafter cited as *Legal Origins;* Barry Friedman, *The History of the Countermajoritarian Difficulty, Part Three: The Lesson of Lochner*, 76 N. Y. U. L. Rev. 1383 (2001).

127. Horwitz, Transformation, *supra* note 46, at 33.

128. See Kahn, Legitimacy, *supra* note 108, at 117–30; Purcell, Crisis, *supra* note 29, at 74–94; Purcell, Brandeis, *supra* note 124, at 38.

129. Wiecek, Law and Ideology, *supra* note 22, at 7–8; Novak, *Legal Origins*, *supra* note 126, at 7.

130. Bernstein, *Revisionism, supra* note 42, at 5–9; see Albert W. Alschuler, Law without Values: The Life, Work, and Legacy of Justice Holmes 48–49 (2000); Philip P. Wiener, Evolution and the Founders of Pragmatism 176–77 (1969); cf. Vincent Blasi, *Holmes and the Marketplace of Ideas*, 2004 Sup. Ct. Rev. 1, 25–31 (linking Holmes' Darwinism to his views on freedom of expression). The debate continues. Chief Justice Rehnquist contended that *Lochner's* mistake was

to think that "liberty" included a "right to make a contract." *United States v. Lopez,* 514 U.S. 549, 578 (1995) (opinion for the Court by Rehnquist, C. J.). Justice Souter connects *Lochner* with an erroneous faith in unregulated markets to maximize public welfare. *Id.* at 606 (Souter, J., dissenting). Thomas Grey concedes that Holmes's link between formalist methodology and laissez-faire may have been novel, but he thinks it was astute. Grey, *Pragmatism, supra* note 46, at 494. Aviam Soifer contends that if the Court did not relentlessly deploy the Constitution to promote laissez-faire, it did something just as invidious by ceaselessly invalidating statutes said to be paternalistic. Aviam Soifer, *The Paradox of Paternalism and Laissez-Faire Constitutionalism: United States Supreme Court, 1888–1921,* 5 Law & Hist. Rev. 249, 252–55 (1987). Soifer contends that even as the justices denounced social welfare legislation benefiting the laboring classes, they rendered decisions advancing the interests of the comparatively wealthy. Either ground of decision produced the same result. The Court refused to allow legislatures to enact statutes assisting weak and oppressed classes (including not only workers, but racial minorities, sailors, and Native Americans) and thus fortified the capacity of the powerful to perpetuate oppression.

131. 291 U.S. 502 (1934).

132. *Id.* at 537.

133. *Id.* at 554 (McReynolds, J., dissenting).

134. 348 U.S. 483 (1955).

135. *Id.* at 488. Accord *Lincoln Fed. Labor Union v. Northwestern Iron & Metal Co.,* 335 U.S. 525, 536 (1949) (opinion for the Court by Black, J.) (insisting that the Court turned this corner in 1934 when *Nebbia* was decided).

136. See, for example, Howard Gillman, The Constitution Besieged: The Rise and Demise of Lochner Era Police Powers Jurisprudence (1993); Barry Cushman, Rethinking the New Deal Court (1998); Michael Les Benedict, *Laissez-Faire and Liberty: A Re-Evaluation of the Meaning and Origins of Laissez Faire Constitutionalism,* 1 Law. & Hist. Rev. 293 (1985).

137. See Gillman, Constitution Besieged, *supra* note 136, at 7–13.

138. 152 U.S. 133, 137 (1893), quoted in Gillman, Constitution Besieged, *supra* note 136, at 104. According to Professor Karkkainen, this is one place where the idea that police power measures must further the *general* welfare initially had literal application—namely, to foreclose regulatory measures favoring only a portion of the population. Bradley C. Karkkainen, *The Police Power Revisited: Phantom Incorporation and the Roots of the Takings "Muddle",* 90 Minn. L. Rev. 826, 896 (2006); hereafter cited as *Phantom Incorporation.*

139. G. Edward White, The Constitution and the New Deal 241–46 (2000). But see Grey, *Pragmatism, supra* note 46, at 500 n. 121 (insisting that the "revisionist literature" does not "successfully discredit applying the label 'laissez-faire constitutionalism' to the *Lochner* developments"); see also Paul Kens, *Lochner v. New York: Tradition or Change in Constitutional Law?,* 1 N. Y. U. J. L. & Lib-

erty 404 (2005) (questioning the extent to which recent scholarship unsettles traditional accounts).

140. Gillman, Constitution Besieged, *supra* note 136, at 62; David E. Bernstein, *Bolling, Equal Protection, Due Process, and Lochnerphobia*, 93 Gtn. L. J. 1253, 1261–75 (2005).

141. Recall that Justice Peckham set aside the employer's explicit equal protection claim and addressed only the argument that the work-hour law violated liberty of contract. See text accompanying note 50; Bernstein, *Revisionism, supra* note 42, at 13–31; cf. Barry Cushman, *Some Varieties and Vicissitudes of Lochnerism*, 85 B. U. L. Rev. 881 (2005) (contending that no one has yet sorted out the Court's thinking).

142. New Hampshire Const. § 22 (1776), cited in Benedict, *Laissez-Faire and Liberty, supra* note 136, at 321. Cass Sunstein has argued that various provisions in the original Federal Constitution, too, were understood to keep government officers from using their positions to feather their own nests or the nests of their friends. Cass R. Sunstein, *Naked Preferences and the Constitution*, 84 Colum. L. Rev. 1689 (1984); hereafter cited as *Naked Preferences*. See also William E. Nelson, The Fourteenth Amendment from Political Principle to Judicial Doctrine (1988) (arguing that the Equal Protection Clause drew upon equality ideals established before the Fourteenth Amendment was adopted).

143. See Benedict, *Laissez-Faire and Liberty, supra* note 136, at 317; see also Nedelesky, Private Property, *supra* note 87, at 19–20, 51–56, 64 (explaining that Madison hoped to prevent simple majorities from using government to challenge the power of the propertied classes); accord Sunstein, *Naked Preferences, supra* note 142, at 1690–92. Ronald Cass regards a prohibition on rent-seeking legislation to be part and parcel of what early Americans thought to be the rule of law. Ronald A. Cass, The Rule of Law in America 23–24 (2001), relying on "Federalist No. 47" (Madison).

144. The statute in *Slaughterhouse* created a monopoly and thus (according to Justice Field) was not an "equal" or "impartial" law. See text accompanying notes 25–26. See Benedict, *Laissez-Faire and Liberty, supra* note 136, at 323, 328. See also Charles W. McCurdy, *Justice Field and the Jurisprudence of Government-Business Relations: Some Parameters of Laissez Faire Constitutionalism*, 1863–1897, 61 J. Am. Hist. 970 (1975).

145. See Gillman, Constitution Besieged, *supra* note 136, at 10, 46–47, 63.

146. See text accompanying notes 85–86.

147. See notes 66–73 and accompanying text.

148. Gillman, Constitution Besieged, *supra* note 136, at 63. Accord Wiecek, Law and Ideology, *supra* note 22, at 83; Karkkainen, *Phantom Incorporation, supra* note 138, at 899.

149. See notes 118–19 and accompanying text.

150. Consider, for example, that government plainly can collect revenues via

a graduated income tax (thus touching the comparatively wealthy for the lion's share of the take) and then disburse those funds to the poor (or to subgroups of poor people selected according to government's sense of sound public policy). *Dandridge v. Williams*, 397 U.S. 471 (1970).

151. See chapter 4, notes 196–206 and accompanying text.

152. Kahn, Legitimacy, *supra* note 108, at 126.

153. *Missouri, Texas and Kansas Ry. v. May*, 194 U.S. 267, 270 (1904).

154. *Patsone v. Pennsylvania*, 232 U.S. 138, 144 (1914).

155. See text accompanying note 109.

156. For a more complete account, see Matthew S. R. Bewig, *Laboring in the "Poisonous Gases": Consumption, Public Health, and the Lochner Court*, 1 N. Y. U. J. L. & Liberty 476 (2005).

157. 208 U.S. 412 (1908).

158. Felix Frankfurter, *Hours of Labor and Realism in Constitutional Law*, 29 Harv. L. Rev. 353, 364–65 (1916).

159. *Id.* at 367.

160. 211 U.S. 539 (1909).

161. *Id.* at 547–48, 550.

162. James B. Thayer, *The Origin and Scope of the American Doctrine of Constitutional Law*, 7 Harv. L. Rev. 129 (1893). In Thayer's view, the Supreme Court should leave federal enactments standing even if the justices themselves thought Congress had acted unconstitutionally—unless it appeared that a statute constituted clear error. Thayer insisted that hard problems typically admit of more than one plausible answer and that the Court should resist the temptation to have its own way notwithstanding Congress's contrary position. His point was not that the justices should embrace a questionable federal statute as constitutionally valid in some abstract sense, but rather that the Court should sustain a law, despite its own doubts, in deference to Congress's *reasonable* conclusion (*id.* at 144). See Evan H. Caminker, *Thayerian Deference to Congress and Supreme Court Supermajority Rule: Lessons from the Past*, 78 Ind. L. J. 73, 82–83 (2003); cf. Mark Tushnet, *Alternative Forms of Judicial Review*, 101 Mich. L. Rev. 2781, 2797–98 (2003) (arguing that Thayer went well beyond the idea that the Court should let Congress have its way in doubtful cases).

163. See William N. Eskridge & Gary Peller, *The New Public Law Movement: Moderation as a Postmodern Cultural Form*, 89 Mich. L. Rev. 707 (1991) (offering a good first-stop overview).

164. 291 U.S. at 537.

165. 348 U.S. at 488.

166. 348 U.S. at 32.

167. 125 S.Ct. at 2663.

168. John Hart Ely, Democracy and Distrust (1980). Justice Breyer has sketched the different, but consistent, theory that some individual rights are "ac-

tive" in the sense that they contemplate individual entitlements to participate in one's own government. Stephen Breyer, Active Liberty: Interpreting Our Democratic Constitution (2005).

Chapter Three

1. The Supreme Court sometimes talks this way, but not seriously. The joint opinion in *Planned Parenthood v. Casey,* 505 U.S. 833 (1992), declared that "[i]t is a promise of the Constitution that there is a realm of personal liberty which the government may not enter" (*id.* at 847). In context, however, the idea was far different—namely, that due process has a substantive dimension that extends beyond anything specified in the Bill of Rights. See text accompanying notes 55, 114.

2. Ian Shapiro has explained that in any discussion of rights, it "makes sense . . . to ask: *who* is entitled, to *what,* on what *basis,* and for what *purpose?*" Ian Shapiro, The Evolution of Rights in Liberal Theory 14 (1986); emphasis in original.

3. See chapter 1, notes 117–120 and accompanying text.

4. See chapter 4, notes 139–62 and accompanying text.

5. The understanding of substantive rights I am exploring may seem dangerously utilitarian in that it neglects other aspects of life commonly thought to be valuable. Charles Fried has argued that it is a mistake to regard instrumentalism as the only form of rational action to which constitutional doctrine attends. Fried insists that doctrine also responds to "constitutive structures" into which governmental action must fit if it is be constitutionally sound. Charles Fried, *Constitutional Doctrine,* 107 Harv. L. Rev. 1140 (1994). His treatment is abstract, notwithstanding that he addresses doctrine rather than theory. I'm not sure what real-world differences "constitutive" rationality would produce if it were to displace the down-to-earth instrumentalism the Court actually employs. Professor Fried may not give the Court's brand of instrumentalism sufficient credit for exposing relevant questions to the justices for examination. Rational instrumentalism is not a simplistic cost/benefit analysis, but a flexible mechanism for ensuring that individuals are regulated for reasons that bear on the public interest.

6. The Federal Government has no general authority to make public policy, but only explicit powers enumerated in the written Constitution. *United States v. DeWitt,* 76 U.S. (9 Wall.) 41, 44 (1869); *United States v. Lopez,* 514 U.S. 549, 614 (1995). That is why we have Supreme Court decisions working out the contours of discrete congressional powers as an affirmative matter. A particular power must be given some content, else it would not be particular at all, but general. The definition of any given power, in turn, has both an affirmative (power-conferring) side and also a negative (power-limiting) side. The power entitles Congress to

legislate out to the periphery of the authority granted, but not farther. Accordingly, the Court must identify and elaborate "internal" restraints on congressional power—namely, limits that are necessarily part of the definition of a discrete power and thus internal to it. See, for example, Kathleen M. Sullivan & Gerald Gunther, Constitutional Law 178 (15th ed. 2004). Congress also must respect what academicians call "external" limits on its powers. Even if a statute is within one of Congress's discrete enumerated powers to enact, that is, even if it makes no attempt to reach beyond the internal restraints attending that power, still the statute may run afoul of something else in the Constitution—some constitutional proscription that is external to the power on which Congress relies.

7. *Brown v. Maryland,* 25 U.S. (12 Wheat.) 419, 448 (1827). See Ruth L. Roettinger, The Supreme Court and the State Police Power 10–11 (1957).

8. *License Cases,* 46 U.S. (5 How.) 504, 583 (1847), discussed in D. Benjamin Barros, *The Police Power and the Takings Clause,* 58 U. Miami L. Rev. 471, 477 (2004).

9. I set aside the restraints on state power that the Court has inferred from the Commerce Clause. In some contexts, the justices apparently conceive that those structural inferences generate a constitutional "right" in regulated companies. But the real matter in interest remains the proper role of the states in a system that explicitly confers power on Congress to regulate matters of national concern.

10. See *McCulloch v. Maryland,* 17 U.S. (4 Wheat.) 316 (1819). Professor Lessig argues that the conflict between congressional powers and individual rights may not have been apparent when the Constitution was adopted. Yet changes in social and economic life, as well as technological innovations, have caused us to expand both the reach of Congress's affirmative authority and the scope of competing rights—producing the phenomenon captured by the internal/external distinction. Lawrence Lessig, *Translating Federalism: United States v. Lopez,* 1995 Sup. Ct. Rev. 125, 132.

11. See chapter 2, text accompanying notes 108–9.

12. Randy Barnett, Restoring the Lost Constitution: The Presumption of Liberty 322–34 (2004).

13. *Id.* at 345–53.

14. 539 U.S. 558 (2003).

15. See chapter 4, notes 102–9 and accompanying text.

16. Anthony G. Amsterdam, *Perspectives on the Fourth Amendment,* 58 Minn. L. Rev. 349 (1974).

17. *Id.* at 367 (noting that the Fourth Amendment speaks not of "personal rights" but of the collective "right of the people").

18. Richard H. Pildes, *Why Rights Are Not Trumps: Social Meanings, Expressive Harms, and Constitutionalism,* 27 J. Legal Stud. 725, 730 (1998).

19. *Id.* at 729–31, 734; emphasis in original.

20. *Id.* at 725, 733, 754.

21. See chapter 4, notes 6–54 and accompanying text (discussing "standards of review"). Cf. Robert F. Nagel, *The Formulaic Constitution*, 84 Mich. L. Rev. 165 (1985) (offering quite another account of the relationship between doctrine and the Constitution); see chapter 1, notes 13–14 and accompanying text; chapter 2, notes 11–12 and accompanying text.

22. Steven D. Smith, The Constitution and the Pride of Reason (1998); hereafter cited as Pride.

23. *Id.* at 28, quoting Henry Steele Commager, The Empire of Reason 1 (1977).

24. *Id.* at 10, 15, 46–56, 83. This last would be unobjectionable, according to Smith, were it not for our failure to develop a form of moral reasoning that seriously channels judicial decision making about constitutional meaning. Smith despairs of identifying fundamental moral values that demand our respect, apart from their capacity to win public support. Moreover, he sees no reason to think that Supreme Court justices (or judges and lawyers generally) are any better at determining "moral reality" than anyone else (*id.* at 84–98).

25. *Id.* at 91–98, 101, 115–17; 125–42; see also Steven D. Smith, *The Academy, the Courts, and the Culture of Rationalism* 97, 106, in That Eminent Tribunal (Wolfe ed. 2004).

26. David M. Beatty, The Ultimate Rule of Law (2004).

27. *Id.* at 5–15, 34, 44–56, 116, 131, 182–88.

28. See, for example, notes 122, 235–42 and accompanying text; chapter 4, text accompanying note 11.

29. See, for example, Smith, Pride, *supra* note 22, at 101, citing Robert F. Nagel, Constitutional Cultures 106–7 (1989).

30. Cass R. Sunstein, *Naked Preferences and the Constitution*, 84 Colum. L. Rev. 1689 (1984) (listing the Due Process Clause, the Equal Protection Clause, the Privileges and Immunities Clause, the Takings Clause, the Contracts Clause, and the "Dormant Commerce Clause"); hereafter cited as *Naked Preferences*.

31. *Id.* at 1689–92.

32. *Id.* at 1690–91; emphasis added.

33. See chapter 2, notes 136–51 and accompanying text.

34. Sunstein, *Naked Preferences, supra* note 30, at 1731.

35. 410 U.S. 113 (1973) (the abortion regulation decision).

36. Sunstein, *Naked Preferences, supra* note 30, at 1703 and n. 64, 1732. Of course, Sunstein's 1984 essay came well before *Planned Parenthood v. Casey*, 505 U.S. 833 (1992), where the Court assimilated *Roe* into the larger body of substantive due process cases and thus brought the range of "fundamental rights" into the rational instrumentalism fold. I also hasten to say that Professor Sunstein intimated in his paper that the right of free speech might fit within his framework on the theory that free speech is an "indispensable means of ensuring the emergence of public values." Sunstein, *Naked Preferences, supra* note 30,

at 1732. Of course, Sunstein's current views are best pursued in his modern work. See, for example, Cass R. Sunstein, The Partial Constitution 1–39 (1993) (updating the "Naked Preferences" thesis ten years later); hereafter cited as Partial.

37. See chapter 2, notes 68–76 and accompanying text; chapter 4, notes 191–206 and accompanying text.

38. See chapter 2, notes 103–6 and accompanying text.

39. Sunstein, *Naked Preferences, supra* note 30, at 1694, 1710–13.

40. See chapter 2, notes 35–39, 136–48 and accompanying text.

41. I put aside allied substantive rights, specifically the individual entitlements conventionally associated with the Takings Clause, the Bill of Attainder Clause, the Ex Post Facto Clause, and the Contracts Clause. Cf. Sunstein, *Naked Preferences, supra* note 30 (treating some of these). The doctrine the Court offers in cases in those fields overlaps considerably with substantive due process.

42. See chapter 2, notes 77–83, 152–68 and accompanying text.

43. J. C. Holt, Magna Carta 328 (2d ed. 1992) (translating from the original 1215 version); see *Washington v. Glucksberg*, 521 U.S. 702, 757 n. 5 (1997) (Souter, J., concurring in the judgment); Frank H. Easterbrook, *Substance and Due Process*, 1982 Sup. Ct. Rev. 85 (1983).

44. The classic Supreme Court account is *Murray v. Hoboken Land & Improvement Co.*, 59 U.S. (18 How.) 272 (1855).

45. See chapter 2, note 28 and accompanying text.

46. Edward S. Corwin, Liberty against Government 58–115 (1948); see *Glucksberg*, 521 U.S. at 757 (Souter, J., concurring in the judgment) (relying on Corwin). The celebrated illustration is *Wynehamer v. People*, 13 N.Y. 378 (1856).

47. *Dred Scott v. Sanford*, 60 U.S. (19 How.) 393 (1856). See Charles Fried, Saying What the Law Is: The Constitution in the Supreme Court 172–73 (2004); hereafter cited as Saying.

48. Justice Souter takes this view. *Glucksberg*, 521 U.S. at 758 (Souter, J., concurring in the judgment), citing *Fletcher v. Peck*, 10 U.S. (6 Cranch) 87 (1810). See also Peter J. Rubin, *Square Pegs and Round Holes: Substantive Due Process, Procedural Due Process, and the Bill of Rights*, 103 Colum. L. Rev. 833, 838–39 n. 19 (2003), citing *Terrett v. Taylor*, 13 U.S. (9 Cranch) 43 (1815).

49. See *Whitney v. California*, 274 U.S. 357, 373 (1927) (Brandeis, J., concurring) (famously noting that those arguments were persuasive).

50. See *Davidson v. New Orleans*, 96 U.S. 97, 101 (1877). For early accounts of due process as procedural only, see Edward S. Corwin, *The Supreme Court and the Fourteenth Amendment*, 7 Mich. L. Rev. 643, 662 (1908); Charles M. Hough, *Due Process of Law—Today*, 32 Harv. L. Rev. 218, 223 (1918). In this, due process overlapped with the ban on bills of attainder. A legislature might make some act criminal, but it could not impose a penalty for a violation without first providing the usual enforcement process: trial by jury. See Edward S. Cor-

win, *The Doctrine of Due Process of Law Before the Civil War,* 24 Harv. L. Rev. 366, 373 (1910).

51. See Benjamin R. Twiss, Lawyers and the Constitution: How Laissez Faire Came to the Supreme Court 29 (1942).

52. The conventional explanation is that the justices worried that if they allowed that clause any serious content, they would invite Congress to enact civil rights statutes that would displace settled state policies. Section Five of the Fourteenth Amendment gave Congress authority to adopt legislation to enforce the provisions of Section One (including the Privileges or Immunities Clause, the Due Process Clause, and the Equal Protection Clause).

The Court has invoked the Privileges or Immunities Clause to invalidate a state statute on only one occasion. In that case, *Saenz v. Roe,* 526 U.S. 489 (1999), the Court explained that it is a privilege or immunity of United States citizenship to immigrate permanently from one state to another. The validity of state action touching that entitlement turns, as usual, on rational instrumentalism. A state must select a means that serves a permissible purpose (*id.* at 499 n. 11).

Academics occasionally attempt to recruit the Privileges or Immunities Clause to wider duty. See, for example, John Hart Ely, Democracy and Distrust 22–23 (1980). The point of that exercise is far from clear. Textualists are evidently offended that this ostensibly more appropriate provision of the Fourteenth Amendment has been neglected, the work it might have done transferred to the comparatively unlikely idea of substantive due process. See, for example, John Harrison, *Reconstructing the Privileges or Immunities Clause,* 101 Yale L. J. 1385 (1992); hereafter cited as *Reconstructing.* But it is hard to think the Court would have forged the privileges or immunities of national citizenship into limitations different from the rational instrumentalism associated with due process. We do not have the substantive due process we do because of anything in the text of the Fourteenth Amendment but because of the judgments the Court has made over the years. There is no reason to think the Court would have made different judgments if it had purported to proceed from a different textual starting place. If the only point is to achieve some greater fidelity to the text, then, again, the effort is not worth the candle. Shifting to the Privileges or Immunities Clause would only open up another gap between the written document and the real Constitution—this one between the text of this clause and the Court's decisions repackaging the same body of decisions as interpretations of it.

Of course, the Privileges and Immunities Clause in Art. IV, § 2 comes up much more often, typically to fill in gaps left by the doctrine the Court has developed for handling state activities that restrict interstate commerce. In those cases, rational instrumentalism is equally at work. In *New Hampshire v. Piper,* 470 U.S. 274 (1985), the Court offered this summary: A state can discriminate to the detriment of nonresidents only if there is a "substantial reason for the difference in treatment" and the discrimination "bears a substantial relationship to the State's objective" (*id.* at 284). Cf. Sunstein, *Naked Preferences, supra* note 30, at 1708–10.

53. *Slaughterhouse Cases,* 83 U.S. 36, 83–124 (1872).

54. See chapter 2, notes 47–52 and accompanying text.

55. *Collins v. Harker Heights,* 503 U.S. 115, 125 (1992); *Planned Parenthood v. Casey,* 505 U.S. 833, 846 (1992); *Washington v. Glucksberg,* 521 U.S. 702, 719 (1997).

56. See Easterbrook, *Substance, supra* note 43.

57. See Ely, Democracy and Distrust, *supra* note 52, at 18; John Harrison, *Substantive Due Process and the Constitutional Text,* 83 Va. L. Rev. 493, 502 (1997).

58. See chapter 2, text accompanying note 28.

59. See *Glucksberg,* 521 U.S. at 759 n. 6 (Souter, J., concurring in the judgment); *Poe v. Ullman,* 367 U.S. 497, 542 (1961) (Harlan, J., dissenting).

60. See chapter 2, notes 32–33 and accompanying text.

61. See, for example, *Munn v. Illinois,* 94 U.S. 113, 123 (1877); *Mugler v. Kansas,* 123 U.S. 623, 659 (1887).

62. See chapter 2, notes 107–9 and accompanying text.

63. *Lochner,* 198 U.S. at 57.

64. At the time, Felix Frankfurter acknowledged that Peckham's "principle" was perfectly sound. Yet Frankfurter insisted that getting the principle right was "the beginning and not the end of the inquiry." Felix Frankfurter, *Hours of Labor and Realism in Constitutional Law,* 29 Harv. L. Rev. 353, 369 (1916).

65. *FPC v. Natural Gas Pipeline Co.,* 315 U.S. 575, 599–601 (concurring opinion); *FPC v. Hope Natural Gas Co.,* 320 U.S. 591, 619–20 (1944) (concurring opinion). See Tinsley E. Yarbrough, Mr. Justice Black and His Critics 48–55 (1988).

66. 291 U.S. 502 (1934).

67. *Id.* at 511.

68. 372 U.S. 726 (1963).

69. *Id.* at 733 (Harlan, J., concurring in the judgment).

70. Cf. *Roe v. Wade,* 410 U.S. 113, 167 (1973) (Stewart, J., concurring) (noting that Black's treatment of due process in *Skrupa* did not represent the majority position).

71. In *Lingle v. Chevron,* 544 U.S. 528 (2005), the Court refused to employ a general means/ends rationality test borrowed from due process to determine whether a regulation constitutes a taking of private property. Justice Kennedy wrote separately to underscore that, apart from the Takings Clause, a regulation of property might be found unconstitutional on the theory that it is so arbitrary and irrational as to violate due process. See chapter 2, note 120.

72. See notes 176–77 and accompanying text.

73. See, for example, *Casey,* 505 U.S. at 980 (Scalia, J., dissenting).

74. See notes 137–41 and accompanying text.

75. *Cruzan v. Director,* 497 U.S. 261 (1990).

76. *Id.* at 279; emphasis added. Writing separately in *Cruzan,* Justice Scalia first explained (unremarkably) that "the Due Process Clause does not protect individuals against deprivations of liberty *simpliciter,*" but only "against deprivations of liberty 'without due process of law.' " *Id.* at 293 (Scalia, J., concurring). Then, he said (quite remarkably) that "no 'substantive due process' claim can be maintained unless the claimant demonstrates that the State has deprived him of a *right* historically and traditionally protected against State interference." *Id.* at 294; emphasis added.

77. *Washington v. Glucksberg,* 521 U.S. 702 (1997).

78. *Id.* at 723; emphasis added.

79. 410 U.S. 113 (1973).

80. *Id.* at 155; emphasis added.

81. *Planned Parenthood of Southeastern Pa. v. Casey,* 505 U.S. 833 (1992).

82. *Id.* at 846; emphasis added.

83. 539 U.S. 558 (2003).

84. *Id.* at 567; emphasis added.

85. See, for example, *Loving v. Virginia,* 388 U.S. 1, 12 (1967) (referring to the "right" to marry); *Troxel v. Granville,* 530 U.S. 57, 66 (2000) (referring to the "fundamental right of parents to make decisions" for their children).

86. *Glucksberg,* 521 U.S. at 756 (Souter, J., concurring in the judgment).

87. *Id.* at 720 (opinion for the Court).

88. David A. Strauss, *Modernization and Representation Reinforcement: An Essay in Memory of John Hart Ely,* 57 Stan. L. Rev. 761, 769 (2004).

89. See chapter 4, notes 102–9 and accompanying text.

90. 497 U.S. at 278; emphasis added.

91. 521 U.S. at 720; emphasis added.

92. 410 U.S. at 153; emphasis added.

93. 505 U.S. at 846; emphasis added.

94. 539 U.S. at 564; emphasis added.

95. See, for example, *Moore v. City of East Cleveland,* 431 U.S. 494, 507 (1977) (explaining that "freedom of personal choice in matters of marriage and family life is one of the liberties" protected by due process).

96. *Griswold v. Connecticut,* 381 U.S. 479, 500 (1965) (Harlan, J., concurring in the judgment).

97. Most of the first eight amendments to the Constitution conferred procedural rights on defendants in federal criminal prosecutions. John Marshall explained in *Barron v. Baltimore,* 32 U.S. (7 Pet.) 243 (1833), that those rights were not applicable to *state* prosecutions. After the Fourteenth Amendment was adopted, the Court acknowledged that the new Due Process Clause it contained *did* address state criminal cases. Defendants facing death or incarceration certainly stood to be deprived of liberty, and the only question was what process they were "due"—that is, what procedural rights they enjoyed to protect them from an erroneous loss of liberty. Yet the Court insisted that "due" process within the

meaning of the Fourteenth Amendment was not congruent with the procedural rights the Bill of Rights established for federal trials or, indeed, with any particular procedural rights at all. Instead, due process meant only generalized fundamental fairness. A prisoner might focus on some especially troubling aspect of state procedures. But his Fourteenth Amendment right to due process was violated only if all the procedures in state court, taken as a whole, rendered the proceedings unfair. Certainly, the state's failure to recognize some specific procedural right that the Bill of Rights prescribed for federal trials did not, in itself, establish a violation of due process for purposes of the Fourteenth Amendment.

98. *Adamson v. California*, 332 U.S. 46, 71–72 (1947) (Black, J., dissenting). Justice Black relied both on the Due Process Clause and (despite *Slaughterhouse*) on the Privileges or Immunities Clause. Initially, he insisted that the framers of the latter equated privileges or immunities with the entitlements in the Bill of Rights. When Justice Frankfurter pointed out that the Privileges or Immunities Clause worked only for United States citizens, Black responded that the Due Process Clause could take up the slack for noncitizens. See *Bridges v. California*, 314 U.S. 252, 280 (1941).

99. See Harry H. Wellington, *Common Law Rules and Constitutional Double Standards: Some Notes on Adjudication*, 83 Yale L. J. 221, 275 (1973); hereafter cited as *Common Law Rules*. Black concentrated on substantive due process because that aspect of the Fourteenth Amendment had been used to invalidate social welfare legislation that Black and other New Dealers promoted. Consistently, however, he also resisted the recognition of any procedural due process not tied tightly to the safeguards found in the Bill of Rights. See *Goldberg v. Kelly*, 397 U.S. 254, 277 (1970) (Black, J., dissenting).

100. In a single move, Black offered his colleagues a way to employ due process to improve state criminal process (i.e., they could simply hold that the procedural rights that made up due process in state court were the procedural rights set out in the Bill of Rights) and a way to eliminate substantive due process as a restraint on state regulation of markets (i.e., they must cease examining state economic regulation entirely). The Fourteenth Amendment meant the Bill of Rights—nothing less, and also (importantly) nothing more. See Yarbrough, Justice Black, *supra* note 65, at 79–101.

101. Some justices, notably Justices Frankfurter and Harlan, objected both to the idea that the states must conform their processes to all the provisions of the Bill of Rights and to the proposition that the states could necessarily disclaim any procedural safeguards that were not included in the Bill of Rights. Justice Brennan was glad to bring state process up to the standards of the Bill of Rights, but he also insisted that other safeguards, not explicitly listed, were essential to fairness and thus were required in both state and federal cases.

102. Justice Cardozo's account captured the spirit of the thing: procedural rights were "fundamental" if they were "implicit in a concept of ordered liberty."

Palko v. Connecticut, 302 U.S. 319, 325 (1937). Yet by slipping so quickly from "rights" to "liberty" Cardozo may have added some confusion, as well. Criminal defendants plainly had liberty interests that triggered their right to procedural due process, which, in turn, comprised some of the specific procedural rights drawn from the Bill of Rights as well as other procedures found to be essential to fairness. In some minds, the Court's conception of the procedures required by due process did not change. The justices had always acknowledged that due process demanded fundamentally fair process, and now they demanded only that the states adopt Bill of Rights provisions found to be fundamental. Nevertheless, by taking the relatively "specific" provisions in the Bill of Rights as the starting point, they plainly attached new significance to the existence of those provisions. The procedures contained in the Bill of Rights were not irrelevant to the process "due" in state cases. Nor were they merely evidence of the procedural arrangements that due process required. They occupied a virtual default position. Something new was afoot. The Due Process Clause of the Fourteenth Amendment had become a vessel for calling most of the procedural safeguards originally established for federal cases to duty in state court.

103. *Gitlow v. New York,* 268 U.S. 652, 666 (1925); emphasis added (actually purporting only to "assume" this point).

104. See, for example, *Roth v. United States,* 354 U.S. 476, 505 (1957) (Harlan, J., dissenting) (contending that the First Amendment was more demanding of the Federal Government than the Fourteenth Amendment was of the states); cf. Alexander Meiklejohn, Free Speech and Its Relation to Self-Government (1948) (arguing that the First Amendment protected only criticism of government and that due process offered a less encompassing protection for other forms of expression).

105. 381 U.S. 479 (1965).

106. *Id.* at 484 (opinion for the Court by Douglas, J.) (joined by Clark, J.). Douglas conceded that nothing in the Bill of Rights expressly established a "right of privacy" that the Due Process Clause of the Fourteenth Amendment could incorporate in the manner that Justice Black (and Douglas himself) had previously described. Yet he concluded that the express provisions there implied a right of privacy.

107. *Id.* at 508–9 (Black, J., dissenting) (joined by Stewart, J.).

108. Justice Goldberg declared that "the concept of liberty protects those personal *rights* that are fundamental." *Id.* at 486 (Goldberg, J., concurring) (joined by Warren, C. J., and Brennan, J.); emphasis added. Justice Stewart insisted that due process had no bearing on the case for want of a "general *right* of privacy in the Bill of Rights." *Id.* at 530 (Stewart, J., dissenting) (joined by Black, J.); emphasis added. Justice Harlan wrote as though some "right" apart from the right to due process itself was implicated. *Id.* at 499–500 (Harlan, J., concurring in the judgment). Yet he dismissed the idea that the "liberty guaranteed by the Due

Process Clause . . . is a series of isolated points pricked out in terms of [explicit provisions of the Bill of Rights]." *Poe v. Ullman,* 367 U.S. 497, 543 (1961). Justice White also said that "the liberty entitled to protection under the Fourteenth Amendment includes" various "rights." *Griswold,* 381 U.S. at 502 (White, J., concurring in the judgment).

109. See chapter 4, notes 98–136 and accompanying notes.

110. Libertarians disagree. But that is because they reject the distinction the Court draws between market behavior and the more personal decisions involved in "fundamental interest" cases. See, for example, Richard A. Epstein, *Skepticism and Freedom: The Intellectual Foundations of Our Constitutional Order,* 6 U. Pa. J. Const. L. 657, 676–77 (2004).

111. 497 U.S. at 281.

112. 521 U.S. at 728.

113. 410 U.S. at 155.

114. 505 U.S. at 879.

115. 539 U.S. at 578. Even Justice Douglas invalidated the statute in *Griswold* because it breached the "familiar principle" that government cannot achieve its purposes "by means that sweep unnecessarily broadly." 381 U.S. at 485.

116. In *Paul v. Davis,* 424 U.S. 693 (1976), Justice Rehnquist worried aloud that if substantive due process claims against executive officers became routine, due process would become a "font" of tort law grounded in the Constitution. See also *Chavez v. Martinez,* 538 U.S. 760, 774–76 (2003) (repeating that concern).

117. *County of Sacramento v. Lewis,* 523 U.S. 833, 842–43 (1998).

118. *Graham v. Connor,* 490 U.S. 386, 395 (1989).

119. See, for example, *Chavez,* 538 U.S. at 775; *Rochin v. California,* 342 U.S. 165, 172–73 (1952).

120. *Collins v. City of Harker Heights,* 503 U.S. 115, 128 (1992).

121. *Lewis,* 523 U.S. at 846.

122. See text accompanying notes 27–28 (noting that proportionality forms an element of rational instrumentalism).

123. *Atkins v. Virginia,* 536 U.S. 304, 349 (2002) (Scalia, J., dissenting).

124. I do not treat the Fourth Amendment on its own footing because it entails both substantive and procedural limits on governmental action. Cf. *Whitley v. Albers,* 475 U.S. 312 (1986) (finding a due process claim to be essentially subsumed by an Eighth Amendment theory).

125. Rubin, *Square Pegs, supra* note 48, at 870.

126. See Tracey Maclin, *The Central Meaning of the Fourth Amendment,* 35 Wm. & Mary L. Rev. 197, 199–200 (1993) (linking the Court's estimate of Fourth Amendment "reasonableness" to the "rational basis standard" in due process cases).

127. See note 117 and accompanying text.

128. Accord Sunstein, *Naked Preferences, supra* note 30, at 1710–17.

129. Kenneth L. Karst, Belonging to America: Equal Citizenship under the

Constitution (1989). In defense of his general thesis, Professor Karst invokes both the Equal Protection Clause and the Due Process Clause (*id.* at 3).

130. Owen M. Fiss, *Groups and the Equal Protection Clause,* 5 Phil. & Pub. Aff. 107 (1976). Professor Dorf describes this as an "antisubordination" as opposed to an "antidiscrimination" principle. Michael C. Dorf, *Equal Protection Incorporation,* 88 Va. L. Rev. 951, 962 (2002).

131. John Harrison argues that the Equal Protection Clause was meant only to ensure that states grant all persons the benefit of general laws and enforce those laws consistently in all cases. But he advances that claim to diminish the significance of this clause in favor of another he thinks can better do the work that equal protection usually performs: the Privileges or Immunities Clause. Harrison, *Reconstructing, supra* note 52, at 1410–14.

132. Writing for the Court in *New York City Transit Auth. v. Beazer,* 440 U.S. 568 (1979), Justice Stevens said that "[g]eneral rules that apply evenhandedly to all persons within the jurisdiction unquestionably comply with [equal protection]" (*id.* at 587–88). Yet he quickly recognized that a rule barring public employment to anyone using methadone established a classification that warranted equal protection analysis.

133. See chapter 2, text accompanying notes 142–47.

134. See Peter Westen, *The Empty Idea of Equality,* 95 Harv. L. Rev. 537 (1982).

135. Fried, Saying, *supra* note 47, at 209.

136. A rule that drivers must stop at red lights classifies. It distinguishes between those who comply and those who don't. It treats the former better than the latter, but for a purpose—to create predictable breaks in traffic and so to reduce accidents. In view of that purpose, it makes sense to put those who stop in one category and those who don't in another, and to treat only violators in a disadvantageous way. That difference in treatment does not deny equal protection, because the classes are not similarly situated with respect to highway safety and thus are not entitled to be treated equally.

137. See Rubin, *Square Pegs, supra* note 48, at 844. Professor Lupu has identified the confluence of due process and equal protection, but he resists severing equal protection from an exclusive attention to "pure antidiscrimination concerns." Ira C. Lupu, *Untangling the Strands of the Fourteenth Amendment,* 77 Mich. L. Rev. 981, 985 (1979).

138. See William N. Eskridge Jr., *Destabilizing Due Process and Evolutive Equal Protection,* 47 UCLA L. Rev. 1183, 1192 (2000); hereafter cited as *Destabilizing.*

139. Recall that Joseph Lochner himself framed his complaint, in part, as a denial of equal treatment—albeit he did not pitch his argument in this form, but instead contended that he was subject to rules that did not apply to other employers. See chapter 2, note 49 and accompanying text.

140. 347 U.S. 497 (1954).

141. *Id.* at 499. See *U.S. Railroad Retirement Bd. v. Fritz,* 449 U.S. 166, 177 n. 10 (1980). Warren, in fact, initially meant to trace the idea of equality back to liberty as it was held to be protected by due process during the *Lochner* period. Warren dropped most of his historical references in deference to Justice Black, who balked at crediting substantive due process in any form. David E. Bernstein, *Bolling, Equal Protection, Due Process, and Lochnerphobia,* 93 Gtn. L. J. 1253, 1276–81 (2005). Then again, if the idea of equality at work in the old due process cases was the Lockean objection to class legislation, Black surely had a point. See chapter 2, notes 142–48 and accompanying text.

142. Cass R. Sunstein, *Sexual Orientation and the Constitution: A Note on the Relationship between Due Process and Equal Protection,* 55 U. Chi. L. Rev. 1161 (1988).

143. Lawrence Lessig, *What Drives Derivability: Responses to Responding to Imperfection,* 74 Tex. L. Rev. 839, 874 (1996).

144. See, for example, *Hamdi v. Rumsfeld,* 542 U.S. 507, 556 (2004) (Scalia, J., dissenting). See *Schad v. Arizona,* 501 U.S. 624, 650 (1991) (Scalia, J., concurring) (insisting that historically accepted procedures must necessarily count as the process that is due). In *Shafer v. South Carolina,* 532 U.S. 36 (2001), Justice Scalia claimed to be "attached to the logic of the Constitution, whose Due Process Clause was understood as an embodiment of common-law tradition." See chapter 2, text accompanying note 28. Since the common law did not require special jury instructions in capital cases, Scalia argued that the Court cannot hold, as a constitutional matter, that special instructions are required today. *Id.* at 55 (dissenting opinion). More generally, Justice Scalia contends that the provisions in the Bill of Rights were "designed to restrain transient majorities from impairing long-recognized personal liberties." Accordingly, "when a practice not specifically prohibited by the text of the Bill of Rights bears the endorsement of a long tradition of open, widespread, and unchallenged use that dates back to the beginning of the Republic, [the Court has] no basis for striking it down." *Rutan v. Republican Party of Illinois,* 497 U.S. 62, 95 (1990) (Scalia, J., dissenting).

145. *Griffin v. Illinois,* 351 U.S. 12, 20–21 (1956) (Frankfurter, J., concurring), emphasis added; quoted in Eskridge, *Destabilizing, supra* note 138, at 1212. See also James E. Fleming, *Constructing the Substantive Constitution,* 72 Tex. L. Rev. 211 (1993).

146. 347 U.S. 497 (1954). See text accompanying note 140. There was a practical political element in *Bolling.* The Court could scarcely force the states to desegregate but exempt the Federal Government.

147. *Romer v. Evans,* 517 U.S. 620 (1996). Professor Sunstein seems plainly to have fashioned his distinction between due process and equal protection in order to build an argument for invalidating the statute in *Lawrence* without overruling *Hardwick,* where the Court had relied exclusively on due process and footnoted

equal protection away. Now that *Lawrence* is in the barn, Sunstein's argument lacks the strategic value it may have had when it was first offered. But see Cass R. Sunstein, *What Did Lawrence Hold? Of Autonomy, Desuetude, Sexuality, and Marriage,* 2003 Sup. Ct. Rev. 27, 32 (evidently sticking to his guns); hereafter cited as *Lawrence.*

    148. *Railway Express Agency v. New York,* 336 U.S. 106 (1949).

    149. See Fried, Saying, *supra* note 47, at 210.

    150. Donald H. Regan, *Rewriting Roe v. Wade,* 77 Mich. L. Rev. 1569 (1979).

    151. See, for example, Ruth Bader Ginsburg, *Some Thoughts on Autonomy and Equality in Relation to Roe v. Wade,* 63 N. C. L. Rev. 375 (1985); Cass R. Sunstein, Partial, *supra* note 36, at 283–85. Most of the contributors to Jack Balkin's book take something of this approach; see What *Roe v. Wade* Should Have Said (Balkin ed. 2005). But see Reva Siegel, *Reasoning from the Body: A Historical Perspective on Abortion Regulation and Questions of Equal Protection,* 44 Stan. L. Rev. 261 (1992) (discouraging this line of argument).

    152. See chapter 4, notes 202–6 and accompanying text.

    153. *Casey,* 505 U.S. at 856.

    154. *Lawrence v. Texas,* 539 U.S. 558 (2003).

    155. See chapter 4, text accompanying notes 92–94.

    156. *Lawrence,* 539 U.S. at 582–83 (O'Connor, J., concurring in the judgment).

    157. *Id.* at 575 (opinion for the Court). See Laurence H. Tribe, *Lawrence v. Texas: The "Fundamental Right" That Dare Not Speak Its Name,* 117 Harv. L. Rev. 1893, 1905–6 (2004).

    158. *Lawrence,* 539 U.S. at 564.

    159. *Id.* at 574–75.

    160. See William N. Eskridge Jr., *Lawrence's Jurisprudence of Tolerance: Judicial Review to Lower the Stakes of Identity Politics,* 88 Minn. L. Rev. 1021, 1039 (2004) (explaining that Kennedy's opinion "confirmed the view that anti-gay sentiment was no more a rational basis under the Due Process Clause than it had been [in *Romer*] under the Equal Protection Clause"); Sunstein, *Lawrence, supra* note 147, at 30 (suggesting that while "*Lawrence's* words sound in due process" much of its "music involves equal protection"); Trevor W. Morrison, *Lamenting Lochner's Loss: Randy Barnett's Case for a Libertarian Constitution,* 90 Cornell L. Rev. 839, 870 (2005) (contending that Justice Kennedy dealt with "equality-reinforcing liberty").

    161. *Bowers v. Hardwick,* 478 U.S. 186 (1986).

    162. *Id.* at 196 n.8.

    163. *Lawrence,* 539 U.S. at 581 (O'Connor, J., concurring in the judgment). O'Connor's position was a bit more complicated. She would have invalidated the statute in *Lawrence* because it was limited on its face to same-sex behavior (which O'Connor properly understood to count as discrimination on the basis of sexual orientation). She did not reach the question whether a statute neutral

on its face would also be invalid for the reason that Justice Kennedy gave, that is, that any sodomy statute bears especially on gays and lesbians. O'Connor explained that if the states were denied the ability to enact facially discriminatory laws and were forced either to extend prohibitions on sexual behavior to straight couples or abandon them entirely, there would be sufficient political pressure to force the states to take the latter course (*id.* at 585). Accordingly, she relied on the process-oriented thinking that Justice Jackson offered in *Railway Express*. But see Tribe, *Lawrence v. Texas, supra* note 157, at 1910–11 (contending that O'Connor underestimated the symbolic effect of a holding that formally permitted facially neutral sodomy statutes to stand).

164. There is another strategic explanation. Justice Kennedy may have regarded equal protection as the more likely vehicle for an argument he preferred to avoid—namely, that government cannot limit marriage to heterosexual couples. Cf. Mary A. Case, *The Very Stereotype the Law Condemns: Constitutional Sex Discrimination Law as a Quest for Perfect Proxies,* 85 Cornell L. Rev. 1447 (2000) (contending that barring gay marriage constitutes invalid gender discrimination). Justice O'Connor plainly did not think that equal protection opened the door to gay marriage any wider than did due process. *Lawrence,* 539 U.S. at 585 (O'Connor, J., concurring in the judgment). But Kennedy may have thought that marriage, being a more public matter than sex, could be distinguished more readily from intimate sexual behavior in the privacy of the home. See Tribe, *Lawrence v. Texas, supra* note 157, at 1954. I only want to make the pedestrian point that a ban on gay marriage is obviously vulnerable to challenge as both arbitrary and discriminatory. The relevant considerations do not change if the Court shifts from one textual starting point to the other, and rational instrumentalism organizes those considerations under either heading.

165. See, for example, *Soldal v. Cook County,* 506 U.S. 56, 70 (1992), cited on this point in Rubin, *Square Pegs, supra* note 48, at 859.

166. See notes 116–22 and accompanying text.

167. In *Village of Willowbrook v. Olech,* 528 U.S. 562 (2000) (*per curiam*), the Court explained that an equal protection claim can rest on the argument that government has isolated a single individual in a category all his own. The choice between equal protection and substantive due process *would* matter if the Court were to embrace the view that equal protection is a class-based idea condemning the subordination of racial groups. As it is, the Court insists that equal protection, like due process, is an "individual" right. *Richmond v. J.A. Croson Co.,* 488 U.S. 469, 493 (1989).

168. See chapter 2, note 140 and accompanying text.

169. 253 U.S. 412 (1920).

170. *Id.* at 415.

171. 220 U.S. 61 (1911).

172. *Id.* at 78.

173. *Buck v. Bell,* 274 U.S. 200, 208 (1927).

174. 348 U.S. 483, 489 (1955).

175. *New Orleans v. Dukes,* 427 U.S. 297, 303 (1976). Accord *Dandridge v. Williams,* 397 U.S. 471, 487 (1970) (explaining that government spending programs must draw lines to allocate finite resources and that it is enough if a classification is "rationally based and free from invidious discrimination").

176. See, for example, *Metro. Life Ins. Co. v. Ward,* 470 U.S. 869 (1985). See text accompanying note 77.

177. See chapter 2, notes 152–68 and accompanying text.

178. 316 U.S. 535 (1942).

179. *Id.* at 541; emphasis added. Applying that standard, Douglas concluded that the sterilization law plainly did not serve the governmental interest offered to explain it. The state contended that criminal proclivities were inheritable, but failed to explain why the statute subjected some repeat offenders to sterilization while sparing others. The Oklahoma statute was a product of the eugenics movement, which had been given credence by Justice Holmes: "Three generations of imbeciles are enough." *Buck,* 274 U.S. at 207. By the time of *Skinner,* Justice Douglas was obviously dubious. Still, he focused primarily on discrimination at a different level. Oklahoma's statute prescribed sterilization for burglars but not for embezzlers, without any suggestion that only the behavior of the former was genetically grounded. By common account, Douglas suspected that race was at the bottom of things. In Oklahoma at the time, members of the preferred class (thieves who committed their crimes in offices) were very likely white.

180. *Reynolds v. Sims,* 377 U.S. 533, 562 (1964). See *Griffin v. Illinois,* 351 U.S. 12 (1956) (involving criminal procedure rules); *Shapiro v. Thompson,* 394 U.S. 618 (1969) (the classic travel case); *Boddie v. Connecticut,* 401 U.S. 371 (1971) (involving access to the courts for purposes of obtaining a divorce).

181. In *San Antonio Indep. School Dist. v. Rodriguez,* 411 U.S. 1 (1973), Justice Powell purported to explain all these cases on the common theory that they involve "a fundamental right explicitly or implicitly protected by the Constitution" (*id.* at 17). He accommodated voting on the theory that there is a "right . . . implicit in our constitutional system, to participate in state elections on an equal basis" (*id.* at n. 78). That was a bit specious, to be sure. But the Court's pragmatism is easy to understand and accept. There is no independent constitutional home for a right to vote, so the Court needs equal protection to fill the void. See Fried, Saying, *supra* note 47, at 224–25.

182. See chapter 4, text accompanying notes 102–9.

183. Compare *Strauder v. West Virginia,* 100 U.S. (10 Otto) 303 (1880) (invalidating the practice of excluding blacks from juries), with *Plessy v. Ferguson,* 163 U.S. 537 (1896) (the infamous "separate but equal" decision).

184. *Allen v. Wright,* 468 U.S. 737, 756 (1984) (referring to racial discrimination in public schooling).

185. *Johnson v. California,* 543 U.S. 499 (2005); *Adarand Constructors v. Pena,* 515 U.S. 200 (1995). See *United States v. Virginia,* 518 U.S. 515, 524 (1996) (gender); *Graham v. Richardson,* 403 U.S. 365, 371 (1971) (alienage); *Oyama v. California,* 332 U.S. 633, 646 (1948) (ancestry). Some classifications according to illegitimacy have also been closely examined. See, for example, *Levy v. Louisiana,* 391 U.S. 68, 71 (1968). But see *Clark v. Jeter,* 486 U.S. 456, 461 (1988) (explaining that the standard for illegitimacy cases is somewhat less demanding).

186. *Grutter v. Bollinger,* 539 U.S. 306, 326 (2003).

187. *Arlington Heights v. Metro. Housing Develop. Corp.,* 429 U.S. 252, 265 (1977).

188. See chapter 4, text accompanying notes 74–82.

189. See also *United States v. Armstrong,* 517 U.S. 456 (1996) (regarding "selective prosecution"). Selective prosecution claims are not impossible, but they demand heroic showings of factual proof. Richard H. McAdams, *Race and Selective Prosecution: Discovering the Pitfalls of Armstrong,* 73 Chi.-Kent L. Rev. 605 (1998).

190. The Court draws no meaningful distinction between freedom "of the press" and freedom of speech generally. See *Richmond Newspapers v. Virginia,* 448 U.S. 555 (1980). The rational instrumentalism we observe in the run of free speech and religion cases is equally discernible in cases involving the press. See, for example, *id.* at 581 (explaining that the press can be excluded from a public trial only if the court finds that closed proceedings promote an "overriding interest").

191. Cass R. Sunstein, Democracy and the Problem of Free Speech xii (1993); Philip B. Kurland, *The Irrelevance of the Constitution: The First Amendment's Freedom of Speech and Freedom of Press Clauses,* 29 Drake L. Rev. 1 (1979).

192. *New York Times Co. v. United States,* 403 U.S. 713, 715 (Black, J., concurring); see Hugo L. Black, *The Bill of Rights,* 35 N. Y. U. L. Rev. 865, 874–75 (1960).

193. See Harry H. Wellington, Interpreting the Constitution: The Supreme Court and the Process of Adjudication 59 (1990). But see Richard H. Pildes & Elizabeth S. Anderson, *Slinging Arrows at Democracy: Social Choice Theory, Value Pluralism, and Democratic Politics,* 90 Colum. L. Rev. 2121, 2155–57 (1990) (arguing that Black was only contending for an analysis that filled in the meaning of free speech and disclaiming Frankfurter's effort to "balance" speech values against incommensurate governmental interests).

194. See *NEA v. Finley,* 524 U.S. 569, 595 (1998) (Scalia, J., concurring in the judgment).

195. *44 Liquormart v. Rhode Island,* 517 U.S. 484, 517 (1996) (Scalia, J., concurring in part). Dissenting in *Bd. of County Commissioners v. Umbehr,* 518 U.S. 668 (1996), Justice Scalia said that "[t]he constitutional text is assuredly as susceptible of one meaning as of the other" (*id.* at 688). So in his mind other considerations must generally determine results—like, for example, his own view

that long-standing practices should be taken as constitutionally valid for the sufficient reason that they always were (*id*).

196. See, for example, *McIntyre v. Ohio Elections Comm'n,* 514 U.S. 334, 359 (1995) (Thomas, J., concurring); accord *id.* at 374 (Scalia, J., dissenting).

197. See, for example, Leonard W. Levy, Emergence of a Free Press (1985); David M. Rabban, Freedom of Speech in Its Forgotten Years (1997); David M. Rabban, *The Ahistorical Historian: Leonard Levy on Freedom of Expression in Early American History,* 37 Stan. L. Rev. 795 (1985).

198. David A. Strauss, *Freedom of Speech and the Common-Law Constitution* 33, in Eternally Vigilant: Free Speech in the Modern Era (Bollinger & Stone eds. 2002).

199. See text accompanying notes 103–4.

200. The literature classically identifies four values with which freedom of speech is associated—four reasons for valuing this form of individual liberty more than others. First and perhaps foremost, free expression is essential to democratic self-government. Individuals must be able to speak their minds in order to participate in politics. Second, free expression is crucial to the pursuit of truth generally—not only political truth in the sense of good public policy, but an accurate understanding of the universe. Censorship restricts the exchange of ideas necessary to the scientific method. Third, freedom of speech reduces the risk of social upheaval. The freedom to dissent opens a safety valve, releasing tensions that otherwise might fester into rebellion. Fourth, freedom of expression is crucial to self-actualization. The ability to express oneself freely is part of what it means to be human. Only the last of these four contemplates that freedom of speech is intrinsically valuable. All the others sound in instrumentalism. See Wellington, *Common Law Rules, supra* note 99, at 267. I do not contend, though, that rational instrumentalism provides the doctrinal framework for judging speech cases because speech itself is largely instrumental—important because it generates other matters of social value. Rational instrumentalism forms the doctrinal core of freedom of expression for the same reasons it does so for other substantive rights. Government's function is to regulate in the public interest. The values that free speech itself implicates instrumentally enter the analysis when the justices weigh them in the mix of considerations that rational instrumentalism makes relevant.

201. See, for example, *Lovell v. Griffin,* 303 U.S. 444, 451–52 (1938).

202. *New York Times Co. v. United States,* 403 U.S. 713 (1971). See also *Near v. Minnesota,* 283 U.S. 697, 716 (1931) (explaining that previous restraints may be justified in case of dire emergency).

203. Compare *Abrams v. United States,* 250 U.S. 616, 628 (1919) (Holmes, J., dissenting), with *Whitney v. California,* 274 U.S. 357, 372 (1927) (Brandeis, J., concurring). See Pnina Lahav, *Holmes and Brandeis: Libertarian and Republican Justifications for Free Speech,* 4 J. Law & Pol. 451 (1988).

204. *Dennis v. United States*, 341 U.S. 494 (1951).

205. Recall that Vinson explicitly endorsed Judge Hand's account in the circuit court: "In each case [the court] must ask whether the gravity of the 'evil,' discounted by its improbability, justifies such invasion of free speech as is necessary to avoid the danger" (*id.* at 510).

206. *Brandenburg v. Ohio*, 395 U.S. 444, 447 (1969).

207. 521 U.S. 844 (1997).

208. Cf. *Osborne v. Ohio*, 495 U.S. 103, 112–14 (1990) (holding that a state court had saved an overbroad statute by giving it a narrowing construction).

209. *United States v. O'Brien*, 391 U.S. 367 (1968).

210. *Id.* at 377.

211. See chapter 4, text accompanying notes 142–46.

212. *Central Hudson Gas v. Pub. Svc. Comm'n*, 447 U.S. 557 (1980).

213. *Id.* at 566.

214. *Bd. of Trustees of SUNY v. Fox*, 492 U.S. 469, 476 (1989).

215. Thomas H. Jackson & John C. Jeffries Jr., *Commercial Speech: Economic Due Process and the First Amendment*, 65 Va. L. Rev. 1 (1979); Robert Post, *The Constitutional Status of Commercial Speech*, 48 UCLA L. Rev. 1 (2000).

216. 427 U.S. 50 (1976).

217. *Id.* at 71.

218. In *Perry Educators' Ass'n v. Perry Local Educators' Ass'n*, 460 U.S. 37, 45 (1983), Justice White explained that regulations regarding traditional public forums can discriminate on the basis of content only if they are "necessary to serve a compelling state interest" and are "narrowly drawn to achieve that end." Regulations in public places not traditionally open for speech must be "reasonable" and must not constitute "an effort to suppress expression merely because public officials oppose the speaker's view" (*id.* at 46).

219. *Elrod v. Burns*, 427 U.S. 347, 366 (1976).

220. See, for example, *NEA v. Finley*, 524 U.S. 569, 587–88 (1998).

221. *McIntyre v. Ohio Elections Comm'n*, 514 U.S. 334, 357 (1995).

222. *Village of Schaumburg v. Citizens for a Better Environment*, 444 U.S. 620, 636 (1980).

223. *Gibson v. Florida Legislative Invest. Comm.*, 372 U.S. 539, 551 (1963).

224. *McConnell v. Federal Election Comm'n*, 540 U.S. 93, 134 (2003).

225. The abundant literature regarding the origins of the religion clauses makes the field a continuing battleground. See, for example, James H. Hutson, Religion and the Founding of the American Republic (1998); Leonard W. Levy, The Establishment Clause: Religion and the First Amendment (1986); Noah Feldman, *The Intellectual Origins of the Establishment Clause*, 77 N. Y. U. L. Rev. 346 (2002). Witness the inconclusive debate between Justice Stevens and Justice Scalia in the "Ten Commandments" cases. Compare *Van Orden v. Perry,*

125 S.Ct. 2854, 2873 (2005) (Stevens, J., dissenting) (with *McCreary County Kentucky v. ACLU,* 125 S.Ct. 2722, 2748 (2005) (Scalia, J., dissenting). Justice Thomas insists that the Court has slipped the proper historical traces with respect to the Establishment Clause and would do better to return to the "original meaning of the Clause." *Van Orden,* 125 S.Ct. at 2865 (Thomas, J., concurring). By his originalist account, the Establishment Clause only forbids the Federal Government (it does not speak to the states at all) to coerce support for religion—by, for example, mandating church attendance or imposing taxes to pay ministers' salaries.

226. *Lemon v. Kurtzman,* 403 U.S. 602, 612–13 (1971), quoting *Walt v. Tax Comm'n,* 397 U.S. 664, 674 (1970). See Kent Greenawalt, *Quo Vadis: The Status and Prospects of "Tests" under the Religion Clauses,* 1995 Sup. Ct. Rev. 323. Several justices have expressed impatience with this formulation, and by common account the Court occasionally varies from it a bit. See, for example, *Lynch v. Donnelly,* 465 U.S. 668, 673 (1984) (indicating that the key question is whether government endorses or disapproves religion). In the Kentucky "Ten Commandments" case, Justice Scalia excoriated *Lemon* as unprincipled. *McCreary,* 125 S.Ct. at 2750–52. Yet Justice Souter's majority opinion relied on *Lemon* for a summary of the "familiar considerations for evaluating Establishment Clause claims." *Id.* at 2732–33 (opinion for the Court). See chapter 4, notes 156–62 and accompanying text.

227. *Church of the Lukumi Babalu Aye v. City of Hialeah,* 508 U.S. 520 (1993).

228. *Sherbert v. Verner,* 374 U.S. 398 (1963) (holding that a Seventh-Day Adventist who refused to work on Saturday was entitled to an exemption from a state law denying unemployment benefits to anyone who declined to accept work).

229. *Wisconsin v. Yoder,* 406 U.S. 205 (1972) (holding that Amish parents were entitled to an exemption from a state law compelling school attendance until age sixteen).

230. *Employment Div. v. Smith,* 494 U.S. 872 (1990) (holding that members of the Native American Church who used peyote for religious purposes were not entitled to an exemption from a general drug-control law).

231. See Christopher L. Eisgruber & Lawrence G. Sager, *The Vulnerability of Conscience: The Constitutional Basis for Protecting Religious Conduct,* 61 U. Chi. L. Rev. 1245, 1297–1301 (1994).

232. *Good News Club v. Milford Central School,* 533 U.S. 98, 106 (2001). Justice Scalia charged the Court with abandoning this approach in *Locke v. Davey,* 540 U.S. 712, 724 (2004), where Chief Justice Rehnquist allowed a state to deny otherwise generally available scholarship aid to students pursuing "devotional" theology degrees. *Id.* at 728 (dissenting opinion). In that case, though, Rehnquist was pragmatically trying to reconcile the general principle of neutrality associ-

ated with free exercise, on the one hand, with the state's legitimate desire not to tax its citizens for the benefit of religion, on the other. He managed the task by holding that the state did not have to withhold financial aid from students seeking sectarian degrees, but was constitutionally entitled to do so in the absence of any showing of "animus" toward religion." *Id.* at 725 (majority opinion). See generally Kathleen Sullivan, *The New Religion and the Constitution,* 116 Harv. L. Rev. 1397 (2003).

233. 125 S.Ct. 1183 (2005).

234. *Id.* at 1190, 1196, quoting *Atkins v. Virginia,* 536 U.S. 304, 319 (2002).

235. *Id.* at 1190, quoting *Trop v. Dulles,* 356 U.S. 86, 100–101 (1958).

236. Let me be clear that *nothing* about cold-blooded, state-sponsored homicide makes any sense to me. But I promised not to make this book a recital of my personal views.

237. 433 U.S. 584 (1977).

238. *Id.* at 592–93 n.4, 598.

239. Roughly this same means/ends structure is apparent in other cases in the *Coker* line. In *Enmund v. Florida,* 458 U.S. 782 (1982), and *Tison v. Arizona,* 481 U.S. 137 (1987), the justices quarreled over the particular *kind* of homicide (intentional or reckless) that might be punished by death in service of the goals identified in *Coker.*

240. 538 U.S. 11 (2003) (plurality opinion).

241. Justice O'Connor listed the "gravity" of the crime, the "harshness" of the penalty, the sentences dealt to "other criminals in the same jurisdiction," and the punishments imposed for similar offenses "in other jurisdictions." *Id.* at 22, relying on *Solem v. Helm,* 463 U.S. 277, 292 (1983).

242. *Ewing,* 538 U.S. at 29.

243. Justice Scalia thinks that proportionality (i.e., "the notion that the punishment should fit the crime") is uniquely suited for cases in which the governmental objective is retribution. It is unintelligible, in his view, to compare the nature of the offense to the severity of the penalty when other state interests are implicated (e.g., incapacitation and rehabilitation). *Ewing,* 538 U.S. at 31 (Scalia, J., concurring in the judgment). Justice Thomas rejects proportionality even in death penalty cases—because it is "incapable of judicial application." *Id.* at 32 (Thomas, J., concurring in the judgment).

244. *Ewing,* 538 U.S. at 52 (Breyer, J., dissenting).

245. *Id.* at 23 (plurality opinion), relying on *Solem,* 463 U.S. at 288 (Kennedy, J., concurring).

246. Justice Scalia's resistance rests, at least in part, on doubts that the Court can determine whether penalties sufficiently further nonretributive goals without second-guessing legislative policy decisions. Justice Breyer really only argues that the wide range of considerations defies any structured analysis and thus is suited to an entirely *ad hoc* approach. Professor Ristroph hopes to break the tie to retrib-

utive penal theory by recharacterizing proportionality as an external restraint on governmental power. Alice Ristroph, *Proportionality as a Principle of Limited Government*, 55 Duke L. J. 263, 270 (2005). That move allows Ristroph to address a wider range of explanations for the imposition of punishment and to argue, in turn, that courts are positioned to employ proportionality as a test for constitutionality. There is something to that, but in the end (in my view) the "external restraint" approach misconceives the doctrinal framework actually at work in these cases—that is, rational instrumentalism (of which proportionality forms a part).

247. James Liebman has explained that the NAACP Legal Defense and Education Fund recognized early on that the Court was unlikely to rule capital punishment unconstitutional generally and thus adopted the strategy of protecting defendants via procedural safeguards. The Court declined to derive special death penalty procedures from the Due Process Clause—see *McGautha v. California*, 402 U.S. 183 (1971)—but later built them into the Eighth Amendment. James S. Liebman, *The Overproduction of Death*, 100 Colum. L. Rev. 2030, 2032–38 (2000). So these cases also illustrate that it typically makes no difference which provision of the written Constitution provides the starting point. In the end, the Court itself supplies the necessary content, which invariably turns out to be rational instrumentalism.

248. 428 U.S. 153 (1976).

249. 438 U.S. 586 (1978).

250. Justice Scalia, for his part, contends that there is an irreconcilable tension between "guided discretion" and "individualized consideration." *Johnson v. Texas*, 509 U.S. 350, 373–74 (1993) (Scalia, J., concurring).

Chapter Four

1. Ray A. Brown, *Due Process of Law, Police Power, and the Supreme Court*, 40 Harv. L. Rev. 943, 945 (1927).

2. 96 U.S. 97 (1877).

3. *Id.* at 104, cited on this point in Brown, *Due Process, supra* note 1, at 957.

4. See Dale Carpenter, *Is Lawrence Libertarian?* 88 Minn. L. Rev. 1140, 1160–61 (2004) (arguing that a single standard across the board would either revive *Lochner* or dilute personal liberty).

5. Laurence H. Tribe, *Lawrence v. Texas: The "Fundamental Right" that Dare Not Speak Its Name*, 117 Harv. L. Rev. 1893, 1916–17 (2004); hereafter cited as *Lawrence v. Texas*.

6. Michael C. Dorf, *Equal Protection Incorporation*, 88 Va. L. Rev. 951, 966 (2002); Andrew Koppelman, Antidiscrimination Law and Social Equality 15 (1996). Not everyone agrees. Professor Roosevelt argues that the standards of review reflect the level of deference the Court accords to other branches of the

Federal Government and the states. Kermit Roosevelt III, The Myth of Judicial Activism: Making Sense of Supreme Court Decisions 32–35, 43–46 (2006). Robert Nagel regards these standards of review as a part of the doctrine the Court claims to apply to cases. Robert G. Nagel, *The Formulaic Constitution*, 84 Mich. L. Rev. 165 (1985). That accounts to some extent for his understanding that the Court actually employs a variety of doctrinal formulae in substantive rights cases. The better understanding is that standards of review are not an essential part of the baseline doctrine at work, nor even a very serious part of that doctrine. Nagel regrets that arguments over the appropriate test in any particular case often occupy far too much attention at the expense of what should be the more important task of grappling with the case at hand, under whatever test (*id.* at 204–7). He is right about that. But he is not right that the justices take responsibility primarily for the standard of review they announce for a case, not for the analysis that follows. At least, we can and should hold them to account for the latter. If we don't, the fault is in ourselves.

7. *Massachusetts Bd. of Retirement v. Murgia*, 427 U.S. 307, 318 (1976) (Marshall, J., dissenting). See also *San Antonio Ind. School Dist. v. Rodriguez*, 411 U.S. 1, 71 (1973) (Marshall, J., dissenting).

8. *City of Cleburne v. Cleburne Living Center*, 473 U.S. 432, 452 (1985) (Stevens, J., concurring). See also *Craig v. Boren*, 429 U.S. 190, 212 (1976) (Stevens, J., concurring).

9. See chapter 3, text accompanying notes 26–28.

10. *Planned Parenthood v. Casey*, 505 U.S. 833, 849 (1992).

11. *Murgia*, 427 U.S. at 312.

12. *New Orleans v. Dukes*, 427 U.S. 297, 303 (1976).

13. *Cleburne*, 473 U.S. at 440.

14. *Williamson v. Lee Optical Co.*, 348 U.S. 483, 488 (1955).

15. Chief Justice Hughes famously put it this way: "Times without number we have said that the legislature is primarily the judge of the necessity of such an enactment, that every possible presumption is in favor of its validity, and that though the court may hold views inconsistent with the wisdom of the law, it may not be annulled unless palpably in excess of legislative power." *West Coast Hotel Co. v. Parrish*, 300 U.S. 379, 398 (1937).

16. *Cleburne*, 473 U.S. 432 (1985).

17. 517 U.S. 620 (1996).

18. 539 U.S. 558 (2003).

19. See Michael C. Dorf, *Foreword: The Limits of Socratic Deliberation*, 112 Harv. L. Rev. 4, 50 n. 256 (1998) (explaining that "shrewd lawyers" forage for alternative ways of presenting claims in hopes of inviting a more demanding standard of judicial review); hereafter cited as *Foreword*.

20. *Skinner v. Oklahoma*, 316 U.S. 535, 541 (1942). See, for example, *Kramer v. Union Free School District*, 395 U.S. 621 (1969) (involving the interest in vot-

ing); *Johnson v. California,* 543 U.S. 499 (2005) (involving a classification on the basis of race).

21. *Adarand Constructors v. Pena,* 515 U.S. 200, 227 (1995).

22. *Id.* at 227.

23. *Richmond v. J. A. Croson Co.,* 488 U.S. 469, 493 (1989).

24. *Id.* Accord *Kramer,* 395 U.S. at 632.

25. *City of Boerne v. Flores,* 521 U.S. 507, 534 (1997).

26. *Adarand,* 515 U.S. at 237.

27. See, for example, *Grutter v. Bollinger,* 539 U.S. 306 (2003).

28. See, for example, *Moore v. City of East Cleveland,* 431 U.S. 494, 499 (1977) (explaining that when government regulates the living arrangements of blood relatives, the Court must "examine carefully the importance of the governmental interests advanced and the extent to which they are served by the challenged regulation"); *Zablocki v. Redhahil,* 434 U.S. 374, 388 (1978) (invalidating a limitation on the "right to marry" because it was not "closely tailored" to achieve "sufficiently important state interests").

29. *Washington v. Davis,* 426 U.S. 229 (1976); see notes 74–86 and accompanying text.

30. *Akron v. Akron Center for Reproductive Health,* 462 U.S. 416 (1983).

31. *Id.* at 463 (O'Connor, J., dissenting).

32. Kenneth L. Karst, *Justice O'Connor and the Substance of Equal Citizenship,* 2003 Sup. Ct. Rev. 357, 423 (noting this shift). Of course, Justice O'Connor's initial position in *Akron* may have been tailored to the then-prevailing "strict scrutiny" framework from *Roe,* while her position in *Casey* may have reflected her own superseding doctrinal adjustment. In *Akron,* she used the "undue burden" test (which seems to go to the state's means) to describe what was "fundamental" about a woman's interest in abortion, thus to identify, in turn, the circumstances in which governmental regulation should be examined carefully.

33. *United States v. Virginia,* 518 U.S. 515 (1996); referred to as *VMI.*

34. *Id.* at 524.

35. *Id.* at 533.

36. See *Goesaert v. Cleary,* 335 U.S. 464 (1948) (assuming that a straightforward gender classification would be valid); *Reed v. Reed,* 404 U.S. 71 (1971) (insisting that a general classification according to gender is "arbitrary" in the absence of some other explanation); *Frontiero v. Richardson,* 411 U.S. 677 (1973) (plurality opinion for the Court by Brennan, J.) (drawing the analogy to race discrimination); *Craig v. Boren,* 429 U.S. 1909 (1976) (opinion for the Court by Brennan, J.) (adopting the "important-interest/substantially-related-means" test); *Michael M. v. Superior Court,* 450 U.S. 464 (1981) (plurality opinion for the Court by Rehnquist, J.) (arguably attempting to dilute the *Craig* standard); *Virginia,* 518 U.S. at 531 (acknowledging that the precedents have not equated

gender and race classifications but explaining that the former evoke "skeptical scrutiny").

37. Prior to *VMI*, it was common to describe the standard of review in gender cases as "intermediate" scrutiny—occupying a "middle tier" within the standard-of-review hierarchy. Justice Scalia described the standard that way in *VMI* itself and declared himself satisfied. 518 U.S. at 573 (Scalia, J., dissenting). Then again, Scalia and others often remark on the Court's generally dissatisfying attempts to articulate ever more subtle distinctions among standards of review. See, for example, *Madsen v. Women's Health Center,* 512 U.S. 753, 791 (1994) (Scalia, J., dissenting) (ridiculing the Court's use of "intermediate-intermediate" scrutiny in a free speech setting).

38. *United States v. O'Brien,* 391 U.S. 367 (1968).

39. *Central Hudson Gas v. Pub. Svc. Comm'n,* 447 U.S. 557 (1980).

40. *O'Brien,* 391 U.S. at 377.

41. *Central Hudson,* 447 U.S. at 564.

42. *Ward v. Rock Against Racism,* 491 U.S. 781, 798 (1989) (taking this position with respect to regulations of symbolic expression); *Bd. of Trustees of SUNY v. Fox,* 492 U.S. 469, 476 (1989) (taking the same position with respect to commercial expression).

43. *Fox,* 492 U.S. at 480, quoting *Posadas de Puerto Rico Associates v. Tourism Co. of Puerto Rico,* 478 U.S. 328, 341 (1986), and *In re R. M. J.,* 455 U.S. 191, 203 (1982).

44. *Fox,* 492 U.S. at 480.

45. Cass R. Sunstein, *What Did Lawrence Hold? Of Autonomy, Desuetude, Sexuality and Marriage,* 2003 Sup. Ct. Rev. 27, 46 (lamenting that "[t]he conventional doctrinal categories and terms are simply missing"); hereafter cited as *Lawrence.*

46. *Lawrence,* 539 U.S. at 578.

47. See Sunstein, *Lawrence, supra* note 45, at 47–48.

48. Tribe, *Lawrence v. Texas, supra* note 5, at 1893–94. Accord Carpenter, *Lawrence, supra* note 4, at 1150–51.

49. Mary Anne Case, *Of "This" and "That" in Lawrence v. Texas,* 2003 Sup. Ct. Rev. 75, 83–84.

50. See Cass R. Sunstein, One Case at a Time 148 (1999) (explaining *Cleburne* and *Romer* in part as illustrations of the Court's practice of deciding as little as possible).

51. See, for example, *Romer v. Evans,* 517 U.S. 620, 636 (1996) (Scalia, J., dissenting); *Grutter,* 539 U.S. at 357 (Thomas, J., dissenting).

52. See *Rowland v. Mad River Local Sch. Dist.,* 470 U.S. 1009, 1014 (1985) (Brennan, J., dissenting); *Grutter,* 539 U.S. at 344 (Ginsburg, J., concurring).

53. See Dorf, *Foreword, supra* note 19, at 52; emphasis added.

54. See notes 139–206 and accompanying text.

55. *Perry Ed. Ass'n v. Perry Local Educators' Ass'n,* 460 U.S. 37 (1983).

56. Compare, for example, *R. A. V. v. City of St. Paul,* 505 U.S. 377, 391 (1992) (opinion for the Court by Scalia, J.) (suggesting that a cross-burning ordinance discriminated on the basis of viewpoint), with *id.* at 434 (Stevens, J., concurring in the judgment) (insisting that the ordinance was neutral with respect to viewpoint).

57. *Members of City Council v. Taxpayers for Vincent,* 466 U.S. 789 (1984).

58. *Id.* at 828–31 (dissenting opinion).

59. See chapter 3, text accompanying notes 148–49.

60. *R. A. V.,* 505 U.S. 377 (1992).

61. 538 U.S. 343 (2003).

62. *Id.* at 382–84.

63. *Id.* at 382 (dissenting opinion). During oral argument in *Black,* Justice Thomas insisted that cross-burning has only the purpose of intimidation. His impassioned remarks altered the atmosphere in the chamber and signaled the result the Court would reach. See Linda Greenhouse, *An Intense Attack by Justice Thomas on Cross-Burning,* N.Y. Times, A1 (Dec. 12, 2002).

64. See Richard A. Primus, *Equal Protection and Disparate Impact: Round Three,* 117 Harv. L. Rev. 493, 505 (2003) (giving some of these examples and contending that an "'express racial classification'" is not a "self-defining term"). See also note 206 below (discussing the consideration of race as a factor in university admissions decisions).

65. See, for example, *Adarand,* 515 U.S. at 227; see also *Grutter,* 539 U.S. at 326 (the law school admission case).

66. See Ian F. Haney Lopez, *Institutional Racism: Judicial Conduct and a New Theory of Racial Discrimination,* 109 Yale L. J. 1717, 1835–38 (2000) (arguing that the Court's account of race-sensitive cases is overinclusive). Justice Stevens made this point vividly in *Adarand* when he insisted that a race-sensitive affirmative action plan cannot sensibly be examined in the manner appropriate for a statute forbidding African American children to attend school with whites. *Adarand,* 515 U.S. at 243 (Stevens, J., concurring), cited on this point in Lopez, *supra* at 1837–38.

67. 388 U.S. 1 (1967).

68. A similar argument came up in *Goodridge v. Dep't of Pub. Health,* 440 Mass. 309 (2003), where the state contended that a ban on gay marriage does not really keep gays and lesbians from getting married, because they are free to choose partners of the opposite sex. Gays and lesbians can marry; they just can't marry the people they love. The Supreme Judicial Court of Massachusetts summarily rejected that argument.

69. *Cleburne,* 473 U.S. 432 (1985).

70. *Id.* at 448–50.

71. *Id.* at 450.

72. 118 U.S. 356 (1886).

73. See, for example, *Castaneda v. Partida*, 430 U.S. 482 (1977).

74. 426 U.S. 229 (1976).

75. *Id.* at 239.

76. *Arlington Heights v. Metro. Housing Develop. Corp.*, 429 U.S. 252 (1977).

77. *Id.* at 266.

78. See Elena Kagen, *Private Speech, Public Purpose: The Role of Governmental Motive in First Amendment Doctrine*, 63 U. Chi. L. Rev. 413, 439 n. 78 (1996), endorsing Laurence H. Tribe, *The Mystery of Motive, Private and Public: Some Notes Inspired by the Problems of Hate Crime and Animal Sacrifice*, 1993 Sup. Ct. Rev. 1, 33 n. 79. Accord Cass R. Sunstein, *Naked Preferences and the Constitution*, 84 Colum. L. Rev. 1689, 1714–15 (1984); hereafter cited as *Naked Preferences*. Professor Brest insists that even an "illicit motive" that is "subordinate" in a "decisionmaker's mind" still can control "the outcome of the decision." Paul Brest, *Palmer v. Thompson: An Approach to the Problem of Unconstitutional Legislative Motive*, 1971 Sup. Ct. Rev. 95, 119. That is surely right as a logical matter; even a modest invalid impulse can constitute that final, dispositive straw. Yet the point of the Court's doctrine is that when a valid purpose or series of valid purposes overwhelms anything illegitimate in the mix, that should be enough. The Court's thinking is again pragmatic. The alternative is unattractive. The Court cannot very well invalidate a "law conscripting clerics" because "an atheist voted for it." *Davis*, 426 U.S. at 253 (Stevens, J., concurring).

79. See notes 137–40 and accompanying text.

80. See notes 147–48 and accompanying text.

81. *Davis*, 426 U.S. at 242.

82. *Arlington Heights*, 429 U.S. at 265.

83. See Constitutional Law 616 (G. Stone, L. M. Seidman, C. Sunstein & M. Tushnet eds., 3rd ed. 1996); chapter 2, note 78.

84. Charles Fried, Saying What the Law Is: The Constitution in the Supreme Court 226 (2004).

85. *Davis*, 426 U.S. at 254 (Stevens, J., concurring).

86. *Id.* at 253.

87. See, for example, *Guinn v. United States*, 238 U.S. 347, 364–65 (1915) (involving a grandfather clause exempting descendants of registered voters from a literacy test).

88. 528 U.S. 495 (2000).

89. *Personnel Administrator of Massachusetts v. Feeney*, 442 U.S. 256, 274 (1979).

90. 500 U.S. 352 (1991).

91. Writing separately in *Hernandez*, Justice O'Connor insisted that "[n]o matter how closely tied . . . to race the explanation for a peremptory strike may

be, the strike does not implicate the Equal Protection Clause unless it is based on race." *Id.* at 375 (O'Connor, J., concurring). See Lopez, *Institutional Racism, supra* note 66, at 1837 (arguing that *Hernandez* shows that the Court's understanding of race discrimination is also underinclusive).

92. *Lawrence,* 539 U.S. 558 (2003).

93. The state argued that the statute did not classify according to the status of *being* gay, lesbian, or bisexual and thus eluded the difficulties the Court had recently found with that kind of classification in the Colorado Proposition 2 case, *Romer v. Evans,* 517 U.S. 620 (1996). See Case, *Of "This" and "That," supra* note 49, at 89.

94. See Karst, *Equal Citizenship, supra* note 32, at 434–42; Sunstein, *Lawrence, supra* note 45, at 52. Professor MacKinnon argues that the classification was more nuanced still. Since the statute made criminality turn on the sex of the participants, it could fairly be considered a classification according to sex, thus vulnerable to attack under precedents like *United States v. Virginia,* 518 U.S. 515 (1996). Catharine A. MacKinnon, *The Road Not Taken: Sex Equality in Lawrence v. Texas,* 65 Ohio St. L. J. 1081, 1083 (2004).

95. *Renton v. Playtime Theaters,* 475 U.S. 41 (1986).

96. *Madsen v. Women's Health Center,* 512 U.S. 753 (1994).

97. *City of Los Angeles v. Alameda Books,* 535 U.S. 425, 447 (2002) (Kennedy, J., concurring in the judgment).

98. See chapter 3, notes 75–89 and accompanying text.

99. See chapter 3, notes 97–102 and accompanying text. Cf. Peter J. Rubin, *Square Pegs and Round Holes: Substantive Due Process, Procedural Due Process, and the Bill of Rights,* 103 Colum. L. Rev. 833, 842 (2003) (treating "incorporation" theory as a "form of fundamental rights analysis").

100. *Casey,* 505 U.S. at 848.

101. *Albright v. Oliver,* 510 U.S. 266, 275 (1994) (Scalia, J., concurring). See chapter 3, note 144.

102. *Washington v. Glucksberg,* 521 U.S. 702 (1997).

103. *Id.* at 720; emphasis added.

104. *Id.* at 768 n. 10 (Souter, J., concurring in the judgment).

105. *Id.* at 722 n. 17.

106. See chapter 2, notes 47–55 and accompanying text.

107. See Fried, Saying, *supra* note 84, at 185–87 (explaining that Rehnquist's approach in *Glucksberg* illustrates the Court's caution in developing substantive due process doctrine); Sunstein, *Lawrence, supra* note 45, at 37–38 (reading *Glucksberg* to proclaim: "'Thus far, but no further!'"); Tribe, *Lawrence v. Texas, supra* note 5, at 1923–24 (2004) (contending that Chief Justice Rehnquist's opinion in *Glucksberg* was "a gambit toward hacking away not just at substantive due process but also at the nature of liberty itself"); Nelson Lund & John O. McGinnis, *Lawrence v. Texas and Judicial Hubris,* 102 Mich. L. Rev. 1555, 1573 (2004)

(reading *Glucksberg* as an attempt at "freezing" substantive due process as it stood at the time). Cf. *Glucksberg*, 521 U.S. at 790 (Breyer, J., concurring in the judgment) (suggesting that everybody has in mind the same fundamental matters but dresses them in different language). I do not mean to make this simpler than it is. Most justices employ the label "right" for the emphasis I describe, but some use it in a way that can only be regarded as Lochnerian in flavor and Lockean in foundation. Despite his commitment to incorporation theory in *Griswold*, Justice Douglas said he was dealing with a "right" of privacy "older than the Bill of Rights." *Griswold*, 381 U.S. at 486. John Harlan was a comparative conservative in the ranks of Warren Court justices. Yet he proclaimed that substantive due process vindicates "rights" that are "fundamental" in the sense that they "belong [to] the citizens of all free governments." And he insisted that liberty includes "freedom from all substantial arbitrary impositions and purposeless restraints." *Poe v. Ullman*, 367 U.S. 497, 541 (1961) (dissenting opinion). Justice Stevens, for his part, is not afraid to invoke natural law by name. In his telling, the liberty protected by due process is "one of the cardinal unalienable rights" conferred on "all men" by "their Creator." *Meachum v. Fano*, 427 U.S. 215, 230 (1976) (Stevens, J., dissenting), cited in *Glucksberg*, 521 U.S. at 710 n. 10 (1997) (Stevens, J., concurring in the judgment). Justice Harlan did not intend to go so far and probably meant only to say that any kind of individual freedom counts as "liberty" and thus triggers some kind of due process analysis. Justice Stevens has promoted natural law as the foundation for liberty in cases in which the majority is disinclined either to bring due process to bear at all or to give the idea much bite. Still, you have to think that this kind of rhetoric scares the daylights out of other justices, who acknowledge the existence and value of substantive due process but still are sensitive about its potential.

108. Justice O'Connor joined Rehnquist's opinion for the Court because she agreed "there is no generalized right to 'commit suicide.'" *Glucksberg*, 521 U.S. at 736 (O'Connor, J., concurring). Justice Stevens also mingled "liberty" with "rights," insisting that "the 'liberty' protected by the Due Process Clause does not include a categorical 'right to commit suicide.'" *Id.* at 741 (Stevens, J., concurring in the judgment).

109. *Lawrence*, 539 U.S. at 588 (Scalia, J., dissenting).

110. See, for example, Lund & McGinnis, *Judicial Hubris, supra* note 107, at 1578–79.

111. See, for example, Tribe, *Lawrence v. Texas, supra* note 5, at 1898, 1934–35.

112. Randy E. Barnett, *Justice Kennedy's Libertarian Revolution: Lawrence v. Texas*, 2003 Cato Sup. Ct. Rev. 21. Accord Lino A. Graglia, *Lawrence v. Texas: Our Philosopher-Kings Adopt Libertarianism as Our Official National Philosophy and Reject Traditional Morality as a Basis for Law*, 65 Ohio St. L. J. 1139 (2004).

113. Carpenter, *Lawrence, supra* note 4, at 1150–56.

114. Lund & McGinnis, *Judicial Hubris, supra* note 107, at 1595 (arguing that *Lawrence* at most indicates a willingness to look closely at statutes affecting "sexual autonomy"); accord Carpenter, *Lawrence, supra* note 4, at 1152.

115. 410 U.S. 113 (1973).

116. *Id.* at 154.

117. *Id.* at 153.

118. *Cruzan v. Director, Missouri Dep't of Health*, 497 U.S. 261 (1990).

119. *Id.* at 278.

120. *Glucksberg*, 521 U.S. at 723.

121. See *id.* at 736 (O'Connor, J., concurring) (noting that the Court did not reach the question whether a prohibition on assisted suicide would be sustained in a case in which the individual's interest is conceived in this way).

122. *Michael H. & Victoria D. v. Gerald D.*, 491 U.S. 110 (1989).

123. *Id.* at 127 n.6 (expressing a minority view on this point).

124. Laurence H. Tribe & Michael C. Dorf, On Reading the Constitution 73 (1991).

125. *Michael H.*, 491 U.S. at 141–42 (dissenting opinion).

126. *Id.* at 127–28 n. 6 (plurality opinion).

127. The joint opinion in *Casey* explicitly disclaimed Scalia's argument. *Casey*, 505 U.S. at 847. Chief Justice Rehnquist appeared to revive it (at least in part) in *Glucksberg* when he made it sound as though "rights" are "fundamental" only if they enjoy solid support in "tradition." *Glucksberg*, 521 U.S. at 710. That view seemed to have majority support. Yet in *Lawrence*, Justice Kennedy clearly relied on maturing modern attitudes rather than anything with such strong historical footing.

128. This point is independent of a different one, which goes to the entire enterprise of gearing the constitutional protection to which an interest is entitled to the respect the interest enjoys in society. The idea is to keep government from departing from deep-seated values. Yet if society really treasures something all that much, it seems unlikely that a legislature would abandon it. The very existence of a statute limiting some freedom is evidence that the public does *not* regard the freedom as especially worthy. Harry H. Wellington, *Common Law Rules and Constitutional Double Standards: Some Notes on Adjudication*, 83 Yale L. J. 221, 287 (1973).

Some academics contend that the Court cannot sensibly ascribe the policy embedded in a statute to society at large if the statute is old, at best the product of an ancient generation's sense of the public good. Professor Wellington himself argues that legislatures are not good at monitoring shifts in public attitudes about morality and keeping relevant statutes up to date. Old laws based on outdated thinking may remain in place out of inertia and the hesitancy of elected officials to revisit touchy issues. See Wellington, *supra* at 287–91; cf. David A.

Strauss, *Modernization and Representation Reinforcement: An Essay in Memory of John Hart Ely*, 57 Stan. L. Rev. 761, 762 (2004) (explaining that "laws on the books" may "no longer reflect popular opinion" for a variety of reasons). There may be something to that, but it is hard to think there is much. Some current enactments do infringe upon sensitive personal interests. Both the state constitutional amendment in *Romer* and the antisodomy statute in *Lawrence* were quite recent.

129. *Michael H.*, 491 U.S. at 141 (Brennan, J., dissenting).

130. *Lawrence*, 539 U.S. at 571–72. See Cass R. Sunstein, *Liberty After Lawrence*, 65 Ohio St. L. J. 1059, 1060 (2004) (explaining that *Lawrence* establishes that "the reach of liberty interests extends well beyond what tradition supports").

131. *Michael H.*, 491 U.S. at 137 (Brennan, J., dissenting).

132. Tribe & Dorf, Reading, *supra* note 124, at 106.

133. *Id.* at 98, 101. See also J. M. Balkin, *Tradition, Betrayal, and the Politics of Deconstruction*, 11 Cardozo L. Rev. 1613 (1990).

134. *Michael H.*, 491 U.S. at 127–28 n. 6.

135. *Bowers v. Hardwick*, 478 U.S. 186, 190 (1986).

136. Carpenter *Lawrence*, *supra* note 4, at 1153.

137. *U.S. Railroad Retirement Bd. v. Fritz*, 449 U.S. 166 (1980).

138. *Id.* at 177 (opinion of Rehnquist, C. J.); see *id.* at 186–87 (Brennan, J., dissenting); accord *id.* at 180 (Stevens, J., concurring in the judgment). See generally Ashutosh Bhagwat, *Purpose Scrutiny in Constitutional Analysis*, 85 Calif. L. Rev. 297, 303 (1997) (tracking the Court's examination of "purpose" as well as "means").

139. See Victoria F. Nourse & Jane S. Schacter, *The Politics of Legislative Drafting: A Congressional Case Study*, 77 N. Y. U. L. Rev. 575 (2002).

140. See chapter 1, notes 117–20 and accompanying text.

141. See chapter 1, notes 237–39 and accompanying text.

142. *O'Brien*, 391 U.S. at 383.

143. See, for example, *Palmer v. Thompson*, 403 U.S. 217 (1971).

144. No one in Congress seriously proposed that additional legislation was needed to ensure that potential conscripts kept their cards in order. But when protesters burned cards in public in a show of defiance, a bill was immediately introduced, rifled to the floor without hearings, and passed and signed within nine days. The sponsors openly declared that the point of the measure was to punish anyone who had burned his card to demonstrate opposition to the war. Lawrence R. Velvel, *Freedom of Speech and the Draft Card Burning Cases*, 16 U. Kan. L. Rev. 149 (1968).

145. *O'Brien*, 391 U.S. at 377. See Fried, Saying, *supra* note 84, at 122. In the flag-burning case, *Johnson v. Texas*, 491 U.S. 393 (1989), the Court declined to rely on the *O'Brien* standard for the express reason that the government's stated

interest was very much related to the suppression of speech. Preserving the flag as a symbol of national unity is speech-related. It appropriates the flag for one message and denies its use for any other. Dean Kagen has suggested, accordingly, that *O'Brien's* blanket disclaimer of any interest in legislative purpose is due for "reinterpretation." Kagen, *Private Speech, supra* note 78, at 442.

146. See *McCreary County v. ACLU*, 125 S.Ct. 2722, 2737 n. 14 (2005) (invoking Holmes' epigram in this context).

147. See, for example, *Church of the Lukumi Babalu Aye v. City of Hialeah*, 508 U.S. 520, 558 (1993) (Scalia, J., concurring).

148. *Edwards v. Aguillard*, 482 U.S. 578, 636–38 (1987) (Scalia, J., dissenting). See chapter 1, notes 117–20 and accompanying text.

149. *Fritz*, 449 U.S. at 179 (opinion for the Court by Rehnquist, C. J.); see text accompanying notes 137–38. See also Note, *Legislative Purpose, Rationality, and Equal Protection*, 82 Yale L. J. 123, 128 (1972) (making this point).

150. See, for example, *Levy v. Louisiana*, 391 U.S. 68, 69 (1968).

151. See, for example, *U.S. Dep't of Agriculture v. Moreno*, 413 U.S. 528, 534 (1973).

152. See, for example, *Fritz*, 449 U.S. at 173.

153. See text accompanying notes 181–90.

154. *Edwards*, 482 U.S. 578 (1987).

155. *Lukumi*, 508 U.S. 520 (1993).

156. *McCreary County*, 125 S.Ct. 2722 (2005).

157. *Id.* at 2757–58 (Scalia, J., dissenting). Recall that Justice Scalia objects to the *Lemon* test in its entirety, in part on the ground that it is subject to manipulation and does not foster consistent results (*id.* at 2750–51).

158. *Id.* at 2734–35 (majority opinion).

159. *Id.*

160. *Van Orden v. Perry*, 125 S.Ct. 2854 (2005).

161. *Id.* at 2869–71 (Breyer, J., concurring in the judgment).

162. See Erwin Chemerinsky, *Why Justice Breyer Was Wrong in Van Orden v. Perry*, 14 Wm. & Mary Bill Rts. J. 1, 15 (2005) (charging Breyer with ignoring the "basic reality" of the case); William Van Alstyne, *Ten Commandments, Nine Judges, and Five Versions of One Amendment—The First ("Now What?")*, 14 Wm. & Mary Bill Rts. J. 17, 25 (2005) (describing Breyer's opinion as so much "breast beating").

163. It is hard to find a case in which we can safely say that government took truly mindless action. In *Glickman v. Wileman Bros.*, 521 U.S. 457 (1997), Justice Souter could discern no reason why Congress had prescribed a generic advertising system for some agricultural crops but not others. In that case, it made no sense to distinguish onions and tomatoes from cucumbers and garlic. Well, maybe some sense, but not much. The only explanation was that some growers asked for a generic advertising scheme and some did not. Then again, that ex-

planation reflected something akin to a political market account of what happened. In *Bush v. Gore,* 531 U.S. 98 (2000), Justice Souter saw no basis at all for allowing Florida counties to use different standards for reading "dimpled" ballots. There, however, a plausible state interest was available at a higher level of generality—namely, the interest in vindicating the intentions of individual voters. Souter's (fair) complaint was that the state needed a more specifically defined explanation for using a decentralized system for determining voter intentions. In *Schweiker v. Wilson,* 450 U.S. 221 (1981), Justice Powell found it utterly irrational that Congress had *failed* to distinguish between Social Security and Medicaid and thus applied standards designed for the one to the other. In that case, however, a majority of the justices rejected Powell's appraisal and sustained the statute.

164. See Mark Kelman, *Law and Behavioral Science: Conceptual Overviews,* 97 Nw. U. L. Rev. 1347, 1355–56 (2003) (making this point to describe rational-choice theory regarding the behavior of private individuals).

165. In dissent, Justice Brennan insisted that the "equitable claim" argument was contrived and that the real explanation for denying benefits to workers who had left the industry earlier was that the actual drafters (employers and unions) had simply decided to carve non-union retirees out. *Fritz,* 449 U.S. at 189–91.

166. *Moreno,* 413 U.S. 528 (1973).

167. *Id.* at 535. Professor Sager offers a different account of *Moreno.* In that and other cases, he contends, the Court actually recognized a constitutional right to "minimum welfare" but hesitated actually to announce and enforce that right openly. Instead, the Court found other, less controversial grounds on which to rest. Lawrence G. Sager, Justice in Plainclothes: A Theory of American Constitutional Practice 99–100 (2004).

168. *Grutter,* 539 U.S. 306 (2003).

169. *Croson,* 488 U.S. 469 (1989). The issues in *Croson* were more complicated. Since Richmond contended that its purpose was remedial, Justice O'Connor insisted that the city itself must have been at least a "passive participant" in the historical discrimination that produced the effects to be redressed. That accounted, at least in part, for her refusal to accept the argument that the set-aside scheme was addressed to the consequences of race discrimination beyond the local vicinity (*id.* at 492; 499–500). See also text accompanying notes 178–79.

170. The dissenters in *Grutter* rejected the means/ends connections the law school advanced, dismissed the "critical mass" link in the chain as an effective "quota," and insisted that the immediate purpose the law school identified (obtaining the educational benefits of racial diversity) could be achieved by other means. *Grutter,* 539 U.S. at 346 (Scalia, J., concurring in part and dissenting in part); *id.* at 354 (Thomas, J., concurring in part and dissenting in part); *id.* at 378 (Rehnquist, C. J., dissenting); *id.* at 387 (Kennedy, J., dissenting).

171. But see Suzanne B. Goldberg, *Morals-Based Justifications for Lawmaking: Before and After Lawrence v. Texas*, 88 Minn. L. Rev. 1233, 1235 (2004) (arguing that the Court has never allowed government to regulate in the name of general morality apart from some independent interest "tied to demonstrable facts").

172. *Lawrence*, 539 U.S. 558 (2003).

173. Dale Carpenter thinks Kennedy meant that the state interest in protecting public morality was legitimate but insufficient to justify a criminal statute barring all sodomy—to which a demanding standard of review was applicable because the individual interest at stake was fundamental. Carpenter, *Lawrence, supra* note 4, at 1157–58. It is easier to understand *Lawrence* as a case in which the state pressed an interest at a much more specific level of generality—namely, the desire simply to punish what the individuals did in the circumstances in which they did it. That attempt to equate the state's purpose with its means defied means/ends analysis and thus could not supply the legitimate interest necessary. Accordingly, the state had to lose.

174. Steven D. Smith, The Constitution and the Pride of Reason 101–4 (1998).

175. See chapter 2, text accompanying notes 51–52, 123–28.

176. *Grutter*, 539 U.S. at 327–33.

177. See text accompanying note 168.

178. *Croson*, 488 U.S. 469 (1989).

179. *Id.* at 500, quoting *Wygant v. Jackson Bd. of Ed.*, 476 U.S. 267, 277 (1986).

180. *Sable Communications of Calif. v. FCC*, 492 U.S. 115, 131 (1989) (Scalia, J., concurring).

181. See John Hart Ely, Democracy and Distrust 145–46 (1980).

182. See text accompanying notes 147–48.

183. *Croson*, 488 U.S. at 493. In fact, Justice O'Connor explained in *Croson* that "strict scrutiny" unmasks "illegitimate uses of race by assuring that the legislative body is pursuing a goal important enough to warrant use of a highly suspect tool" (*id*). Yet it is fair to understand the point to be that "strict scrutiny" is meant to unmask a use of race that serves no public purpose. See Sunstein, *Naked Preferences, supra* note 78, at 1714–15.

184. See, for example, *Croson*, 488 U.S. at 501; *City of Lakewood v. Plain Dealer Publishing Co.*, 486 U.S. 750, 758 (1988). See Fried, Saying, *supra* note 84, at 118–22, 125, 210–11 (2004); Kagen, *Private Speech, supra* note 78, at 430.

185. In *Erznoznick v. Jacksonville*, 422 U.S. 205 (1975), for example, a city ordinance required drive-in movie theaters to erect walls to prevent drivers on an adjacent freeway from seeing nude scenes on the screen. The chief explanation was highway safety. Drivers distracted by nude movies were likely to pile up their vehicles. Of course, movies of any kind might be distracting, and it made no serious sense to single out scenes depicting performers in the nude. Justice Powell

did not say so, but he and everybody else knew perfectly well that the city did not expect theater operators to respond to the ordinance by building expensive walls. After all, they had their own economic incentives to do anything practical to keep people from watching their movies for free. The point of the ordinance was to get operators to change their fare—a purpose to discourage expression of which the city disapproved.

186. Occasionally, counsel is foolish enough to confess that governmental action is meant to further constitutionally illegitimate ends. That happened in *Cleburne*, 473 U.S. 432 (1985), where the city's lawyers argued that a home for the "mentally retarded" had been denied a permit because of the "negative attitudes" of abutters (*id.* at 448). Justice White responded that city officials could no more act on the prejudices of others than they could act on their own.

187. Fried, Saying, *supra* note 84, at 211 (referring to the analysis in *Moreno*).

188. *Cleburne*, 473 U.S. at 450.

189. *Romer*, 517 U.S. at 643.

190. *Lawrence*, 539 U.S. 558 (2003). *Amici* argued that the statute in *Lawrence* was a health measure meant to discourage sexual practices that might transmit communicable disease (read AIDS). Professor Carpenter argues that if Justice Kennedy had credited that argument, he might have been forced to articulate a rigorous standard of review. After all, if the "rational-basis" standard was applicable, even an extremely weak explanation for the statute should have saved it. Carpenter, *Lawrence, supra* note 4, at 1158–59. Then again, Justice Kennedy probably would have concluded that a criminal statute banning gay sodomy was so grossly over- and underinclusive with respect to health risks that an explanation along those lines was specious. And he would still have deduced that the only serious possibility was animus toward gays and lesbians.

191. *C.B. & Q. R.R. Co. v. McGuire*, 219 U.S. 549, 569 (1911).

192. See, for example, Albert M. Kales, *Due Process, the Inarticulate Major Premise and the Adamson Act*, 26 Yale L. J. 519, 520–21 (1917).

193. *McCreary County*, 125 S.Ct. at 2733.

194. *R. A. V.*, 505 U.S. at 386. See Kagen, *Private Speech, supra* note 78, at 443.

195. *Croson*, 488 U.S. at 493.

196. *Moreno*, 413 U.S. at 534; emphasis added.

197. See notes 188–90 and accompanying text.

198. *United States v. Virginia*, 518 U.S. 515 (1996).

199. Justice Ginsburg explained that the state had "trained [its] argument on 'means' rather than 'end,' and thus misperceived" the Court's precedents. The state's argument was "circular" inasmuch as it assumed that women were not equipped for the Virginia Military Institute and, on that basis, purported to justify their exclusion (*id.* at 545).

200. 477 U.S. 399 (1986).

201. *Id.* at 409.

202. *Cleburne*, 473 U.S. at 440; emphasis added.

203. Cf. *Weber v. Aetna Casualty and Surety Co.*, 406 U.S. 164 (1972) (explaining that it is "illogical" to punish illegitimate children "for the sake of punishing the illicit relations of their parents"); *Jimenez v. Weinberger*, 417 U.S. 628, 637 (1974) (making the same point); *Levy v. Louisiana*, 391 U.S. 68, 72 (1968) (invalidating a state policy forbidding illegitimate children to file wrongful death actions on the theory that "no action, conduct, or demeanor" of the children could "possibly" be relevant to "the harm that was done the mother").

204. *Mississippi University for Women v. Hogan*, 458 U.S. 718, 725 (1982).

205. Ely, Democracy and Distrust, *supra* note 181, at 150–70.

206. Even affirmative action cases can arguably be explained on this basis. If, for example, government reserves some percentage of public contracts for minority-operated companies, the affected firms *can* react—not by changing their essential character, but by making business choices in light of the new environment. Minority-operated companies can pursue contracts more aggressively in the knowledge that their chances of success are improved; white-operated companies may be equally vigorous in the knowledge that they no longer enjoy their previous advantages. And the result may be more robust economic activity generally—in furtherance of the public interest. But arguments along those lines prove too much. Any adjustment in the status quo, however senseless, can nonetheless generate reactions that may be socially beneficial. Cases in which the Court has allowed government to use race-conscious policies (i.e., *Grutter*) stand on a different footing. Genuine public objectives are served notwithstanding that the individuals who bear the costs (whites who do not receive similar treatment because of their race) cannot improve their position by changing their behavior. Then again, the admissions program sustained in *Grutter* did not simply prefer minority applicants and thus exclude others on the basis of race alone. The program directed admissions officers to consider race as one factor among many and, into the bargain, to read every application in an effort to identify candidates whose catalogue of talents and experiences would contribute to the intellectual life of the school. No candidate's file was set aside and no candidate was rejected exclusively on racial grounds. The character of the law school's means thus both mitigated the negative effects of the program on nonminority applicants and defused concerns that minority candidates who were admitted might be stigmatized.

Conclusion

1. Ludwig Wittgenstein, Philosophical Investigations § 271, 95 (G. E. M. trans. 1965), quoted in Richard Rorty, Consequences of Pragmatism xxxv (1982).

2. *Planned Parenthood v. Casey*, 505 U.S. 833, 849 (1992); emphasis added.

3. *Van Orden v. Perry,* 125 S.Ct. 2854, 2869 (2005) (concurring opinion); emphasis added.

4. *Roper v. Simmons,* 125 S.Ct. 1183, 1191 (2005), emphasis added; quoting *Atkins v. Virginia,* 536 U.S. 304, 312 (2002), quoting *Coker v. Georgia,* 433 U.S 584, 597 (1977).

5. With apologies to Andre Gide, The Immoralist 7 (D. Bussy trans. 1930).

Index